ARTHUR
And the Fall of Roman Britain

ARTHUR
And the Fall of Roman Britain

By

Edwin Pace

Invermark Books

First published by Invermark Books in 2008

Invermark Books
20 Ladysmith Road
Cheltenham
GL52 5LQ

www.invermarkbooks.co.uk

Typeset by Invermark Books in 12 point Times New Roman

British Library Cataloguing in Publication Data:
A catalogue record for this book is available from the British Library

ISBN: 9780955420146

Printed and bound by: CPI Antony Rowe
Chippenham, Wiltshire

Cover Design: Elafius

Photograph of the Deurne helmet used with permission of the Rijksmuseum van Oudheden, Leyden, the Netherlands

Table of Contents

ACKNOWLEDGEMENTS

The number of people who have helped with this book, directly or indirectly, is very large, but I wish to thank in particular my publisher, Niall Angus, and the staff of Invermark Books for their tireless efforts on my behalf. I also wish to give special thanks to Christopher Gidlow for having read the manuscript at a critical stage in its evolution. Although he has his own carefully considered views on many aspects of this issue, his comments and criticisms were invaluable.

Thanks as well to my copy-editor, Allison Hill, for her meticulous work on the project.

Permission to reproduce an image of the Late Roman *dracostandarte* from the Museum of Koblenz has been generously provided by the Generaldirektion Kulterelles Erbe, Direktion Archäologie, Koblenz.

Permission to reproduce an image of the Late Roman ridged helmet from the Museum of Worms has been generously provided by the Stadtarkhiv, Institut für Stadtgeschichte, Worms.

Permission to use an image of a half-scale model of the Sutton Hoo ship under sail was generously granted by Joyce and Edwin Gifford, its re-constructors.

Use of numismatic images of the emperors Theodosius II, Marcian, Valentinian III, and Anthemius was generously granted by Joseph Sermarini, president of 'Forum Ancient Coins'. (www.forumancientcoins.com)

Use of a numismatic image of the emperor Constantine wearing a *pilleus* was generously granted by Zachary Beasley, of 'Beast Coins'. (www.beastcoins.com)

The image of the Deurne Late Roman ridged helmet is reproduced by kind permission of the Rijksmuseum van Oudheden, Leyden, the Netherlands.

The image of Dido and Aeneas, found on folio 100v of the *Vergilius Romanus* (cod. lat. 3867), is reproduced by permission of the Vatican Library.

The image of Tintagel Castle viewed from the air was provided courtesy of Cornwall County Council.

The image of Richborough fortress was provided courtesy of Skyscan and English Heritage.

Most of the topographical details found in the maps of the Badon Campaign and the environs of Thanet are taken from *An Atlas of Roman Britain*, by Barri Jones and David Mattingly, published in 1990 by Basil Blackwell, Oxford. Dr. Mattingly generously granted permission to use and simplify the excellent maps contained in that work.

Howard Wiseman kindly granted permission to quote his translation of Gildas' 'Badon passage'.

Unless otherwise noted, quotations from Gildas are reproduced by kind permission from Arthurian Period Sources, volume 7, *Gildas: The Ruin of Britain and Other Works*. (ed. and trans. M. Winterbottom) published in 1978 by Phillimore, Madam Green Farm, Oving, PO20 2DD Chichester. (www.phillimore.co.uk) Unless otherwise noted, quotations from the *Historia Brittonum* and the *Annales Cambriae* are reproduced by kind permission from Arthurian Period Sources, volume 8, *Nennius: British History and The Welsh Annals.* (ed & trans. John Morris), published in 1980 by Phillimore as above. Quotations from St Patrick are reproduced by kind permission from Arthurian Period Sources, *St. Patrick: His Writings and Muirchu's Life.* (ed. and trans. A.B.E. Hood), published in 1978 by Phillimore as above.

Quotations from Sidonius Apollinaris are reproduced by kind permission from *Sidonius, Poems and Letters,* 2 vol. (trans. W. B. Anderson.), published in 1936 by Harvard University Press.

The quotation from 'The Gallic Chronicle of 452' is reproduced by kind permission from *The Later Roman Empire*, 3 vols., by A.H.M. Jones, published in 1964 by Blackwell, Oxford.

Permission to quote from *Zosimus: New History, The Decline of Rome* (trans. James J. Buchanan and Harold T. Davis), published in 1967, was generously granted by Trinity University Press, San Antonio.

Quotations from the Venerable Bede are reproduced by kind permission from *Bede, A History of the English Church and People* (trans. Leo Sherly-Price), published in 1968 by Penguin Books Ltd., Harmondsworth.

Quotations from the *Anglo-Saxon Chronicle* are reproduced by kind permission from *The Anglo-Saxon Chronicle* (trans. G.N. Garmonsway), published in 1972 by Dent, London.

Quotations from the Gallo-Roman hagiographer Constantius are reproduced from *The Western Fathers. Being the Lives of SS Martin of Tours, Ambrose, Augustine of Hippo, Honoratus of Arles, and Germanus of Auxe*rre (ed. and trans. F.R. Hoare), published in 1954 by Sheed and Ward, London and New York: by kind permission of Continuum.

Permission to quote from *Epitome of Military Science*, (trans.N. P. Miller), published in 1993, was generously granted by Liverpool University Press.

Although fully noted in the references section, the author would also like to explicitly acknowledge his debt to the work of Geoffrey Ashe and Nikolai Tolstoy, whose insights underpin a significant part of this book.

Finally, I would like to thank the staffs of the British Library and Huntingdon Library, Cambridgeshire, for their unfailing courtesy and helpfulness.

FOREWORD

This book was written to demonstrate that the earliest sources, above all Gildas, provide sufficient evidence for a valid narrative history of post-Roman Britain. However, this book was also written for several different audiences, and there are thus several ways to approach it. A general reader interested in the story of fifth century Britain is best advised to simply read from page one. Readers having some familiarity with the relevant sources and issues will doubtless also wish to delve into the footnotes and appendices. Here many of the alternative theories about this era are addressed in detail.

Finally, those few (mostly scholars) with an interest in the arcane issue of Late Roman and British timekeeping would be best advised to begin with the epilogue and appendices. Although often tedious, these form the intellectual basis for the book's hypothesis, and best illustrate the author's assertion that *all* of the earliest sources ultimately derive from the same series of fifth century events.

INTRODUCTION

The thesis of this book is simple. Not only did a British ruler called Arthur exist—he was one of the most powerful rulers in mid-fifth-century Western Europe. Indeed, his reign was a crucial time in British history, marking a violent transition from Late Roman times to the early medieval era. Most significant, however, is the fact that the evidence for this has been in our most reliable sources all along, but unrecognized by observers for the last 1500 years.

This is *not*, of course, what most previous studies say about Arthur. Those who contend that Arthur existed usually place him in later times, depicting him as a very minor figure who by some bardic alchemy became the 'Once and Future King'. Contemporary scholars, on the other hand, tend to ignore him altogether, claiming that even considering the possibility of his existence can only distort 'serious' study of this era. More to the point, they also assert that the earliest documents that mention him are probably the fabrications of later times, or at the very least 'inadmissible' in any serious historical research.

The author in no way desires to belittle past efforts by either amateurs or professionals. As will be plain in the following pages, even the most sceptical scholars have provided invaluable insights into this problem—insights without which this book simply could not have been written. But, as the author will also demonstrate, too often quite valuable sources have been dismissed on the basis of fragmentary, anecdotal evidence.

Inconvenient data have been ignored because of supposed 'scribal errors' that are impossible to verify.

The best explanation for the earliest data from this period is much more simple. Not only do we have documentary proof of Arthur's existence, but practically all of the earliest sources speak of him. He was neither a myth nor an obscure warlord. *Every* early source—Gildas, the *Anglo-Saxon Chronicle*, Bede, the *Historia Brittonum*—places him at the very centre of events in the fifth century. Indeed, the author would argue that the reason that so little is known about fifth-century Britain is because scholars have failed to notice the underlying connections between the extant sources. On a superficial level each seems to tell a different story: a story that appears to contradict all the rest. But if we take a careful look at these sources *together*, we begin to see astonishing similarities between citations. Passages that seem to be talking about entirely different things are suddenly found to be recounting the same events. For the first time in 1500 years we begin to see what really occurred in fifth-century Britain.

Yet this confusion is in no way due to any deficiency on the part of modern observers. The records appear contradictory for a very good reason. The 'Once and Future King' was a controversial figure. He brought prosperity and peace to a stricken island. He launched powerful naval expeditions against Britain's enemies. But the end of his reign saw a catastrophe so complete that many Britons forgot his achievements and remembered only his failures. Others who continued to honour him as the great British war leader glossed over the events that led to Roman Britain's collapse. In the end the two views could never be reconciled.

The reason that Arthur failed is not, however, due to some arcane situation peculiar to the fifth century. Instead, it stems from a challenge that we face in the twenty-first. This was the time of the *Völkerwanderung*, the 'Wandering of the Nations'.

In the fifth century the Roman Empire was required to adapt to an unprecedented influx of barbarians. Some came as peaceful immigrants, some as marauding invaders. Rome's attempts to meet this challenge ended in the empire's demise. But in Britain the encounter ended not only in violence and hatred, but in a separation between Britons and barbarians that was more complete than in any other part of Western Europe. To see Arthur therefore as simply a British champion against Saxon invaders is to diminish him greatly. He fought Saxons, yes. But he also *used* Saxons—and many other peoples—to achieve his design. And if that design had succeeded, our world would be a far different place.

But in the end he failed. The battle of Camlann destroyed both his kingdom and most of what had been preserved from Roman times. The little that did survive served only to confuse the issue; to make scholars, quite understandably, see this whole era as little more than myth. But now the sources are beginning to speak with one voice, and the story they recount is far grander and more tragic than anything found in Malory or Tennyson.

1.

'CONFLICT WITH THEIR CRUEL ENEMIES'

THANET

On a cold autumn morning in the year 469 two armies made ready for battle. As the sun rose above the alders to the east, rank after rank of men gathered beneath brightly coloured banners. Some fingered the edges of well-forged swords. Others fitted arrows to bowstrings. Still others made one last test of linden-wood shields. Both sides knew that the time for talk had long passed. Only blood could settle this dispute. But both sides could still agree on one thing: this would be the final battle, the encounter that would decide the fate of the island of Britain.

An expanse of several hundred yards separated these two armies. On past battlefields such a distance would have been a minor hindrance, something that a spirited charge could cover in a matter of moments. But what lay before these soldiers of Late Antiquity was no well-ploughed field, no grassy pasture. This ground was different. It was a ford: a ford over a shallow salt sea of reeds. Whichever army made the first move would wade through treacherous waters that reached to knees and waists. With each step the attackers would sink into bottom mud, while all the time exposed to a rain of missiles. Even the most seasoned campaigners looked down in apprehension, cursing the dark waters they would soon traverse.

One man, and one man only, had brought these two armies together. A few months before, soldiers on both sides would have followed him without question; would have laid down their lives for him. He had been the *Dux Bellorum*, the battle leader who had united the island of Britain as never before. But now warriors in one army saw this man as nothing less than a traitor. He had beggared the men of Britain with his taxes and foreign wars. He had allowed pagans into this Christian island, permitted them to thrive and multiply. He and his barbarian henchmen must be destroyed, or Britain would die.

Men on the other side took a rather different view. To them this man was still the *Dux Bellorum*. He was the leader who had turned former enemies into faithful allies. He had constructed one of the strongest states in western Europe. In battle after battle, in crisis after crisis, he—and only he—had found a way to snatch success from even the most hopeless situation. Now, with their backs to the wall, his followers hoped this man might achieve one last miracle.

The sun was now well above the trees. It bathed the soldiers to the west of the channel in a dazzling light. Swords and helmets gleamed. A young man on horseback appeared. To rapturous cheers he dismounted, donned a gilded helmet with cheek-pieces and a nose-guard. He took his place in the line of armoured spearmen. A chill breeze swept across the marsh, rippling the dragon banners above his head. The young man raised his hand, then let it fall. Trumpets sounded. Cheers grew louder. Then his entire army stepped off, splashing its way forward through the shallow, sun-flecked waters…

The goal of this young man and his army was a place called Thanet. In the year 469 it was an island at the very eastern tip of Kent, separated from the rest of the British mainland by a salt-water channel known as the Wantsum. Thanet itself was an unprepossessing place. Flat and windswept, it was a country bordered by brackish marshes. Sources from this period speak of tidal streams, of fords across mudflats. Later writers would call it the Isle of the Dead. But Thanet also lay near the mouth of the Thames, and the outflow from that great river was slowly silting up the Wantsum. Eventually the channel would run dry. Thanet would become part of mainland Kent. The island would quite vanish away, as ephemeral as the mythical Isle of Avalon.

But Thanet was no myth. It was a place of real strategic importance. To the north lay the mouth of the Thames: the gateway to the city of London and the heart of Lowland Britain. To the south lay the Gallican Straits (the modern Straits of Dover), one of the most vital sea-lanes in western Europe. In the third century the Romans had raised a fortress called *Rutupiae* near here—the modern Richborough. It was a powerful maritime citadel that had guarded the eastern approaches to Roman Britain for more than a century. And even after the Romans abandoned Richborough, Thanet was to remain the linchpin of a sophisticated naval strategy devised to defend Britain from barbarian attack. For two decades Thanet had brought security to Britain. But now, at this stream and on this island, the destiny of what remained of Roman Britain was to be decided.

For it was here that the man called Arthur won his last and most devastating victory—a victory that destroyed his world.

DIOCESE

The period in which Arthur flourished corresponds with a much larger event, an event that is often called the Fall of the Roman Empire. At the beginning of the fifth century a unified imperial government ruled over most of western Europe. At its close this same area had disintegrated into a collection of warring states, none of which could really be called Roman. This process was no less wrenching for Britain. During what is sometimes called the post-Roman period, an imperial diocese that was heir to the Classical tradition was somehow transformed into a dozen petty Germanic and Celtic kingdoms. Britain had taken on many of the traits of a modern 'failed state'. This was a change even more profound than that brought on by either the Roman or the Norman Conquest. But in order to understand why this transformation occurred, and why Arthur was so crucial to it, it is necessary to understand fifth-century Britain's place in the Roman world.

At the beginning of the fifth century Britain was an integral part of the Roman Empire. A British *decurio*, one of the local officials of a Roman town, was indistinguishable from his counter-part in any other province of the empire. He would take his seat in the same *ordo*, or council, as a *decurio* in Egypt. He would argue the finer points of public administration in the same Latin as a lawyer in Carthage. He would go to church and pray to the same God as a Christian in Syria. And, if caught in some bit of malfeasance, he would be tried under the same legal system as a fellow malefactor in Gaul. Across the empire all educated men read the same books, enjoyed the same paintings, and practised the same arts of public speaking. Even bathing had been elevated into an art form shared by all Romans of any status. Although no longer a political whole—the empire was now split into eastern and western halves—the territories that made up the Roman world were unified in a way that would not be seen in Europe for another fifteen centuries.[1]

The Latin name for Britain, *Britanniae*, is also significant. It is a plural noun, meaning 'the Britains', reflecting the fact that it was a Roman diocese made up of four separate provinces. The ruler of this diocese, the *vicarius*, sat in London and was subordinate to a higher official in Gaul, the Praetorian Prefect. With regard to taxation, administration and military affairs, 'the Britains' were no different from any of the provinces in Greece, Egypt or North Africa.[2]

In one crucial sense, however, this diocese *was* different. Alone of all the major imperial possessions, Britain was an island, set in the midst of the great World Ocean that Romans believed encircled the four continents. Gaul, Spain and Germany might find ships useful for trade and communication, but for Romano-Britons this 'wooden bridge' across Ocean was indispensable. With it, they might trade their bountiful harvests for the consumer goods produced by the rest of the Roman world. Without it, their links with the empire were severed. They literally ceased to be a part of civilization.

For the first three centuries of Roman rule Britain prospered. Goods from as far away as Antioch and Constantinople poured into the island. Local landowners built magnificent villas, leading lives not dissimilar to those described in Fielding and Austen. *Romanitas*—the Roman way of doing things—was unchallenged south of Hadrian's Wall.

But in the third century a new threat appeared. Maritime barbarians—Saxons, Picts and 'Scots'—captured ships on the high seas. They raided coastal villages, stealing away the young and fit to be slaves. The Romans responded by building a series of massive fortifications on Britain's eastern and southern coasts. A sleepless watch was maintained over the surrounding waters—to include that most critical passage, the mouth of the Thames. Britain became a fortress under siege.

In a sense, though, Rome itself was under siege. *Romanitas*, that complex of ideas and beliefs that underpinned this mighty empire, was disappearing. Or rather, it was being converted into something unrecognizable to the early Caesars. In the past 'barbarians' (i.e. those who stood outside Roman culture) had been eager to enter the empire. In the first centuries of the Christian era they could only be impressed by it. The great buildings of marble, the numberless soldiers encased in iron, the cunningly wrought artworks so akin to life itself—all testified that the Roman way was the best way, the *only* way. The new immigrants had adopted Roman names, had learned Roman speech; in short, had adopted every aspect of *Romanitas*. The empire became a vast machine, transforming foreign peoples and foreign ideas into something that could be used for the greater good of Rome. It could take the sons of Germanic warriors and turn them into generals as loyal to the emperor as any Italian or Gaul. It could take a foreign religion, Christianity, and make it the core of a revitalized imperial ideology.

But by the fifth century *Romanitas* had become a different proposition. The grand public buildings and great literary monuments were things of the past. Barbarians were entering the empire in ever-larger numbers, often with arms in their hands. They were finding less and less that awed them, and more and more that aroused their greed. The empire, beset on every side, was forced to build fortresses to command the rivers and seas. It deployed vast mobile armies, increasingly made up of expensive cavalry, to counter the multiple threats to Rome's long, winding borders. The empire had to come to terms with a world where the imperial way did not always prevail. Grand monuments and grand ideas were things of the past. Now *Romanitas* was only another word for survival.

For Britain this was particularly ominous. Civil wars between rival Roman generals on the continent often made travel by land a very dangerous proposition. Overland trade fell off dramatically. This in turn depressed the Roman economy, shrinking the imperial tax base. But of even greater significance for Britain, barbarian piracy was cutting into maritime trade. By the dawn of the fifth century the consumer goods that had once flowed across the Gallican Straits had dried to a trickle. Of no less significance, the number of ships engaged in this trade declined as well. By the year 406 the 'wooden bridge' that had linked the diocese with the rest of the Roman world had become a rickety structure indeed.[3]

1. 'Conflict With Their Cruel Enemies'

GRANDEES

Two sorts of men ruled this island. The first were officials sent out from Rome, colonial administrators whose power and wealth lay in estates far away. Their interest in the diocese extended only to whether or not they could satisfy the expectations of the emperor in Rome. Such men ran the government from London. Their main concern was how much tax the island could yield and how much of this tax was required to defend Britain from her unfriendly neighbours.

Below these men from far off were other, more local leaders. They were landowners for the most part, the Romano-British elite. From them came the *decuriones*, the officials who sat on the *ordines*, the local governing councils. It was they who appropriated the money to build and maintain the fine town halls (*basilicae*) and the defensive walls with which every major city had been ringed since the third century. Many of these landowners had taken up large-scale farming and stock breeding, selling their produce to an army that required vast amounts of grain and meat. As the army became the central focus of Roman life, a few of these locals had grown quite wealthy. By the middle of the fourth century, villas of unprecedented opulence had appeared, particularly in those areas of Lowland Britain that now correspond to Somerset and Gloucestershire.[4]

Life was not all roses for the *decuriones*, however. They were responsible for the prompt payment of taxes. If there was any shortfall, the difference came out of their own pockets. Further, by this time most men were legally required to follow the trade of their fathers, so that even if a *decurio* wanted to resign his lofty position, often he could not do so. There are even reports of *decuriones* attempting to escape their responsibilities by absconding to far-off places and living under assumed names.[5]

That things were beginning to change for Romano-Britons of all classes is found in the archaeology. By the end of the fourth century the construction of impressive Roman monu-

11

ments in stone and brick tails off, or ceases altogether. Even existing public buildings are given over to other, often industrial functions. Most strange, the villas erected with such cost and effort begin to fall into ruin.[6]

Economic factors certainly had something to do with this. By the fifth century the economy of the empire was very much a shrinking pie. Taxes were eating further and further into the income of every citizen; the cost of maintaining the army had become a crushing burden for all but the very highest nobility— who, ironically, were often exempt from taxation.[7] Further, a barbarian invasion in 367 and a British general's rebellion in 383 had done much to undermine the island's social stability. But these factors alone cannot explain what we see in Britain. This was not merely a society being impoverished. It was a society facing a serious and growing threat.

And that threat came from the sea.

2.

'CAVALRY BY LAND AND MARINERS BY SEA'

RAID

4 00. Autumn. Southeastern Britain. It was well past midnight. The current of the British river was strong, and the barbarians were tired. They had been rowing for more than an hour. But now they could see it: on the dark shore to their left they could just make out the great *Weala* house, larger than anything in their home country. The fisherman they had captured had told the truth. By the time he died he had been far too frightened to lie.

The barbarians beached their craft, then waded ashore. They surrounded the house, guarding all exits. Most had been on such raids before, and each man knew his place. An hour passed. In the east the sky began to redden. Their leader looked up, drew his sword, then gave an unearthly yell. Two men sprinted forward, shattering the strong oaken doors with axes. The rest poured in after them. Moving from room to room they roused the groggy *Weala* from their beds. Soon a dozen people stood shivering in the largest room of the house. Two of the marauders brought in a white-haired old man, a gatekeeper. A third intruder, a red-haired man with a wide grin, calmly slit the ancient's throat. As the old gatekeeper shuddered, then collapsed into a pool of his own blood, a stout woman of about forty grew hysterical. Flickering torches showed fear on every *Weala* face. But the raiders were well pleased. The sight of blood always weakened the will to resist.

Now the barbarians began to comb the house in earnest, emptying chests and jars, searching for valuables. Others lined up the captives outside. In the gray light of morning the barbarian leader, a man of fifty with bright blue eyes, chose a likely looking girl of fourteen, then a tall young man of sixteen. As the girl was led away the stout woman began to shriek. The red-haired man laughed, then struck her so hard that she fell to the ground.

The leader now strode up to a balding man in his forties. The raiders had not found the silver trays and golden coins that all wealthy *Weala* owned. In broken Latin the leader asked where these riches might be. The red-haired barbarian kicked the stout woman as she lay sprawled on the ground, to emphasize the point. The leader's bright blue eyes widened as he threatened to kill them all if the loot was not produced.

The balding man stammered so much that his words were incoherent. But with an unsteady gait he led the marauders out into the garden. At the foot of a pear tree he pointed downward. Like hungry dogs digging at a rabbit hole, the barbarians grubbed at the dark soil with what tools they could find. But even after the pit was waist deep nothing turned up. The leader snarled at the balding *Weala* and struck him—hard. If he were playing for time it would go ill with him.

The sun was now well above the trees. A short young man with a scraggly beard ran up, breathless. He reported that the *Weala* on the other side of the river had seen their ship. This brought a frown to the barbarian leader's face. He had not expected this so soon. But the next moment the ginger-haired warrior arrived—and his news was far more disturbing. Horsemen were coming, at least a score of them. The leader ground his teeth, looked away. They might just be locals. But they might be something far worse. In a few seconds he made up his mind. With one smooth motion he slashed the throat of the balding *Weala*. Noiselessly the man fell to the ground, quivering for a few moments in the shade of the pear tree. In the next instant the raiders were moving. Taking whatever they could carry, they raced to the ship. The vessel slid from the shingle bank with a minimum of effort. Rough hands shoved the two young *Weala* on board. A moment later the oarsmen were rowing with all their strength.

In the full light of day they passed fields dotted with peasants. The farmers looked up, gazing curiously until the vessel disappeared from view. But the barbarian leader kept his bright blue eyes fixed firmly ahead, following every bend in the twisting channel. Gradually the waters grew wider. Ahead he could see a broad estuary. Beyond it was a deep blue, as pleasing as a clear summer sky back in his homeland. It was Ocean, the place where his ship would find safety.

The men pulled hard as they reached the open sea. But now the barbarian leader heard a cry from behind him. He turned. A young man pointed off to the north. The leader's eyes were old and what he saw was little more than a blur on the blue-grey horizon of Ocean. But all the same, he knew what they were: *picati*, Roman warships.

The barbarian leader gave a curse in his own tongue. The sun was still high in the sky. His men were tired, while the *Weala* were fresh. The barbarians would have many hours of hard rowing before the night would hide them. Fleetingly, he also wondered if the sacrifice he had made to his gods had been enough.

He gazed back at the two *Weala*. The boy was healthy. He would make a good slave, perhaps a swineherd. The girl was fair, and under other circumstances the old barbarian would have made her his own. But this raid had not been a success. Besides these two, the only other booty was a pile of *Weala* clothes and a handful of trinkets. The leader had come to a harsh but firm conclusion: the days of single-ship raids were over. The danger was too great. The *Weala* Caesar had many riders and many ships. The next time the barbarian came he would bring others—many others...

ARMY

An attack by barbarian sea marauders is not the first thing that springs to mind when we think of Arthur. The most authentic sources we have testify that he fought all his battles on land. But for Britons in the fifth century, these raids were *the* great threat—a threat as deadly as the one terrorism poses for us today. *Every* British witness speaks of them. It is thus no coincidence that seven of Arthur's battles took place on rivers accessible from the sea. Nor is it by chance that two others, Chester and Bath, were fought in areas long ravaged by pirates. Even Arthur's death near an island called Avalon speaks to a naval dimension in his battles. Indeed, it is this dynamic between land and sea, Ocean and Island, that is the crucial factor in understanding fifth-century Britain. Put simply, Arthur used his victories on land to halt the threat from the sea.

But the victor in these battles did not just appear out of nowhere. Arthur was very much a man of his time. We find military leaders like him all over the fifth-century Roman world. By this period war had become the empire's main business. The military writer Vegetius expressed it best when he asked: 'Who can doubt that the art of war comes before everything else, when it preserves our liberty... extends the provinces and saves the Empire?'[1]

Arthur lived at a time when Britain was no longer part of the Roman Empire. But Vegetius' words still hold true. Arthur's great achievement was to adapt Rome's military *and* naval doctrine to a post-Roman world. If we can understand how imperial forces fought and won their wars, we can understand how Arthur was able to save his world from the sea barbarians.

CAVALRY

War as practised by Late Roman armies was a very different thing from what we see portrayed in movies and television documentaries. By the fifth century battles of annihilation like Cannae and Alesia were things of the past. The empire was on the defensive, threatened on every side by barbarians. The best that Rome could do was to hold on to what she had. But this required a whole new strategy. Instead of defeating invaders on her frontiers, Rome now sought to lure them deep into the imperial hinterland. Here the invaders were to be defeated by a new kind of Roman force, the *comitatenses*, or mobile field armies. Where once legions of heavily armoured foot soldiers had advanced relentlessly in rank after orderly rank, the new field armies practised a much more flexible kind of warfare. Instead of the savage head-on battles of Julius Caesar's day, fifth-century Roman commanders carefully husbanded their forces, fighting only at times and places of their own choosing. It was a strategy of the indirect approach, and it had transformed the once-despised cavalry into the premier branch of the Late Roman Army. With smaller but more mobile forces, Rome could defeat whole armies of invaders. Examining just how this was done in the early fifth century can give us crucial insights into how Arthur was to do the same thing many decades later.

For any barbarian army that violated the imperial frontier the first day would have been the most exhilarating. They had expected a fierce battle with the greatest military power on earth. But the *limitanei*, the Roman border troops, had made no effort to dispute their passage. Instead, the *Weala* soldiers had simply withdrawn inside their fort—and watched as the invaders marched past. The barbarians were both astonished and delighted. It was plain the *Weala* were cowards. They had given up without a fight. The empire's riches were theirs for the taking.

The barbarians made good time as they marched down the fine Roman roads. Each day they passed broad fields, far larger than the tiny plots tilled in their dark northern forests. They passed stately villas, far grander than even royal residences in free Germany. But they also found nothing that resembled riches. The fields and villas were bare of all sustenance—and bare of all *Weala*. Where the Romans had gone was not hard to guess. Every town the barbarians passed was ringed with high walls. They knew that the *Weala* and their riches lay inside those walls. But they also knew that they had no means of breaching such strong defences. Frustrated, they marched further south, the summer sun growing hotter with each passing day.

Soon the invaders encountered the first elements of the *Weala* field army. For now, these were only small detachments of riders—horse archers and other light cavalry. These Romans proved no more willing to fight than the *limitanei* had been. But the horsemen also took an uncanny interest in where the intruders went. They shadowed the barbarians from every hilltop, never letting them out of their sight. One day a foraging party left the great horde and did not return. It was found hours later, arrows protruding from every corpse. A sense of unease spread through the ranks.

As days turned into weeks, something else began to spread: hunger. Disgruntled men left the main force in ever-larger numbers, searching over the bare landscape for food. Many did not return. Ordinary warriors grumbled about their leaders. Leaders complained of their followers. Famished, exhausted men lay down each night to a sleep that brought no rest.

Then, on the morning of a particularly fine day, the barbarians caught the glint of something in the distance. It was a column of *Weala* infantry, moving at a quick march—moving towards them. Men rose from their slumber, dazed. There was no time to call in foraging parties. There was barely time to form ranks. Within a very short time the Romans had spread out into a long, disciplined line of battle. The invaders braced themselves for the attack.

But the attack never came. The *Weala* simply stood there, silent. Warriors breathed easier. Leaders regained their courage. These new foes might have iron helmets and breastplates, but the *Weala* were still outnumbered by many thousands. Men clashed swords against shields, daring the Romans to attack. The bravest boasted of how they would shed much *Weala* blood this day.

It was only then that warriors in the rear ranks began to shout out a warning. Clouds of dust were rising above the trees off to their flanks. Soon there was the glint of armour—and, every so often, strange, bright banners in the shape of dragons. This was followed by the sound of horse hoofs: many horse hoofs. The *Weala* heavy cavalry had arrived. But they were coming from a direction that no one had anticipated. Barbarian leaders cursed; called out desperate, contradictory orders. Men jostled one another as they tried to re-form ranks to face the new threat. But it was far too late. An avalanche of armoured riders was already bearing down on the rearmost warriors...

Using infantry to fix an enemy army and then employing heavy cavalry to destroy it is an obvious enough tactic. But what may be much less obvious is why Rome chose to lure her foes so deep inside imperial territory in the first place. Why would she expose her richest provinces to barbarian depredations? This was no accident. On the contrary, it was the linchpin of Rome's strategy.

And it all had to do with walls.

Since the third century every major Roman town had been ringed with strong fortifications. But these were intended not simply to keep the barbarians out, but to keep everything else of value *in*. The local *decuriones* ensured that enough supplies for a long siege were always on hand.[2] Then, when trouble arose, they ordered anything that might feed the intruders to be put to the torch. In this way the barbarians soon faced a cruel dilemma. Possessing neither a baggage train nor a siege train, they could neither feed themselves nor get at the food stored in the towns. Very quickly most invading armies broke up into foraging parties, scouring the countryside for food.

Now the imperial forces played their best card. These same fortified towns not only denied food to the enemy; they acted as supply bases for the Romans. The imperial field armies could remain concentrated at all times, ready at the first sign of barbarian weakness to deliver a knockout blow. Vegetius gives the essence of this doctrine in a single line: 'By this strategy the enemy, if they collect together suffer famine, and if they disperse, are readily beaten by frequent surprise attacks.'[3] As we shall see, the sieges reported during Arthur's time are not evidence of desperate Romano-British civilians cowering behind high walls. Rather, they testify that much of Rome's defensive doctrine remained alive and well in Britain.

On paper, and in many of the early encounters, this system worked beautifully. Time and again we read of barbarian armies stymied by walls and eventually either annihilated or forced to make peace on Roman terms. Like certain twenty-first-century American military reformers, Late Roman leaders were gambling that smaller, highly mobile units could do the same job as larger armies of the past—and at less expense. In an empire whose tax base was diminishing with every year, it was an attractive proposition.

But it is important to remember that this revenue crunch was affecting not just imperial military doctrine, but recruiting policies as well. By the fifth century the Roman economy was dangerously distorted. The bulk of government revenues went to finance the army. But this was an army that depended above all on its elite cavalry arm. It required not just raw recruits, but masses of skilled archers and crack riders. It made little sense to spend years training up Gallic and British peasants in these skills—not when a pool of ready-made recruits lay just across the frontier.

And this brings us to a very special group of barbarians.

ALANS

Just how Rome solved her cavalry recruitment problems actually sheds light on some important aspects of the Arthurian legend. The story begins late in the fourth century. It concerns a foolish young ruler—and some of the most potent symbols in world literature.

In the year 377 a new emperor ascended the western throne, a young man called Gratian. The new Caesar appears to have had a taste for the exotic—and in 377 nothing seemed quite so exotic as the Alans. They were a group of barbarians who were beginning to enter the empire in large numbers. They spoke a language that was akin to modern Iranian. Their original home had been on the steppes of what is now Ukraine. But circumstances had forced them to migrate westward. Mounted on sleek blooded horses and clothed in gaudy shirts of tooled buckskin, they were expert bowmen—precisely the sort of warriors that the Late Roman army required. Very soon, large numbers of them were being hired to staff the imperial cavalry.

But to the newly crowned Gratian these nomads were much more than just soldiers. Their 'wild west' esprit intrigued him. Their hunting skills captivated him. He recruited the best of them into his own personal guard. But this was only the beginning. Very soon Gratian himself was sporting the tall cap and double-curved bow of his bodyguards. More ominously, the new emperor began to spend less time looking after imperial affairs and more time occupying himself with the thrills of the chase.

For several years all went well. Using his newly acquired skills in archery and horsemanship, Gratian shot hecatombs of game in the forests of Gaul. But just across Ocean, in Britain, a talented general by the name of Maximus was carefully observing the young emperor's every move. The crafty officer knew that the rest of the army took a different view of Gratian's Alans. Most infantry units were composed of Germanic recruits, men who with each passing day were growing more jealous of Gratian's equestrian pets.[4] In 383 Maximus saw his opportunity. Rallying his own units in Britain, he crossed the Channel and proclaimed himself emperor. When the German foot soldiers in Gaul learned of the coup, they deserted *en masse* to Maximus. Desperate, Gratian fled westward towards Rome. But long before he reached Italy he was assassinated by one of his own generals. Maximus seized all imperial possessions north of the Alps. For a time it even seemed that the eastern emperor, Theodosius the Great, might recognize the usurper as his co-ruler.[5]

The Alans however, were destined to have their revenge— and it was Theodosius who would give them the opportunity.

The eastern Caesar knew how to seize the moment even better than Maximus. Theodosius bided his time for five years. Then, in 388, he made his move. Marching his forces westward, he encountered Maximus' army dug in behind a seemingly un-fordable barrier on the present River Save. For a time the Alans bore the taunts of the German and British insurgents without complaint. But then Theodosius devised a clever stratagem. He ordered a commando of Alanic and Hunnish riders to swim the flood, surprising and outflanking the rebel defences. Caught in a storm of arrows, Maximus' force disintegrated.[6] The soldiers from Britain who had sought empire became a hunted rabble. Maximus, like Gratian before him, turned fugitive. Pursued to Italy, the British usurper was captured and executed. The empire was once more united.

Every province welcomed the end of civil war. But Theodosius' victory may also have had some important consequences for Britain in particular. Defeated Roman mutineers were often transported far from their home bases as punishment. If this happened in Britain after 388, it is logical that significant numbers of Alans would have been deployed to the island as replacements. The steppe warriors had, after all, proved their worth and loyalty on the battlefield. Indeed, there is evidence that this is precisely what happened.

We have seen how the everyday dress and behaviour of the Alans intrigued the unfortunate emperor Gratian. But other aspects of their culture also appear to have found their way into Arthurian legend. To take but one example, the Alans had traditionally worshipped a naked sword plunged point-first into a mound.[7] This was considered to be a powerful symbol of their war god. Indeed, the king of another steppe people, Attila the Hun, would claim that his own sword—*found on a mountaintop*—was the 'sword of the war god'.[8] It was one of his main claims to kingship. Later generations would transform this idea of a royal sword buried in the earth into that most potent of literary motifs, Arthur's Sword in the Stone.

The Alans influenced other aspects of Roman military culture, too. Their battle standard from time immemorial had been a kind of windsock painted to resemble a dragon. As the Roman army came to rely more and more on steppe riders such standards became the norm for imperial troops, with a gilded dragon's head added to the windsock design to make it more realistic and threatening.[9] Not coincidentally, in legend Arthur's standard is described as a golden dragon. Moreover, his putative father is called Uther Pendragon ('Supreme Dragon'). Indeed, the medieval Welsh word *dragon* signifies, quite simply, 'military commander'.[10]

Another everyday item used by the Alans' Roman commanders may be even more surprising. The Gallo-Roman aristocrat Sidonius Apollinaris describes the table at which he dined with the emperor Majorian as an *orbis*, or circle.[11] The *Vergilius Romanus*, a fifth-century work which many believe may have been produced in Britain, actually gives a picture of this Late Roman *orbis*. On folio 100v of this work we find an illustration of Dido and Aeneas feasting from a *circular* table. It is this commonplace Roman item that is the most likely explanation for the literary artifact we know as the Round Table.[12]

All of this strongly suggests that much of the later legend of King Arthur comes from the Late Roman period. First the story was filtered through a Celtic lens, exemplified by such works as the Welsh *Triads* and the *Mabinogion*. Then it was filtered through a medieval lens, via such writers as Geoffrey of Monmouth and Chrétien de Troyes. But the bedrock of this legend is the very real account of the rise and fall of a Late Roman general.

MARINERS

We have seen how Rome's new doctrine was changing the face of the empire as a whole. But in a diocese surrounded by Ocean, Rome's mobile strategy was modified to a maritime environment. As elsewhere in the empire, Britain possessed its own field army, and strong defensive walls circled its major cities. But the island also had another layer of protection. This was a very sophisticated system of defence called the *Litus Saxonicum*—the Saxon Shore. Today, the remains of this system are visible in the massive walls of such seaside citadels as Portchester, Pevensey (or *Anderida*) and Richborough (or *Rutupiae*). In Roman times a chain of these fortresses guarded the southern and eastern coasts of Britain (Map 1).

But Richborough and its companion forts would have been little more than a Roman Maginot Line if they had been meant to guard only their own small portion of Britain's immense coastline. Rome had other assets to combat the sea barbarians.

The first of these was the field army stationed in Britain. Made up of the same highly mobile infantry and cavalry units found elsewhere, it acted as a quick-reaction force to counter incursions by sea. Even if it could not catch the marauders on land, its very existence sharply limited the time barbarians could loiter on shore. As we shall see, Arthur would turn back the sea barbarians' greatest challenge with a British version of a Roman field army.

The other major component in Britain's sea defences was her fleet of *picati*. These were small ships propelled by a single bank of oars. They were built expressly to catch the raiders at sea. Both their hulls and their crews' uniforms were painted a bluish grey—designed to achieve the same effect as the 'battleship grey' camouflage of modern warships. Again, it is Vegetius who offers the best insight into how Rome used these warships:

> Just as in land warfare, descents are made upon sailors who are unsuspecting, and ambushes are laid about suitable narrows between islands. This is done with the idea of destroying them more easily, being unprepared. If the enemy sailors are weary from lengthy rowing; if pressed by head-winds; if the tide is flowing against the ships' 'beaks'; if the enemy are asleep, suspecting nothing; if the anchorage that they hold has no other exit; if a desired opportunity for battle occurs, one should take Fortune's favour in one's hands and give battle...'[13]

The operative word here is 'just as in land warfare'. On both land and sea, Rome's strategy was now to avoid costly head-on encounters, and instead to use surprise and key terrain to the maximum extent possible. But on Ocean key terrain was at places like the Gallican Straits, and on the other side of this narrow body of water was a kind of mirror image of the Saxon Shore. Here the Romans had established a similar chain of naval fortifications that stretched along the western coast of Gaul, whose *picati* cooperated closely with those in Britain to control the Straits. Richborough in particular had an analogous Gallic maritime stronghold just across the narrows near the modern Boulogne. Indeed, the best description of these seaside fortresses is quite simply 'naval bases'. Impregnable to barbarian assault, they provided the naval stores and foodstuffs to enable the Romans to operate their *picati* in all seasons.[14] We will see how Arthur established post-Roman 'naval bases' to achieve this same end.

It was at just such strategic 'choke points' that the *picati* could carry out their naval ambushes. The Roman galleys, swift and nearly invisible because of their blue camouflage, could often pounce before their foes were even aware of the danger. In theory, at least, Rome had produced a winning combination that could neutralize the barbarian threat.

That cavalry and ships would work together in this way may seem like mere speculation. But imperial doctrine was now based on the use of highly mobile elements, and in Britain these could only be the cavalry and the *picati*. Remarkably, evidence from the next century suggests that close cooperation between cavalry and warships was a commonplace idea among Britons. The sixth-century British writer Gildas gives a vivid description of how he believed the empire had dealt with Pictish and Irish marauders. The Romans, he writes, 'send forward, like eagles, their unexpected bands of cavalry by land, and mariners by sea, and, placing their terrible swords on the shoulders of their enemies, they mow them down like leaves'.[15] For Gildas, the best way—the *Roman* way—to deal with seaborne invaders is with a combination of cavalry and ships. Significantly, he is writing in a time *after* the floruit of Arthur. Indeed, there is substantial evidence to suggest that one of Arthur's main objectives was to establish a kind of post-Roman version of the Saxon Shore.

There was also an offensive component to Rome's maritime strategy. Indeed, earlier Roman commanders had set a rather high standard. In 368 Theodosius the Elder had defeated a coordinated attack by a number of barbarian peoples that almost overwhelmed Britain. But his repulse of the invaders was only the first stage. Theodosius then launched naval attacks on 'Orcades, Hibernia, and Thule': the Orkneys, Ireland, and Scandinavia.[16] These seem quite audacious expeditions, but the strategic thinking behind them is eminently sound. The barbarians raided primarily for material gain. Taking the fight to the enemy destroyed far more of his wealth than he was likely to obtain from raiding, removing any incentive to attack the empire. It is thus important to remember that this would always be Rome's preferred naval strategy: attack and destroy the enemy's bases. Many decades later, we find a number of Arthur's subordinates doing precisely the same thing.

But the Saxon Shore was far from a perfect defence. Small groups of raiders were easily dealt with. But larger fleets could be a real problem. Records of the time speak of a victory against the Picts and Irish in about 382. But we hear of other such 'victories' against Saxons, Picts and Irish in 398 and again in 400.[17] In 405 the High King of Ireland, Niall of the Nine Hostages, died in a Channel battle with the Romans. This implies the ambush and destruction of a very large Irish fleet at the most strategic of Britain's 'choke points'.[18] But we read of another Saxon incursion only a few years later.[19] This suggests that the struggle with the sea barbarians had become a kind of naval guerrilla war, and, as in many modern guerrilla conflicts, the stronger side was not necessarily guaranteed to win. On land or sea the Romans could beat any barbarian force in a head-on fight. The Channel victory over Niall was proof of that. But imperial forces could not be everywhere, and the pinprick raids continued year after year. By the beginning of the fifth century the Saxon Shore was beginning to show more than a few cracks in its masonry.

Still, even at this late date, Britain's sea defences formed one of the most sophisticated military systems in existence. Success required close cooperation between very different forces on both land and sea—and on two sides of Ocean. Great amounts of cash were needed just to keep the whole system functioning.[20] Essentially this was a machine: a highly complex machine with many different parts. But, as with any machine, failure at any one of a number of critical points could bring the whole mechanism to a standstill.

And in the year 406 this great defensive system came to a sudden and dramatic halt.

3.

'LEFT WITHOUT A SHEPHERD'

FALL

4 06. *New Year's Eve. The Rhine.* The night was cold, and the snow reflected a ghostly light in every direction. A single torch flickered in the gloom, then another. Soon knots of men began to emerge from the treeline. More followed. Within a short time long columns of warriors stretched across the snowy fields, numbered in the thousands. Garbed in thick wraps and weighed down by heavy bundles, few had any idea where they were. Still fewer knew where they were going. It was enough that an occasional rider cantered by, growling out an order to close up, to turn left or right. At any other time the march of this barbarian host would have been barred by a chain of frontier Roman forts—and by the dark waters of the Rhine itself. But this was an unguarded spot. No Roman or allied force patrolled here. More important, what had been a barrier was now a bridge.

The Rhine was frozen.

Behind them rode men in fine woollen garments, cloaks glittering with golden brooches, swilling wine from leather flasks. These were their leaders, the great men who had taken many months to prepare for this night. They had buttonholed Syrian traders about the Roman roads and the Roman forts. They had sworn extravagant oaths to their gods, both old and new.

They had exchanged favourite daughters in marriage—all so that this great army could cross into Gaul.

Hours passed. The day finally broke. Men struggled forward under an ice-blue sky, fighting a wind that cut like Egyptian glass. Few had any idea where the straight Roman roads would take them. Most had no thoughts beyond plunder and adventure. But a handful dreamt of the warmth of a Mediterranean sun; of an easy life in Spain or Africa. Many would end their days there.

Riding among the Vandals was a slight, silent horseman, wrapped in furs. He talked little and smiled less. His name was Geiseric. He was a Vandal of noble birth. Yet men laughed at him behind his back. They laughed because his mother had been a slave. They laughed because he limped whenever he dismounted his horse, his gait as comical as a dwarf's. Now, he was little more than a stripling. But already Geiseric was clever—and ruthless. His pale blue eyes were constantly searching: searching for the weaknesses in both barbarian and Roman. He knew that this was the way a warrior survived. He knew that this was the way a warrior became great. And then no one would ever laugh at him again…

When this army of Vandals, Suevi and Alans crossed the Rhine on New Year's Day of 407, the whole Roman world was thrown into disarray. On past occasions the elite elements of the Roman army—swift-riding Alans and hardy Germans—would have made short work of such a force. But in 407 the cream of Rome's military was elsewhere, fighting off two other barbarian armies that threatened Italy itself. One group of invaders was quickly defeated by Stilicho, a talented Roman marshal, himself of Vandal stock. But the other barbarian force, a disciplined army of Germanic Visigoths, was not so easy to deal with. The Goths had fought as Roman allies before, and Stilicho had hopes that they might do so again. So he put off a final showdown, fearing that a head-on battle would fatally weaken both his own army and these potential allies. Like any Late Roman commander, Stilicho believed that the best way to halt the latest barbarian incursion across the Rhine was with other barbarians. *Divide et impera.*[1]

Most Romans did not see it that way at all. The Goths were barbarians. They were ravaging Italy itself, looting villas, freeing slaves. Worst of all, they were Arian Christians. This meant they believed that Christ was not made of the same (Greek *homo*) substance as His Father, but only made of a similar (Greek *homoi*) substance. Humorists might jest that there was only an *iota*'s difference between the two positions, but it would be a crucial factor in the next eighty years. The burning and pillaging might one day be forgotten. But neither side could ever give up its own narrow view of Christianity.

Each time Stilicho tried to reason with the Goths, he merely ended by exasperating the Romans. Many came to suspect that he secretly sympathized with his fellow Germans. In the end the marshal was assassinated. But this only made things worse. Without any coherent leadership the Romans fell back and hid behind their defences at Rome. The Goths marched on the capital. After a confused series of political manoeuvres the unthinkable happened.[2]

In 410 Rome fell.

This was not the end of the western empire by any means. But the sack of the greatest city in the known world, the cradle of *Romanitas*, shook the confidence of every imperial citizen. Civilization itself was threatened.[3] In faraway North Africa, Saint Augustine began to contemplate a world in which Rome, 'the City of Man', no longer existed. Instead he foresaw a future in which Christians must look to its Platonic equivalent, 'the City of God'.

But what was the Roman army in Britain doing at this time? Where were they when the Goths broke through the Salarian Gate and into the Eternal City? The answer is simple. Earlier—

in the same year that the great barbarian army had breached the Rhine—they had sailed across the Channel to Gaul, where they proceeded to do battle with the Roman forces stationed there. Instead of destroying Rome's enemies, the two field armies of the Prefecture of Gaul were doing an excellent job of destroying themselves.

MUTINY

His name was Constantine. In the end that was all that mattered. The Roman army in Britain, rebellious and super-stitious at the same time, had chosen him in the year 406 to be their new emperor. Constantine was no officer, only a simple soldier. But he bore the name of Constantine the Great, the most famous Roman ruler within the last hundred years. To both pagan and Christian this was auspicious, a sure sign that this new Constantine, the third of that name, would lead his followers to victory. Coins were struck in his honour. Preparations began for war. Then, in 407, soldiers from the army of Britain sailed to Gaul. Like Maximus before them, they were going to march on Rome.[4]

Just why the Roman army in Britain mutinied in 406 is far from clear. One obvious motive is greed, for the army of a successful usurper could expect to be well rewarded. Another factor is that few Roman soldiers by now felt anything resembling a sense of Roman patriotism. Most were barbarians. Strong loyalties did not extend much beyond officers and comrades. Further, the example of Maximus' near-successful usurpation in 383 can only have encouraged the army in Britain to make a new attempt. The feeling may have been: 'this time we'll do it right'.

It is also important to remember that these soldiers had been conducting sustained combat operations over many years. Cavalry troopers had galloped out on cold, windy nights to repel real or imagined landings. Men assigned to the *picati* had spent days at a time on treacherous seas, scanning the horizon for the barbarian ships that all too often eluded them. If they had grievances, their only real recourse was to march on Rome and force the bureaucrats to give them their fair share.

One of the early ringleaders of the rebellion appears to have been a British civilian, indicating that ordinary Romano-Britons may have shared in the army's resentment. The reason is simple. The cornerstone of Rome's military effectiveness lay in her logistics. As noted above, the main reason Roman forces could win against well-armed and well-led opponents was often because it could keep its troops in the field indefinitely. But there were drawbacks to this strategy. To operate effectively the soldiers required huge reserves of food stored in many strategic places. The field army in particular was a cavalry-heavy force, requiring swarms of grain-fed horses.[5] The drain on British agriculture must have been enormous, and in bad years perhaps unsustainable. Many civilians in Britain, both peasant and *decurio*, would have had perfectly rational reasons to desire a change.

There is, however, one final piece of evidence that may give us an insight into the soldiers' mood at the time. The Saxon Shore fort of Richborough, that fortress at the very eastern tip of Britain, has revealed an archaeological anomaly. Most other British military sites show a sharp decline in the number of coins discovered from the fourth and early fifth centuries. But in the 1930s, digs at Richborough yielded hundreds of low-value bronze coins.[6] Many were from the very end of the Roman period, and for some reason may not even have been issued. This might or might not have been the final straw for the mutiny that followed. But what were the soldiers of Britain to think of a government that paid them in *pennies*?

USURPERS

Once the British insurgents landed in Gaul they did a very curious thing. The usurper Constantine's marshal, or military commander-in-chief, was an officer called Gerontius. As soon as Gerontius disembarked, his first act was to invite some of the barbarians who had lately crossed the Rhine to join him. He even recruited the best of them into Constantine's new imperial guard, called the *Honoriaci*.[7] This is a strange course of action for ostensibly Roman troops to adopt, and it demands some explanation.

We have already seen some of the factors that led to the revolt. But Gerontius and his fellow insurgents may have been motivated by one more hope. Although never explicitly stated, we may suspect that in many of his units a particular kind of barbarian predominated: Alans and Huns in the cavalry, Franks and other Germans in the infantry. These recruits would have spoken at best a very basic form of Latin on duty, and probably their own native language after hours. The corollary to this is that a number of soldiers from Britain may have still had strong ties with the Alans, Suevi, and Vandals who had crossed the Rhine in 406. If so, Constantine and Gerontius would have had good reason to think that at least part of the great barbarian host might rally to their own side. The incident of the *Honoriaci* suggests that these hopes were not unreasonable.

Gaul soon gave in, with little fighting. In 408 Gerontius crossed the Pyrenees and conquered Spain for his master. Then Constantine III embarked on the most crucial phase of his campaign—the march on Rome. The would-be Caesar must have felt confident as he descended into the rich fields of Italy. He held Britain, Spain and Gaul. Only the Roman heartland remained. But what raised Constantine's spirits even more was something only he and a few others knew: a senior general in Rome, one Alanicus, was ready to betray the legitimate emperor Honorius. As the insurgents rode through the gates of Verona this third Constantine was dreaming of a second Milvian Bridge.

Devious Alanicus may have been, but he was not devious enough. His plot was discovered. As Constantine drew near, the emperor Honorius ordered that a ceremonial procession take place in the capital, with Alanicus riding in a place of honour. But the moment the event ended the emperor coolly ordered the conspirator set upon and killed. Alanicus' death was a decisive blow to Constantine's hopes. When word reached Verona of the assassination, the usurper lost heart and retreated across the Alps.[8]

The setback soon caused a rift between Constantine and his general Gerontius. In 409 the latter raised a puppet emperor of his own to the purple. He then moved against his former sovereign. A many-sided civil war was in full cry. Several more astonishing turns of fate occurred—including the proclamation of yet another emperor. But for the men of Britain the end was tawdry. Constantine was executed after capture by imperial troops. The British insurgency melted away, just as it had after Maximus' defeat on the Save River.

Gerontius' fate is more interesting, however, for it may tell us something about the Roman army in Britain. After turning on Constantine, Gerontius allied himself with a group of Roman soldiers from Spain. But a series of setbacks soon convinced the Spaniards that the man from Britain was not their kind of general. They made a surprise attack on his residence one night, when only Gerontius, his wife, and one other companion were present. But whatever the quality of Gerontius' generalship, he was a skilful soldier. Or, more correctly, like any steppe warrior he was a deadly bowman. In a shoot-out that resembled something out of *Butch Cassidy and the Sundance Kid*, he and his loyal companion used their bows to deadly effect. The morning sun revealed literally dozens of dead or mortally wounded Spaniards lying around the refuge. But in the end the pair could not prevent the house from being set alight. Gerontius, his wife, and his compatriot all perished.

And the name of this brave companion? Alanus—'the Alan'.[9]

It is thus very interesting that in Gerontius we find a man who deals intimately with Alans, who fights like an Alan, and who has close relations with two people who almost certainly were Alans themselves (Alanicus and 'the Alan'). Further, it is of interest that when Gerontius and Constantine fell out, the latter sent a general of his, Edovicus, to recruit Franks and Alamanni from beyond the Rhine.[10] This suggests that Edovicus, and perhaps Constantine as well, were infantry soldiers of Germanic origin. Taken together, these facts explain much about the events of 406–12. That the infantry units of the British forces would have been primarily German, while the cavalry units would include many Alans, should not surprise us. This was the usual ethnic make-up of the Late Roman army. That a simple infantry soldier chosen to be emperor would select an Alan to lead his cavalry seems only good politics. Finally, that the insurgents would eventually fall out along ethnic lines also seems plausible.

This is substantial evidence that a large and influential part of the Late Roman army in Britain was made up of Alans and other steppe peoples. They probably formed a significant segment of the field army and would have been present in more static formations stationed on Hadrian's Wall and the Saxon Shore. The ease with which they accepted barbarian recruits suggests that they were not far removed culturally or linguistically from their original ethnic groups. But, like most immigrants, they were also beginning to meld with the larger culture. They would have had a basic command of Latin, and would have begun to intermarry with Celtic speakers in Britain. They had come to look upon themselves as citizens of the empire and, when the tie with Rome was broken, would see themselves as Britons. Whether Arthur himself was an Alan is unknowable. But the 'steppe *élan*' that these immigrants brought to the Late Roman army was something that would survive in the military forces of post-Roman Britain.

For the western empire as a whole, however, the events of 406–12 proved to be a kind of 'perfect storm'. Not only did several barbarian groups overwhelm Rome's mobile defences, but the remaining imperial troops had fought one another instead of the barbarians. Still worse, all of this had taken place deep inside Gaul and Spain. Many of these areas would never be brought back under imperial control, and others remained wasteland for years. The western imperial economy, already in decline, would never completely recover. It was, quite simply, a disaster.

But for Britain the result was even worse. By 413 most of western Europe had fallen into barbarian hands. Goths, Burgundians and Franks ruled in what had been Gaul and Germany, while Alans, Suevi and Vandals held large tracts of Spain. Rome had lost control of nearly all her possessions north of the Alps.[11] Not only was the 'wooden bridge' over Ocean severed, but a vast stretch of barbarian-infested land separated the island diocese from what was left of the western empire. Britain stood alone.

VITALIS

The names of most of the Romano-Britons who lived through these chaotic times have been lost to us. But we do know something about at least one of them. His name was Vitalis. His profession is not certain, but because his son was a soldier, and because by now most sons were legally required to follow the trade of their fathers, it is most likely that Vitalis followed the imperial dragons as well. It is also very possible that he was not of British origin. We know that in addition to his Latin name of Vitalis he was known as Catel Durnluc, which could be a corruption of some barbarian name. But even so, Vitalis almost certainly would have taken a wife from among the local Britons. We know that this union produced at least one son.[12] But whatever his profession or origin, Vitalis was almost certainly an eyewitness to the unrest that eventually made Constantine III master of Britain. If a soldier, he may even have followed Constantine and Gerontius across Ocean to Gaul.

But whatever Vitalis' role in the rebellion, it is unlikely that he ever spoke of these events with anything but extreme reluctance. He knew what the army of Britain had done. It had turned a mutiny into a catastrophe. It had effectively cut Britain's ties with the civilized world. Indeed, when the first account of Britain's post-Roman history was written a century later, no mention would be made of either Constantine III or his fatal adventure.

Vitalis' fate, however, was far from unenviable. In later centuries he would be counted as the founder of a dynasty—the first in a lineage of powerful kings who came to rule over a large part of Wales. But it was this son of his who would be the real founder of the line.[13] As the boy grew to manhood in this new Britain, he would learn how Roman strategy and Roman expertise had once protected the diocese. He would learn the art of war in a very tough school.

And—for one brief moment—he would make Britain the strongest state in western Europe.

4.

'THE PROUD TYRANT'

SOURCES

The Romano-British stage has been set for this drama. But what about its main actor? Who was Arthur, and did he really exist? Most scholars insist that the answer must be no. They argue that the evidence for him is simply too slight. Even those who concede someone named Arthur may have flourished somewhere, sometime in Dark Age Britain see him as a very minor figure. He is great not because of his deeds, but because later bards somehow moulded him into a figure of greatness. More to the point, almost all observers are unanimous in the conclusion that he played no part in the two major events of fifth-century Britain: the decision to invite Saxon mercenaries into the island, and its sequel, the Saxon Revolt. At best, Arthur is seen as somehow slowing the Saxon tide of conquest that followed the Revolt. At worst, he is dismissed as the fantasy of credulous medieval clerics.

That Arthur may not have existed is a possibility that can never be wholly discounted. The sources for this period are fragmentary and contradictory, so much so that one might even make a plausible case that the central event of post-Roman Britain, the Saxon Revolt, never occurred. But the fact that the evidence appears to be so contradictory may be an important clue in itself. It may indicate that a very significant piece of the evidence is missing, a factor of such importance that any explanation that ignores it makes very little sense. In short, scholars *may* be doing the equivalent of trying to write a history of the Napoleonic Wars without Napoleon.[1] To test this hypothesis we must first examine what evidence we do possess.

The most important single source for this period is a work by a British cleric called Gildas. He wrote sometime around 520 or 530 AD, more than a century after Britain's break with Rome. Gildas' account, commonly called the *De Excidio Britanniae* (*DEB*), gives a very sketchy outline of history down to his own day. Once the Romans left, he claims, Britain was beset by Irish and Pictish raiders, raiders who in the end almost conquered the island. The Britons were forced to abandon many of their cities. But then, miraculously, they were able to defeat their foes. For a while there was even 'a time of plenty'. But he goes on to say that a new Picto-Irish threat appeared, worse than any previous danger. To counter it a certain 'Proud Tyrant' recruited Saxon mercenaries to help drive back the invaders. While this may have disposed of the Picts and Irish, the new set of barbarians turned out to be worse than the old. The Saxons revolted, on the pretext of unpaid wages. Turning against their masters, they spread fire and sword throughout the island. After some years of fighting, a Briton called Ambrosius Aurelianus finally fought the Saxons to a standstill and saved part of the country from the invaders.

Gildas is a problematical source for early British history. There is little evidence that he consciously falsifies anything. But it is also important to stress that he is using history for a very specific purpose: to show that the success of the Saxon invaders was due to the sins of the Britons. He subordinates everything to this main theme, giving us very few historical details. Yet the very fact that his work has survived suggests that his is an accurate reflection of how educated sixth-century Britons saw their recent past. It is doubtful that any society would accurately copy and transmit a work of 110 chapters over many centuries if its author were known to be a crank. Still less would they call him 'Gildas the Wise'.

There are also peculiarities in Gildas' account. He seems to think that only Pictish and Irish raiders were threatening Britain before mid-century, when archaeology tells us that Saxons had settled large tracts of the diocese much earlier than this. He thinks that Hadrian's Wall was built in the fifth century. He portrays the Romano-Britons as cowardly and inept, while the Byzantine historian Zosimus—and Gildas himself—testify that British armies could sometimes be highly effective. But these very mistakes may actually help us gain a better understanding of this period. Once we remove Gildas' misconceptions and hyperbole, we find underneath a narrative that gives a coherent, consistent picture of fifth-century Britain—and of the man who dominated it.

Another potentially useful source is a biography of the Gallo-Roman bishop of Auxerre, St Germanus. Written in the late fifth century, it recounts a short visit this cleric made to Britain in 429. Although his biographer's main goal is to recount the good works of a holy man, it is our only source with potential eyewitness information of conditions in Britain during this period.

Still another source comes from the writings of a second Gallo-Roman cleric who lived later in the century: Sidonius Apollinaris. His main concern is not with Britain, but with the fate of his own region in southern Gaul. But at times the two stories overlap and become subordinate to the larger drama of Rome's fall. Indeed, many contend that he wrote a letter to Arthur, a letter which still survives. A fascinating character in his own right, Sidonius also gives important insights into everyday life of the period.

We have as well a number of short references in various chronicles and histories. They are not much. Armies and fleets make sudden appearances and then vanish again forever. Yet they are accounts that give us 'hooks' for a sensible chronology.

Finally, there are two other sources of some length, both of which appear centuries later. One is the *Anglo-Saxon Chronicle* (*ASC*). In earlier times this was treated as primary source material, and its chronology searched assiduously for clues to the conflict between Briton and Saxon. But in the last quarter of a century many scholars have questioned how Saxons who were both pagan and illiterate could preserve anything of historical value.[2]

The second work is the *Historia Brittonum*, traditionally attributed to one 'Nennius'. The *Historia* is in no sense sober history. In places it might better be termed a romance which incorporates some of Gildas' account. It is also very much an exercise in character assassination, condemning one of the most important rulers of this period, a certain Vortigern, who seems to be identical to the Proud Tyrant whom Gildas mentions. The *Historia*'s very elaborate chronology is also contradictory, hiding a number of fundamental errors. But one key section has the first mention of Arthur in any detail. This citation is not a narrative, merely a listing of battles fought by this ruler. But it is crucial to our story; in this author's opinion a careful reading of the *Historia Brittonum* shows precisely when and how the perception of Arthur first went wrong—and why this misunderstanding has lasted down to our own time.

Remarkably, at one time or another the veracity of each of these sources has been called into question. And there is a good reason for this. Taken together, the information gleaned from this material stubbornly refuses to meld into a larger picture. Serious scholars and amateurs alike have come up with highly conflicting treatments using the same basic data. Moreover, implicit in *all* previous studies, from the most sceptical to the most visionary, is a requirement that some or all of the above evidence be false, or be interpreted in very unlikely ways. A cynic might say that observers of this period attempt to make the facts fit the hypothesis, rather than the other way around. In the end most scholars now believe that, while Gildas is a genuine product of the early sixth century, such sources as the *Historia Brittonum* and the *Anglo-Saxon Chronicle* are simply too unreliable to use in any serious examination of fifth-century Britain. Without a 'paper trail'—a transparent line of transmission—a 'rigorous' discipline must automatically reject them.

But it is this very lack of a 'paper trail' that presents another problem. Because of our complete ignorance of how the *ASC* and *Historia Brittonum* were compiled, there is no certainty that the information they contain is false either. Both quote Gildas and other sources quite accurately, and, with regard to most of their other citations, we simply have no better evidence that they came from anything other than genuine fifth-century sources independent of Gildas.[3] 'Rigour' may demand that we reject them. But in doing so we are simply using our complete ignorance of the origin of these sources to reach an analytical conclusion. By doing this we are introducing into our investigation not 'rigour', but something called *bias*. True rigour would require us to make no conclusion either way on their veracity. It also means that any hypothesis that contradicts the *ASC* or the *Historia Brittonum* can never be secure. We rapidly reach a state where we can say nothing about fifth-century Britain with any certainty.

A better alternative might be to consider a methodology employed by other disciplines that actually do make discoveries about observable reality. One thing police forces, intelligence analysts, and reporters do *not* do is employ a single investigator to consider a single piece of evidence in a vacuum, and then use his findings to make sweeping pronouncements about its authenticity. Instead, serious disciplines accept the fact that different pieces of valid evidence may not always be consistent—at least at first glance. Such disciplines employ a method called 'all-source analysis'. They gather all available evidence, prioritize it according to reliability, and then work from the known to the unknown. They use the scientific method to isolate the most likely alternatives. As a noted reporter recently put it, they try to obtain 'the best available version of the truth'.

It is this methodology that the author has used to try and construct an accurate historical framework for this period. By using *all* the sources—written, linguistic, archaeological—and carefully prioritizing them, we can take a source likely to be true, such as Gildas, and use him to evaluate other sources, such as the *Anglo-Saxon Chronicle*. Very soon we find that Gildas actually corroborates much of the *ASC*. Moreover, the latter often gives us a fresh perspective on the more reliable evidence, answering riddles that have puzzled scholars for years. Time and again we find that apparently contradictory accounts are actually different versions of the same event. It is only the different perspectives used in writing each source that conceal the under-lying similarity.

In the end this methodology has produced one particular hypothesis. It is a powerful hypothesis. Instead of using supposed anomalies within sources in order to dismiss them, this hypothesis offers coherent, consistent *explanations* for the provenance of these sources. It is also a very simple hypothesis, and can be stated in a few words. If we accept it, virtually all of the earliest data for fifth-century Britain turns out to be valid. If we reject it, we are condemned to a discipline whose written sources are ever in doubt, but where any conclusion that contra-dicts these same sources can never be secure. As with the Napoleonic Wars, we too may have to accept that a single personality casts his shadow over all the significant events of an era.

TYRANT

If Arthur were an historical figure, we might expect to find his name somewhere in the record. But Gildas, a near-contemporary source, mentions only two British rulers from this period, and neither has a name that remotely resembles the name Arthur. One is someone we have already encountered, the unlucky Proud Tyrant. He is often called Vortigern, although there is no evidence that this was the name he bore during his lifetime. Indeed, as we shall see, the name 'Vortigern' does not even appear in his own regnal list. Lacking a contemporary name for him, we will use the title Gildas gives him: the Proud Tyrant. He ruled over Britain in a time of unprecedented prosperity. He countered the threat from the Picts and Scots by hiring Saxon mercenaries to fight them. But in the end the mercenaries grew arrogant, demanding more than the Proud Tyrant could possibly pay. They revolted, spreading fire and sword across the whole island.[4] An idea that had worked for the Romans in the past—divide and rule—had gone horribly wrong.

At face value this seems to be a story of Britons too cowardly to fight and a foolish ruler who hires treacherous foreigners to protect his demesne. Certainly the later Anglo-Saxon writer Bede read Gildas in this way.[5] But just before Gildas tells us about the Proud Tyrant he says something rather different about the Britons, and it is worth quoting at length.

> Others of them, however, lying hid in mountains, caves, and woods, continually sallied out from thence to renew the war... And then it was, for the first time, that they overthrew their enemies, who had for so many years been living in their country; for their trust was not in man, but in God... the boldness of the enemy was for a while checked.[6]

Now, Gildas is often very hard on his fellow Britons, past and present. Time and again he accuses them of cowardice and stupidity, employing the thundering rhetoric of Old Testament prophets. But here he talks of a victory over Britain's foes. It is almost in passing, surrounded by paragraphs of invective, but it is there. The question thus becomes: who attained this victory, and why did the Proud Tyrant afterwards feel the need to call in Saxon mercenaries? Indeed, who was this Proud Tyrant in the first place?

It is sometimes argued that he was merely a local or regional ruler. However, two pieces of evidence argue against this. One is that the Proud Tyrant is only one of two Britons that Gildas names. Moreover, he is much more important than that other fifth-century Briton, Ambrosius Aurelianus, who ruled over only a pale shadow of the Proud Tyrant's demesne. The other piece of evidence is that the sheer scale of the uprising makes it doubtful that there was any other ruler equal to the Proud Tyrant. He may have been a fool to hire Saxons, but for Britain to suffer the sort of catastrophe that Gildas describes would have required that *every* other ruler be just as foolish. The Proud Tyrant's Saxons devastate Britain from sea to sea. But if his alleged 'rivals' employed largely native Britons, or even foreign mercenaries from a different ethnic group, it is difficult to see how the Revolt could have affected every part of the island. Raiding and local depredations would have been possible. But the whole thrust of Gildas' narrative argues for a nationwide calamity occurring without warning. The Revolt was on a national scale, and for some mysterious reason the Britons had no means to counter it.

The *Historia Brittonum*'s author (traditionally known as Nennius) gives the same account as Gildas, but adds some spice to the tale. *This* Proud Tyrant, by now called Vortigern, is presented as a foolish old man. He marries the daughter of the Saxon mercenary leader to seal their alliance. But then

Vortigern's pretty young wife turns his head, making him neglect his duties. The Saxon chief, by now given the name of Hengest, invites Vortigern and his nobles to a feast. All are supposed to be unarmed. But at a signal from Hengest, the Saxons produce hidden knives. They kill the British leaders and take Vortigern prisoner. Then they harry the island of Britain for many years.[7] The beautiful temptress and the treachery in the feasting hall are probably little more than Dark Age romance. But the story does show how decisively Gildas' original story had tainted the memory of the Proud Tyrant even three centuries later. For Gildas—and all succeeding historians—this native tyrant was the arch-traitor, the man who brought death and ruin to Britain.

We have a fairly firm date when these Saxons were hired. The date Bede gives, around 450, is by far the most likely time for this event.[8] Moreover, this is a year based on a date from Late Antiquity, the first regnal year of the western emperor Valentinian III, who became senior Augustus in 450. Just as 7 December 1941 and '9/11' are dates that have entered the popular imagination, so too it is likely that both Saxon and Briton would have remembered this Roman date when all others had been forgotten.[9] This is only confirmed by what Gildas tells us had happened only a few years before: that the Britons had asked for aid from the Roman marshal Aetius, during his third consulship in 446. This tells us little about the Proud Tyrant himself, but it does give us two vital hooks by which to try to date other events. The most plausible period when unaided Britons 'overthrew their enemies' was between 446, the year of desperation, and about 450, after which any victory would have involved Britons and Saxons fighting side by side—in other words, just at the time when the Proud Tyrant was in power. This raises a very interesting question: did this British 'traitor' actually have something to do with the British success that Gildas describes?

The good churchman says nothing one way or the other about this. But this in itself is curious. It has often been said that 'Gildas is very sparing with names.'[10] But this is not strictly true if we mean naming the *agents* of historical events. He gives credit twice to the Romans and once to the Saxons for victories, as well as naming the author of the final victory over the Saxons: Ambrosius Aurelianus. But concerning this victory in the late 440s, Gildas merely states that the Britons put their trust 'not in man, but in God'. This implies that there was a very good reason not to mention its victor: that this victor may have been none other than the Proud Tyrant himself. Note, Gildas does not lie about this. But neither does he mention something that would greatly weaken the force of his sermon.

This has some interesting implications. If the Proud Tyrant were exercising power at this time, he cannot have been a very young man. Most likely he would have been born in the early part of the century, just at the time when Rome lost control of Britain. He would have had a role that gave him overall control of Britain's military forces and used it to gain some kind of victory over the 'barbarians'. Whether he himself was a soldier is uncertain. If we are to believe Gildas, however, the Proud Tyrant was the most significant personality of mid-century Britain. Moreover, he failed, and failed greatly, after a time of plenty. Indeed, by the 800s his downfall had been connected with the actions of a beautiful but treacherous woman.

And, as far as legend goes, this sounds like someone we all know quite well.

ARTHUR

Perhaps no legendary figure has had so much research devoted to him as Arthur. We have had claims for a Scottish Arthur, an Irish Arthur, a Welsh Arthur, and a Bronze Age Arthur, as well as candidates from the second through the sixth centuries. It is easy to laugh at such claims. After all, one version must be true and the rest necessarily false. But for the sober historian of post-Roman Britain Arthur has become a curse. Gildas speaks of two post-Roman leaders, and two only: the Proud Tyrant and Ambrosius Aurelianus. The earliest evidence for Arthur, however, does not seem to agree with the exploits of either of these two historical actors. One source, the *Historia*, tells us that Arthur fought twelve memorable battles, ending with the battle of Badon. Another, the *Annales Cambriae*, or *Welsh Annals*, relates that he fought a disastrous encounter called Camlann some two decades after Badon. These citations appear not in legends, but in sources that purport to be historical and certainly contain much information that is genuine. Yet they seem to clash so directly with Gildas' account that many have dismissed them as fabrications. Perhaps Arthur's name may shed some light on the problem.

One recent exhaustive examination of the names encountered in the earliest Brythonic literature has yielded an interesting result. Its conclusion is that the most likely provenance of the name Arthur is a combination of two early Brythonic words: *arth* ('bear') and *ur* ('man'). It appears to have been a kind of rallying cry for Arthur's Brythonic speakers, a short, sharp name that would convey a sense of confidence to his followers, and of menace to his enemies. Unfortunately, this study also concludes that 'Bear Man' was probably not a given name, but a *nom de guerre* used in the heat of battle. Arthur's given name remains unknown.[11] This unfortunately means that even if we met with an inscription or citation bearing the Bear Man's real name, we would have no means of connecting it with Arthur.

In searching for Arthur perhaps a better method might be to establish where he is *not*. First of all, Gildas makes no mention of Arthur. This may not seem decisive—until we recall that the cleric also tells us that no battles in any way resembling Arthur's have taken place for quite a while. Not only is Britain currently at peace with the Saxons, but the whole generation that witnessed Ambrosius' victories over the Saxons has grown old and died. 'These had departed', he tells us, 'and a new race succeeded, who were ignorant of this troublesome time.'[12] Of interest, the date that the *Anglo-Saxon Chronicle* gives for the last battle with Hengest's Saxons is 473. In a word, not only is there no evidence in Gildas for Arthur, but there is plenty of counter-evidence that no warlord was winning twelve spectacular battles between the latter part of the fifth century and the first third of the sixth.

This has led the more hopeful to conclude that Arthur must have flourished sometime later in the sixth century. This is a time when large areas of Britain were being brought under Saxon control, and the Britons were retreating into Wales and Cornwall. The image of a minor warlord gallantly holding back the Saxon tide has captivated any number of writers, both of fiction and non-fiction. Indeed, it is probably the dominant image most people in the English-speaking world now have of Arthur. Unfortunately, one piece of evidence—or rather four pieces of evidence—argues decisively against this. After the mid-sixth century at least four different elite personalities suddenly appeared in Britain, each bearing the name of Arthur. Moreover, it is difficult to see how their names could derive from anywhere save that of some famous personage. Indeed, it has been argued that this is the earliest evidence for literature about Arthur.[13] But if this is so, then 'the four Arthurs' would have been christened with this name not long after the time that Gildas was writing: that is, *in the time of peace between Saxon and Briton*. Not only this, but Gildas tells us that Arthur's greatest victory, the battle of Badon, *has already occurred*. In other words, the victor of Badon cannot fit into *any* period after about 475. There is simply no room for him.[14]

Many argue that Ambrosius Aurelianus is the most likely candidate for Arthur. After all, he assuredly did fight Saxons, and at what seems to be about the right time. But the only citations we have that tie Arthur to history tell us two things: first, that he fought and won twelve battles; and second, that he died in a disastrous encounter at a place called Camlann. We have nothing to indicate that Ambrosius won twelve battles, nor that he died fighting at Camlann. Indeed, the last battle he fights seems to be a resounding victory. It is not impossible that he is Arthur, but there is no *evidence* to prove it.

In looking at Ambrosius, however, there may be one small clue that has been overlooked: one small but very significant statement by Gildas that may lead us in an entirely new direction. The wise cleric first tells us about the wars of Ambrosius. He then goes on to say that Badon was 'almost the last, but not the least slaughter of our foes'.[15] This implies that Ambrosius fought battles *after* Badon—and thus *after* Arthur's last battle. Instead of preceding Arthur, this suggests that Ambrosius may well have *succeeded* him. This is strengthened when we remember that the only other British victories that Gildas mentions are prior to Ambrosius, and by quite some time. The victory in which the Britons 'overthrew their enemies' brings on a time of unprecedented plenty. This earlier dating also makes it more likely that the Britons were using Roman military expertise to fight and win twelve far-flung battles. In a word, the best candidate for Arthur *may* be Ambrosius' predecessor—and Gildas' arch-villain—the Proud Tyrant.

Some will charge that this is mere speculation, impossible to prove. But, as we shall see, this simple hypothesis has the potential to transform our understanding of fifth-century Britain. Sources previously at loggerheads suddenly come into harmony. Events and personalities that until now have been inexplicable make perfect sense. Most crucially, it enables us to produce a consistent, reliable chronology for this period, which for the very first time helps us to write a detailed history of fifth-century Britain. Until now this story has been submerged, buried beneath revision after revision, each taking us farther away from the man called Arthur, either blackening his memory or erasing him from history. Ironically, it is only in legend, where Arthur fights his last fatal battle with the traitor Mordred, that some small hint of the real story is found.

For, as we shall see, in the end it was not Arthur who wrote the history books, but Mordred.

5.

'THE ROMANS THEREFORE LEFT THE COUNTRY'

PATRICK

I was taken into captivity in Ireland with so many thousands. And we deserved it, because we drew away from God... The Lord brought on us the fury of His anger, and scattered us among many peoples even to the ends of the earth...[1]

So says the one authentic British voice from the fifth century. The Britons called him Patricius, and we know him by the name of St Patrick. That he became a prisoner of the sea raiders is our best indication of what really happened in the years after Britain gained her independence. In some sense Patrick speaks for all the nameless British captives who made their dismal voyages to Ireland, Scotland or Germany.

The simple fact is that a storm struck Britain following her break with Rome. It lasted not for a matter of years, but for decades. The *Historia Brittonum* is very precise on this: 'After... the termination of the Roman power in Britain they were in alarm for forty years.'[2] Significantly, the only other authentic text that can be attributed to St Patrick is a bitter denunciation of a British ruler's 'slave-napping' of Irish Christians.[3] For Patrick and the men of his generation the seaborne threat was *the* great issue of their lives. An annoying problem in Roman times, it had now become a crisis. In the end this crisis would be solved, and the man who solved it would be remembered as Britain's saviour. But first the island would undergo a trial of forty tragic years.

The seaborne raids were not as immediately catastrophic as the Roman or the Norman Conquest. Their effects were cumulative, spread out over many years. But they touched every facet of British life. Some sixty treasure hoards have been found all over Lowland Britain, most likely buried by wealthy Britons anxious to hide their family plate and coinage from barbarian depredations.[4] Nearly all the coins date from before the break with Rome. This tells us that even the elite feared for their security at this time. It also suggests that a great deal of good money was being taken out of circulation, and not being replaced by new coinage. This raises our suspicions that the money economy of Roman times was beginning to break down, morphing into a barter system. Cross-channel trade plummeted, and even trade within the diocese became a dangerous affair. Soon it was all but impossible to support urban artisans. Archaeology reveals that during this period the mass-produced pottery of Roman times greatly declined, if not disappeared. So did other British manufactures.[5] Much that was specifically Roman seems to have gone into irremediable decline after the imperial connection was severed. Indeed, some have argued that Britain experienced a kind of 'Year Zero', where the material culture of Roman times completely disappeared.[6]

This threat from the sea radically changed *where* Britons lived, as well. We see the last of the great villas collapse into ruins in the years following the break with Rome. One very important reason for this 'Fall of the Villas' surely has to do with the fact that they were built not for defence, as in other parts of the empire, but for show.[7] Easily accessible by the fine Roman road system, they can only have been a magnet for the depredations of Saxon, 'Scot' and Pict. Very quickly, members of the *decurio* class learned that the very last place to live was high on a hill, in a house filled with precious objects. Safety, not status, became paramount for even the most powerful.

But just where could these landowners find safety? The most likely sanctuary was the nearest walled city. Curiously, in the archaeology for this period we find what are often called 'dark earth' layers in many urban areas. This 'dark earth' is essentially a deposit of highly organic soil, much like that found in a fertile garden plot. In the past archaeologists assumed that this signalled a sharp population decline in the cities of Late Roman Britain. It was believed that large tracts of the urban landscape were being used for farming and gardening. But recent thinking argues that this may instead reflect a change in building materials. These 'dark earth' deposits could as easily be the decomposed remnants of buildings made from perishable materials. Where once Romano-Britons had built in stone, now they were raising half-timbered or wattle-and-daub structures.[8] Instead of half-empty ghost towns, Britain's cities may actually have been quite full. And, given the decline in urban industries, one very likely explanation is that they served as refuges from the raiders.

The cities were in no way *ad hoc* refuges, however. Britain's large urban centres had been ringed with powerful fortifications since the third century. Vegetius makes it plain that one important facet of Roman strategy involved the systematic gathering of populations and foodstuffs into the cities during barbarian incursions. That large numbers of persons would be found here during times of emergency should thus be no surprise.

The length of this emergency, however, may have had very important consequences, particularly for Britain's elite. Work by the UNHCR in Bosnia and elsewhere indicates that most refugees are reluctant to return to their old homes after five years. If significant numbers of the *decurio* class (and their entourages) fled to the cities for protection, it is doubtful that they would have returned to their estates if the raiding continued over decades. This does not mean that villa owners would have been cut off from their estates. Quite the contrary: they probably still drew an income from them. Each year they may even have talked about returning, perhaps making serious plans to refurbish their mansions. But each year the rumour of a fresh raid would have postponed the move. True, evidence exists for 'squatter' occupation at some sites, and this *could* reflect the return of a few families.[9] But it could equally reflect the use of bailiffs to administer an increasingly unstable countryside.[10]

If many of the *decurio* class were living in the cities, this also suggests a significant shift in building priorities. Where once artisans had maintained individual villas, now these same workers were better employed repairing city walls. For the *decuriones* and their families this was the highest, indeed the only priority. Even in the far west, whose settlements had never previously been fortified, we see hilltop forts begin to appear. Taken together, the evidence suggests that Britain's rulers were diverting a significant amount of their resources into the construction and maintenance of fortified refuges, whether in earth or stone.[11]

One very important cause for the 'Fall of the Villas' is thus almost certainly the threat from the sea. Gildas, Patrick and Constantius all testify that this was the main danger for Britain throughout this period. But it would be wrong to attribute this destruction to barbarian fire and sword. The archaeology does not support this. Instead it is better to see this as a gradual process. First the villas were abandoned because they were no longer safe. Then the real agents of destruction began their work: wind and rain, rot and mould. Over time their quiet work was far more effective than any invading army. By the time real peace returned, the buildings—and the expertise that created them—had vanished from Britain forever.[12]

RAIDERS

Just who were these raiders who wreaked such havoc on Britain? How could they make life so unbearable? The Irish were the main threat in western Britain. Swooping down the Bristol Channel or harrying the coast of Wales, these corsairs spread fear throughout the west country. Not to be outdone were the Saxon pirates from Germany. They made regular landings on Britain's eastern and southern coasts, carrying off booty in abundance. The third group in this unsavoury troika, the Picts, came from settlements in Scotland. Often allied with either the Irish or the Saxons, they were a threat to both coasts of Britain. A mysterious people, the Picts may have spoken a Celtic language distantly related to that of the Britons.[13]

Each of these nations had its own technology and employed its own tactics. The Irish, or *Scotti*, as the Romans rather confusingly called them, used curraghs for much of their raiding. These were rather small ships, made from hides stretched over a boat-shaped frame. They had a sail and up to fourteen oarsmen to propel them through the rough British seas.[14] Once they made landfall, these light vessels could be manhandled ashore and made as inconspicuous as possible to coastal surveillance. Although much less is known about the Picts, it is likely that they used either curraghs or light galleys. Both groups relied on speed and surprise for their raiding.

The Saxon threat was different. Their vessel of choice was the *cyul*, literally 'keel'. This was a large, multi-oared vessel made of wood, with a high, curving prow. Clinker-built with overlapping timber strakes, it was an ancestor of the Viking ship. *Cyuls*, however, had flatter bottoms than the sea-going *drakkas* of later centuries, and were designed more for coastal and river travel. They were also much larger than Irish and Pictish vessels. Many were over a hundred feet in length, with benches for thirty oarsmen. The largest could probably carry up to sixty warriors.[15] At one time scholars believed that *cyuls* were unable to carry a sail, which would have made any trip to Britain a long and arduous rowing exercise. But recent thinking has reversed this.[16] Ships like the one found at Sutton Hoo were not markedly inferior to later Viking ships in either performance or carrying capacity. Significantly, of these three peoples, only the Saxons migrated *en masse* to Britain, and much of this probably had to do with their ships.

Each of these peoples presented a grim challenge to Britain. The light curraghs and flat-bottomed *cyuls* could travel far up-river, placing much of the diocese under direct threat. Just what these raiders were after we have already seen: gold, silver, anything that was both portable and valuable. Even a small curragh could transport this type of wealth back to Ireland. Some of the precious metals that adorn the Tara Brooch and the Ardagh Chalice may have had their origins in a ransacked villa in Somerset.

We know from the fate of St Patrick that the raiders were after another commodity as well, for it was not just the Britons' glittering coins, but the Britons themselves that were valued prizes.[17] Patrick talks of 'thousands' being carried off beyond the sea. And the motive for these abductions is not hard to understand. Even a single slave like Patrick could ease the hard lot of a Pictish or Irish sheep farmer. Half a dozen young Britons could clear new land, make him wealthy. A likely-looking British girl could make his nights much merrier. The importance of slaves in Ireland is exemplified by the *cumal*, the standard monetary unit for the island. It was the price of three cows—or one slave girl.

Although an analogy with the later Vikings is in part appropriate, it would be an overstatement to imagine fleets of stately dragon ships sailing up the Thames for loot. A better analogy might come from the methods employed by English and French buccaneers on the Spanish Main. Instead of the tall galleons we associate with such ruffians, the Brethren of the

Coast usually conducted their raids in small vessels, sometimes even dugout canoes. Speed and surprise were their hallmarks. The less warning a victim had, the better the haul was likely to be.[18] Similarly, when we read of raids by the various seaborne brigands of the fifth century, it is best to imagine a swarm of small ships stealing up the Bristol Channel on a moonless night, out to raid the sleeping farmsteads of Britain.

ARMS

What did the Britons do to counter these raids? If we were to read Gildas in isolation, we might be pardoned for believing that the Roman army in Britain collapsed, and was replaced by a kind of urban militia cowering behind high walls. His characterization of British military prowess is damning enough.

> To oppose them there were placed on the heights a garrison equally slow to fight and ill adapted to run away, a useless and panic-stricken company, who slumbered away their days and nights on their unprofitable watch. Meanwhile the barbed weapons of their enemies were not idle, and our wretched countrymen were dragged from the wall and dashed to the ground.[19]

Superficially, this appears to corroborate another statement that Gildas makes, that in about 410 the Romans 'left the island, never to return'.[20] It is a very famous statement, one that has been dutifully parroted in every popular history and television documentary for the last half century. But, as we have seen, there was no *withdrawal* of Roman forces, at least not in the years 406–12. The troops who left on Constantine's ill-fated expedition fully expected to return in triumph to their homes and families. They sailed the Channel to conquer an empire, not to take part in some exercise in fifth-century military downsizing.

It might be useful to quote a Byzantine historian, Zosimus, who was writing at the same time as Gildas. He is describing the period of Constantine III's failed bid for the purple. But *his* Britons seem to be fighting not on the continent but in their own diocese:

> The barbarians above the Rhine, assaulting everything at their pleasure, reduced both the inhabitants of Britain and some of the Celtic peoples to defecting from Roman rule and living their own lives disassociated from the Roman law. Accordingly the Britons took up arms and, with no consideration of the danger to themselves, freed their own cities from barbarian threat; likewise all of Armorica and other Gallic provinces followed the Britons' lead: they freed themselves, ejected the Roman magistrates, and set up home rule at their own discretion.[21]

This gives a very different picture of the military capabilities of an independent Britain. But it also suggests that quite a bit of the Roman army in Britain may never have left the island in the first place. Getting any significant part of the cavalry across the straits would have been a difficult if not impossible feat. The *picatus* was simply too small to carry many horses. The fact that Constantine's marshal, Gerontius, eagerly recruited barbarian horsemen like the Alans only strengthens this view. Moreover, Britain was Constantine's support base. To leave Britain denuded of troops risked not only a counter-coup, but also the alienation of those British civilians who had favoured his mutiny. Even though Constantine's rebellion failed, we may suspect that significant numbers of organized troops remained in Britain beyond 410.[22]

Zosimus does suggest that some sort of counter-coup may have toppled Constantine's regime in Britain.[23] But again, such a move would have required armed support, and it is doubtful if any political change could have occurred without the aid of some part of the army. Roman civilians were forbidden by law to carry weapons, and the idea that untrained insurgents could suddenly take on and defeat trained Roman soldiers is unlikely in the extreme. Every phase of the complex struggle in Gaul was carried out either by regular Roman soldiers or by experienced barbarian warriors. It is best to see the fall of Constantine's government as simply the Roman army in Britain's third and final rejection of the various usurpers who had plagued the island since 406.

It would thus be quite wrong to assume that the Roman army in Britain simply vanished, to be replaced by either urban militias or heroic-age warbands. No doubt part of Constantine's defeated force disappeared into the Gallic landscape. But others would have returned to a now-independent Britain. That was their home; that was where their families lived.

Moreover, even if most of Constantine's troops ended up marooned on the wrong side of the Channel, there is another factor that must be kept in mind. By the fourth century Roman warfare had become very much a family business. Since the days of Diocletian sons had been expected to take up the trade of their fathers.[24] In addition to soldiers left behind in garrison, there would have been adolescents too young for war, but who had been raised with every expectation of taking their place in the ranks. It may have taken time to rebuild a post-Roman force to a reasonable level of efficiency, but a child born to an Alan father in 407 would still have had every prospect of becoming a soldier in Britain when he came of age.

Finally, in a militarized age and in this most militarized of dioceses, it seems unlikely that whatever political elite emerged from the debacle would have been so short-sighted as to neglect military affairs. The education of the British elite stressed soldierly virtues. The threat from Pict, 'Scot' and Saxon was real and palpable. Perhaps most decisive of all, a government without military force behind it quickly becomes a non-government. Zosimus' characterization of the fighting qualities of Britain's post-Roman military is explicit. They 'took up arms and, with no consideration of the danger to themselves, freed their own cities from barbarian threat.'

But however much of the 'old army' remained, it could not overcome one crucial drawback: the Saxon Shore had essentially disappeared. Given the economic woes cited above, it is doubtful that whatever remained of the old revenue-gathering administration in London would have been able to raise enough cash to support this most complex of mechanisms. Very soon unpaid sailors and shipwrights drifted into other professions. Unpaid coast watchers and signalmen did likewise. Stores to maintain the *picati* were no longer purchased. In a very short time most of the *picati* that had defeated Niall either rotted away or were converted to firewood. Just as crucial, no Romans stood watch on the eastern side of the Channel. The imperial garrisons at the naval forts had been replaced by barbarian Visigoths and Franks. High-prowed Saxon *cyuls* now sailed unmolested through the Gallican Straits.

With the Straits unprotected, nearly all cross-channel trade was effectively halted. This would have had a ruinous effect on both sides of Ocean. Once trade vanished, so too would merchant ships. Ships without cargoes are valueless. The number of ships—and of experienced sailors—would have declined drastically. Within a few years Britain's maritime capability would have quite vanished away.

In the long run the disappearance of the last of Britain's merchant shipping would have had an even more insidious effect on her future. The great American naval strategist A. T. Mahan argued that only nations with a substantial merchant marine can maintain a navy of any effectiveness. The reason is simple. Without reserves of trained sailors and captains, no nation can hope to win a drawn-out struggle with a foe who possesses both.[25] This almost certainly tells us what happened— or rather what did *not* happen—next. In the face of continued attacks from three formidable naval foes, it would have been impossible for the Britons to rebuild any sort of naval capability. There were no ships; no shipwrights; no sailors. The only forces left to defend Britain were soldiers like Vitalis.

That Britain's new army was a competent force is in no way incompatible with the reports we have of successful barbarian raids. In a sense Vitalis and his comrades faced a conflict not dissimilar to the one waged by the American military against Al Qaida prior to 9/11. In both cases the better-armed and better-trained force could win any head-on contest. But however well-armed and mobile they might be, the best they could do was react to the threat. They could neither anticipate the raids, nor destroy the bases from whence they came. As long as Britain's foes ruled the seas, no effective defence was possible. By 418 Britons had begun to accept the bitter fact that each year hundreds of their fellow countrymen would follow Patrick on his gloomy voyage to Ireland.

And then something like a miracle occurred.

RETURN

Gildas' oft-quoted account of a Roman 'withdrawal' from Britain bears no resemblance to the events surrounding Constantine III's usurpation. But it is important to note what he says, for it may be a garbled retelling of something quite different. He first speaks of a Pictish and Irish assault following the suppression of Maximus' rebellion in 388. The Romans successfully halted this incursion. Then, he tells us, 'they returned home in joy and triumph'. Chronologically, this would correspond to the usurpation of 407. But next Gildas testifies that a fresh onslaught of barbarians forced the British to ask for aid once more. It is at this point that the Romans answered the call with 'unexpected bands of cavalry by land and mariners by sea'. Only after this does Gildas give his famous passage: 'The Romans, therefore, left the country, giving notice that they could no longer be harassed by such laborious expeditions.'[26] He notes that just before they departed the Romans built Hadrian's Wall, as well as the Saxon Shore forts. They required the Britons both to finance this work and to provide labour for its construction. They also 'gave the frightened people stirring advice', and left them 'manuals on war training' to help them defend themselves.[27] Again, none of this sounds like events from the first decade of the fifth century. That was a failed rebellion, not a successful pacification of barbarians. So why does Gildas say this?

One explanation may be that Gildas simply has his facts wrong. We know, of course, that the Wall and the Saxon Shore forts were built long before the fifth century. Many scholars see this as a typical muddling of facts, a fault of which Gildas is often supposedly guilty. But why do the Romans come back after 388, then leave, and then come back again? One clue is that there is no mention in Gildas of *political* subordination to Rome during this period. After the Romans leave, the Britons come to them 'like timorous chickens, requesting aid'. For Gildas at least, the political tie has been severed long before the Romans sail away for the last time. Gildas' account also hints at something else. Neither the Wall nor the Saxon Shore forts were built at this time, but the Britons could have rebuilt them in places, under Roman direction. Further, this talk of leaving 'manuals' to teach the Britons how to fight points to something we have often seen in our own day: military advice to a client state. But who were these Romans? Why did they suddenly appear, and then as quickly vanish again? To answer this question we must follow the career of an extraordinary soldier.

CONSTANTIUS

His name harks back to the days of Constantine the Great, for Constantius was the name both of the first Christian emperor's father and of a son who later became emperor in his own right. But in the year 414 a Roman general with this same name was pulling the western empire back together again. While the emperor Honorius cowered behind the walls of Ravenna, Constantius was leading a resurgent Roman Army against the Visigoths in Gaul. Avoiding head-on confrontations whenever possible, he used his naval forces to cut the barbarians off from their food supplies.[28] By the next year the starving Visigoths had retreated into Spain. But here Constantius applied the same naval strategy, bringing the barbarian host to the brink of starvation, while preventing any escape to Africa. At this point he might have given them the *coup de grace*. But Constantius chose diplomacy instead. In exchange for food, the Visigoths agreed to turn on the other barbarian groups in Spain, pacifying much of the peninsula for Rome. It turned out to be an excellent bargain for the Visigoths. In 418 Constantius did something remarkable: he allowed the barbarians to settle in southwestern Gaul, in the province of Aquitania. There they were given the official status of *foederati*, or federates. This meant that they received a portion of the rents from local landowners in exchange for military service. The Germanic Burgundians under King Gundahari—the Gunther of *Niebelungenlied* fame—were given a similar status along the Rhine. Constantius had done the seemingly impossible; he had reasserted Rome's authority in Gaul, Germany and Spain.

The victorious general might have emulated past military strongmen and seized the throne for himself. But Constantius contented himself with the title of *Patricius*, or 'Patrician'. He tolerated the weak-willed emperor Honorius, but was canny enough to marry the latter's sister, Galla Placidia. Within a short time Constantius also performed the dubious act of siring the future emperor Valentinian III. Eventually the general made the title 'Patrician' synonymous with the power behind the imperial throne.[29] While he lived Constantius was the real ruler of Rome, occupying a post not unlike that of a medieval Japanese *shogun*.

Indeed, in 421 he persuaded the nonentity Honorius to make him co-emperor.

All of this suggests that Constantius was the one Roman both willing and able to answer Britain's pleas in the way that Gildas reports. More than any other commander of the age, he demonstrated an ability to use sea power effectively. He would have understood the strategic significance of the Saxon Shore. It would have been clear to him that if the Gallican Straits were undefended, the coastal communities in newly recovered Gaul would also be in danger. Constantius thus possessed both the means and the insight to follow the sophisticated naval strategy that had made both sides of the Straits secure. Since this Patrician was a realist, equally willing to grant concessions to barbarians or Gallo-Romans when it suited him, it is also likely that he would have been ready to work with independent British allies. After the 418 pacification of Gaul we may suspect that quite a few of his 'mariners' and 'cavalry' were sent across the Channel to deal with the barbarian threat. As a by-product the independent Britons would have learned a hard but valuable lesson: only a strong, centralized authority could neutralize the threat from the sea.[30]

Still, is Gildas the only source for this Roman return, or does other information exist that might support him? It well may; it comes from a document called the *Notitia Dignitatum*. The *Notitia* is a list of the military units and commanders in the Late Roman Empire. It was compiled sometime after the beginning of the fifth century, and specifically mentions the Saxon Shore defences, the forts on Hadrian's Wall, and the mobile field army in Britain. But there is a curious gap in the *Notitia*. While it cites units in the north, east and south, it lists *none* for the western littoral of the island. Now, we know from archaeology that Roman troops were certainly stationed in such coastal sites as Caernarvon before the usurpation of 406. So the only sensible explanation is that the British portion of the *Notitia* reflects

Roman dispositions after 406. But since Britain was independent for most of the fifth century, these dispositions at the Wall and at the Saxon Shore can only reflect planning for a *partial* Roman reoccupation of Britain—a reoccupation whose main purpose was to protect Gaul from seaborne attack. And Constantius' reconquest of imperial possessions north of the Alps in 418 is by far the most likely time for Romans to once again stand guard at the Wall and at the Saxon Shore.[31]

If Gildas and archaeology are to be believed, these Romans were needed now more than ever. By 418 the seaborne threat was beginning to change. Barbarians were doing more than just raiding. The first archaeological evidence of permanent Saxon settlements appears at just this time in East Anglia.[32] Pictish legend speaks of a powerful king of Pictland during the same period. His name was Drust son of Erp. He supposedly lived a hundred years and fought a hundred battles.[33] The *Historia Brittonum* also speaks of Irish conquests in Wales.[34] While not all of these were serious attempts at colonization, the sea peoples may still have been trying to establish year-round enclaves in certain key areas—and for very practical reasons. Three centuries later Vikings from Dublin, with much sturdier craft, still found it convenient after their depredations in England to over-winter in southwest Wales. In this way they could avoid the long voyage back to Ireland. Similarly, it would have made good sense for 'Scots', Picts and Saxons to do the same.[35] This would have been particularly true for the Irish and Picts. Given the relative fragility of their vessels, bases in western Britain would have been well nigh indispensable. In these enclaves the marauders could find rest and food. They could repair their ships in safety. Such bases may even have grown into markets for captured booty, both human and otherwise.

Gildas' story about the Wall and the Saxon Shore defences mirrors what is found in the *Notitia Dignitatum.* But he also mentions offensive Roman assets which look suspiciously like units that both Vegetius and the *Notitia* testify were deployed to Britain even at this late date: the *picati* and the mobile field army. It is unlikely that these operated as far as western Britain. Constantius simply did not have enough troops to do this. But he could still conduct vigorous operations in the Channel and at the mouths of Britain's eastern rivers. In the 'Gallican Straits' any hostile barbarian craft was ambushed and sunk using the naval tactics that Vegetius describes. On land, mobile detachments struck at barbarian enclaves, travelling swiftly down a still-functioning Roman road system. Gildas gives an ecstatic vision of the Roman onslaught:

> Planting their terrible swords upon the shoulders of their enemy, they mow them down like leaves which fall at the destined period; and, as a mountain torrent swelled with numerous streams, and bursting its banks with roaring noise... so did our illustrious defenders vigorously drive our enemies' band beyond the sea...[36]

That Romans were active in the diocese later than previously thought may seem only a footnote to the overall story of fifth-century Britain. But it may actually show us how far we may trust Gildas' narrative. While it is often claimed that Gildas bends British history to parallel biblical events, this can in no way explain his story of the military manuals left by the Romans. Military manuals simply do not figure in either the Old or the New Testament. The only safe conclusion is that this account that speaks of leaving military manuals describes the final departure of the Romans from Britain.

Gildas' account of the construction of Hadrian's Wall and the Saxon Shore forts also argues for the authenticity of his narrative. Even a limited Roman rebuilding programme at the Wall and on the Saxon Shore would have made a tremendous impression on the Britons. Gildas tells us that all the Britons had to pay taxes for their construction, and many actually worked on the walls. Thus, even half a century later there would still have been Britons alive who could claim to have 'built' the Wall, either through their taxes or their labour. Memories of any previous building programmes would have been superseded. By the sixth century this would have been the *only* information Gildas and his contemporaries possessed to explain the origin of these impressive structures. He would have come to the logical but erroneous conclusion that this first and only mention of the Wall and the Saxon Shore meant that these defences had been built by the last Romans in Britain.

This has an even larger significance, however. The fact that Gildas is taking information from a specific report and attributing universal significance to it may be the key to understanding his other errors. As we shall see, his information may originally have been perfectly correct, but he may be drawing the wrong conclusions from his data. Indeed, as we shall see, this is the best explanation for *all* of his errors. And once we realize this, our view of British history is transformed. Authentic sources like the *Notitia Dignitatum* actually confirm what Gildas says, giving us confidence that his chronology is sound. In turn, we find that sources like the much later *Historia Brittonum* and the *Anglo-Saxon Chronicle* follow Gildas' narrative rather closely. Once we understand this, we can begin to write a genuine history of fifth-century Britain—and of the man who dominated it.

WITHDRAWAL

This was to be only a brief respite for the Brtions, however. Events on the other side of the Roman world were now coming into play. In 421 Constantius persuaded Honorius to raise him to the imperial purple. But this first required the approval of the emperor in Constantinople—who refused point-blank. Enraged, Constantius resolved on a military confrontation with the Byzantines. He began raising an army to march eastward.[37] At the same time his marshal Castinus was gathering a second force to confront the Vandals in Spain.[38] The manpower required for either of these ventures would have been a sufficient cause to withdraw Rome's forces from Britain. Together, they made the move unavoidable. Remarkably, there is another source that tells us how and when this coalition between Romans and Britons ended—and it suggests that the parting was far from a happy one. The *Anglo-Saxon Chronicle* gives the following citation for the year 418: 'In this year the Romans collected all the treasures which were in Britain and hid some in the earth so that no one afterwards could find them, and some they took with them into Gaul.'[39] When we remember that many of the events in the *Chronicle* are consistently dated two or three years earlier than the accepted dates,[40] the most likely time of this withdrawal is 421—the precise year when the preparations for the two continental campaigns were under way. The citation thus makes perfect sense. For several years the Romans exercised effective control over the Straits and other parts of eastern Britain. But in 421 their forces were withdrawn for operations closer to Rome. The *ASC* also suggests the Romans took much of the portable wealth in and around London with them. Although often dismissed as the product of a much later time, here the *Anglo-Saxon Chronicle* agrees completely with all the other evidence, suggesting that it too contains genuine information about the fifth century.

But why did the Romans not return? Again, the answer lies in events of this same year. By the end of 421 Constantius lay dying, and Castinus' campaign proved a disaster. Routed by Geiseric's Vandals, the unhappy marshal blamed enemies at court for his debacle. While the worthless Honorius lived, he bided his time. But on the old emperor's death in 423 Castinus raised an obscure civil servant to the purple. The next year the marshal himself was named consul. In 424, however, the eastern emperor intervened and overthrew the usurper. Constantius' son by Galla Placidia, the young Valentinian III, was placed on the throne.[41] This brought a measure of stability to the western empire. But from now on Rome's rulers in Ravenna would concentrate on preserving the core of their domain. Peripheral areas like Britain were expendable. If we see a Roman withdrawal in 421, Roman sources and the *Anglo-Saxon Chronicle* only confirm what Gildas says: 'The Romans... therefore left the island, never to return.'

As Constantius' ships sailed home to Gaul, their holds filled with British treasure, Vitalis and his comrades can only have felt despair—and a deep sense of betrayal. Once again their island was bereft of naval support. Once again Britain would have to counter a ship-borne enemy with land-based forces. It was a bleak prospect.

True, there were benefits. The soldiers of the diocese had seen the new Roman army in action. They possessed manuals explaining the doctrine that it used in its operations. Their smiths had seen the latest weapons and armour up close. The idea that a combination of ships and cavalry could overcome the barbarian threat had been reinforced. In the military communities of Britain the problem was understood, as was the solution. Only the ships and crews were lacking.

The children of men like Vitalis, however, may have looked upon all of this rather differently. They had seen the Romans rebuilding the old abandoned forts that had once protected the diocese. They had seen the sleek *picati* and the great warhorses of the imperials. They had been dazzled by the bright weapons and armour. The fact that Romans could still win battles against the barbarians was enormously encouraging for boys who knew that one day they would take their place in the ranks of the island's soldiers. Perhaps most lasting, however, was the knowledge that a strong military leader, the Patrician Constantius, had made all of this possible. In the coming decades news would come of other Patricians' victories over the strongest barbarian armies in Europe. The lesson was clear: a military strongman could defeat the barbarians.

And Vitalis' son began to hope that one day he might be that strongman.

6.

'FORTY YEARS OF FEAR'

ALLELUIA

4*29. Spring. Eastern Britain.* The young soldiers had been waiting in the wet bracken for hours. They were cold. They were sodden. And now most were hoping that the Saxons would not appear. Earlier, at breakfast, they had been filled with the elation of impending combat. They were heroes, ready for any danger. But now they were uneasy. The meal sat in their stomachs like a lump of lead. Many were beginning to contemplate what sharp steel might do against soft body tissue. They had feelings not uncommon in soldiers of all armies in all periods: stultifying boredom mixed with very real terror. They prayed for something to happen—and dreaded what that something might bring.

They heard a rustle in the bracken. A young *draconarius* astride a horse cantered up, a long dragon banner of red silk trailing behind him. His iron helmet and jacket of chain mail only increased the young Britons' annoyance. No helmet protected their heads. Instead, they wore the flat felt *pilleus*, the Roman army service cap. Their 'breastplate' was a simple woollen tunic. Some muttered that all the good equipment went to the officers and rear-rankers. The men who did the fighting had the least protection.

Another man accompanied the *draconarius*. He wore the robes of a priest and immediately began talking to the nearest soldiers. The priest seemed ancient to them, his face withered from a long life of abstinence. They had been told he was a bishop from Gaul. But he acted like no bishop they had ever known, chatting with them like an old campaigner. Only at the last, when he gave them his blessing, were they reminded that he was a man of God.

An hour passed. Then another. A nervous young officer walked past them, telling several to move so that they could not be seen from the road. In the valley below two horsemen flashed by. The riders halted, then galloped off to the right. Moments later their own officer hurried up. 'The pagans are coming,' he hissed. 'Remember the battle cry...'

Soldiers disappeared into the bracken, anxious to relieve themselves one last time. Others checked the balance of their weapons. A few murmured prayers remembered from childhood. Real war was approaching.

Then they saw them. The first few Saxons were scouts. Every so often the pagans left the road, rummaging through the dense brambles beyond. But the barbarians could make little more than a perfunctory reconnaissance. The main column was hard on their heels.

The pagan army was travelling fast and light. At first glance it hardly resembled an army at all. Very few had helmets or armour. Most wore floppy woollen caps; the burdens they carried made them seem more like a throng of pedlars than a military force. But every man had a spear and shield tied to his pack, and their step was purposeful. For some minutes the barbarians filed past. The young men crouching in the bushes realized that they would have no numerical advantage in this fight.

Up ahead a din arose. The young soldiers heard indistinct shouts. The pagans below heard the same noise. Some dropped their bundles, freeing spears and shields for combat. At the same time the Britons' officer gave a loud cry and rose from the bracken. It was a single word: 'Alleluia!' Immediately the young soldiers sprang to their feet, joining in the uproar. They began to march down the slope, anxiously fingering the short swords at their sides. They had practised the *armatura*, the sword exercise, for many weeks. Now they would see whether it worked against living flesh.

Without warning a second battle cry echoed from the other side of the valley. They saw men like themselves suddenly appear from the greenwood, spears and shields at the ready. Some of the pagans below turned to meet this new threat. But in the meantime a confused mass of Saxons appeared on the road from the right, their heads turning in every direction. Some of them raced past the main body. Others faced about, confused, shouting defiance at an enemy that seemed to be everywhere.

The young Britons began to move faster, attempting to keep their ranks straight as they negotiated the irregular slope. At the same time they saw a group of horsemen appear from their right. The bishop was among them. More pagans put down their packs. But this time it was not to prepare for combat. It was to flee. A few individual barbarians still turned to face the enemy. But panic was spreading. The few that stood and fought soon lay face down in the muddy track. Within another minute the whole mass of raiders was melting away like spring snow. The young Britons reached the road, a cry of triumph on their lips. They crowded around the bishop from Gaul, following him as he rode down the broken road. His voice was nearly gone, but still he shouted out: 'Alleluia... alleluia...'

Just why a bishop from Gaul would be leading a force of Britons against Saxons we will discuss shortly. But the above battle is important because it may be the first recorded incident in which Arthur appears. Very much in the foreground of the picture we have just delineated is a man called St Germanus. He was a bishop from Gaul, on a visit to Britain that would last for only a few months. He may rightly be called the central figure in this scene. Yet, as in a crowded photograph, in the background and off to the side we may also detect someone else: Vitalis' son. The above encounter may signal the first imperceptible tread of Arthur onto the stage of British history.

An early-fifth-century chronicler from Gaul gives the first clue as to what brought this bishop to Britain. In his chronicle the writer warns of a dangerous new heresy. Its leader is a cleric from North Africa. This cleric has a dubious past. He has flirted with various pagan beliefs before finally settling on his own peculiar brand of Christianity. For the Gallic chronicler this North African's belief is deeply distasteful. It holds that man is unable to achieve salvation through his own efforts, that he receives it only through the good offices of the Deity Himself. Even the name for these good offices is suspect: *gratia* or grace. After all, *gratia* is the word used to describe the bribery and corruption that is endemic in the empire. A description of the Vatican in our own day as 'God's mafia' gives some idea of the abhorrence that the word 'grace' enjoyed in certain Roman circles. The chronicler concludes that this North African's writings are the source of many of the heresies that have lately arisen in Gaul.[1]

This particular African's ideas, however, were not destined—or, more properly, predestined—for oblivion. His name was Augustine, and the concept of grace he expounded quickly became orthodox theology. This was perhaps inevitable, even useful, given the growing powerlessness of Roman secular authority. Men who might once have sought careers in government or the army increasingly saw their calling within the Church. Rome, the City of Man, might fall, but a Christianized *Romanitas* could still endure within the hearts of the faithful everywhere.

Everywhere, that is, except in Britain. Because of her isolation the island diocese was a place where older values prevailed. For the sons of men who had twice come within an ace of ruling the empire, Augustine's doctrine smacked of something near to spiritual defeatism. And very soon they found their voice. At the same time as this African was developing his theories of grace, a Briton named Pelagius was teaching that men could and must struggle against the world's evil; that neither salvation nor damnation was pre-ordained. Perhaps more importantly, Pelagius and his followers also denounced the abuses of the very rich against the poor. His teachings soon found fertile ground among both Rome's urban poor and his fellow native Britons. But by 429 the pendulum had swung so far in favour of Augustine that Pelagianism was declared a heresy. At the same time, orthodox church leaders in Gaul heard reports that the doctrine was thriving in Britain. They chose to send two men to combat the heretics. Their names were Germanus, Bishop of Auxerre, and Lupus, Bishop of Troyes.

What we know of Germanus and his mission comes from a work of Late Antique hagiography written in 480 by a Gallic clergyman called Constantius (no relation to the earlier Patrician). Considerable doubt has sometimes been cast on the veracity of Constantius' account. It does contain miracles. It was, after all, written to extol the virtues of a saint. But this doubt rests primarily on the notion that a credulous clergyman can never be an accurate witness to historical events. We must remember that this account was written only fifty years after the voyage, when Bishop Lupus was still alive. Further, Constantius appears to have been a man very anxious to preserve the records of his time. He corresponded with the prolific Gallo-Roman writer Sidonius Apollinaris, and urged the future saint to publish his letters for posterity.[2] The information he gives about Gaul is correct as far as can be determined, which implies that the British section also contains valid data.

As to Constantius' 'credulity', one need only point out that it is modern prejudice that sees pagan authors as more reliable witnesses than Christian clergymen. After all, even the Late Roman historian Ammianus Marcellinus blamed the defeat of Julian the Apostate not on poor strategy, but on the emperor's failure to heed his augurs' predictions of disaster.[3] The account of Germanus' visit to Britain is undeniably skewed. Constantius subordinates everything in his narrative to his main theme: Germanus' struggle with a dangerous heresy. The depiction of military and political events is often perfunctory. But it is also not a story fabricated in a monastic cell hundreds of years after the event. If we read carefully and judiciously, we find a perfectly reasonable account of a voyage to Britain in Late Antiquity.

Constantius tells us that Germanus had a sound Roman education. He chose the law as his profession, and may also have had some familiarity with military affairs. But then Germanus was chosen, against his will, to become bishop. Once in office he seems to have been a conscientious shepherd, constantly mortifying his flesh and at times putting his own life in danger to protect his flock.[4] In 428 word came that the Pelagian heresy was rampant in Britain. The next year Germanus and Bishop Lupus crossed the Channel. Of interest is the fact that they encountered stormy weather. This, and the fact that Easter occurred not long after their landing, suggest that it was a winter crossing.[5] This is a bad time of year for a small ship to brave the Channel, and the most likely explanation is that its captain wished to avoid the Saxon pirates they would have encountered in more seasonable months. The good bishop naturally calmed the storm, and the voyage was completed without further danger. But the implication is clear: by 429 neither Roman nor Briton controlled the 'Gallican Straits'. An Ocean voyage was a risky affair.

Upon landing the two bishops were surrounded by throngs of the faithful: so much so that their Pelagian opponents decided to challenge them to a debate. The location is not stated, but it is difficult to see the venue for this debate as anywhere but London itself.[6] This would have been the most logical place for such an event, and the fact that the bishops afterward visited another likely candidate, *Verulamium* (the present St Albans), rules the latter out. The Pelagian debaters duly made their appearance, dressed in fine robes and surrounded by flatterers. This scene could simply be a rhetorical flourish by Germanus' biographer, to emphasize the humility of his hero. Pelagianism had started out as an austere doctrine. But that the 'heretics' possessed fine clothing would still not be out of the question. Any number of austere social movements have succumbed to worldly temptation. Constantius leaves us in no doubt that the debate was a triumph for Germanus and Lupus. The Pelagians were exposed and the worshipful crowds requested immediate baptism. Germanus also found time to heal the daughter of an official who possessed 'tribunic powers'.[7] The result, as Constantius reports it, was total victory for a saintly man.

TRIBUNE

Constantius gives us very little information on what Britain was like in 429. That is not his purpose. But some of the things he says are more than a little tantalizing. First of all, the most likely venue for this debate, London, is certainly not a ghost town. Admittedly, a foreign visitor of such rank was a novelty that would have drawn a crowd. But the old capital does not appear to be a place where large areas have been turned into open fields and gardens.

Yet archaeology suggests that trade, both internal and external, had declined drastically during this period. So had the production of consumer goods. This in turn implies that many of the city's inhabitants were there not for economic reasons but for safety. And the most likely threat to their safety was from the Saxons whom Germanus was shortly to rout.

Of equal interest is this official with 'tribunic powers'. He is literally the only British leader of any rank mentioned, and he may well signify a number of trends in the post-Roman British world. First is his title. In the Roman system there were both military and civilian tribunes. Military tribunes had traditionally led such units as cohorts. But by the fifth century the title could also be borne by civilian officials.[8] Either way, this shows that even in 429 Britain was in no sense ruled by hereditary kings. Men of the *decurio* class still sought and won the offices they had always prized.

Yet it is this tribune's very human concern for his daughter that may be most emblematic of Britain in 429. That his daughter—and his whole family—would be with him inside a walled city gives an insight into the highest priority for Britain's officials at this time: preservation of themselves and their families. This is only natural and human. But it may also be that Britain's rulers were tempted to think more with their hearts than their heads; that they may have been putting the safety of their families ahead of the good of the diocese as a whole.

Or so may have thought the young soldiers who were fighting *outside* those walls.

BATTLE

That Germanus would follow up his spiritual battle against Pelagianism with a very real battle against Saxon marauders may seem odd. It is therefore important to examine this incident in detail, to see what may really have been going on. Germanus' biographer begins by reporting that a band of marauding Saxons and Picts was about to strike. The British soldiers, occupying a camp, were apprehensive about meeting the barbarians in the open field. So they made the unusual request that Germanus lead them into battle. He agreed. But it was Lent, so Germanus first baptized his forces, following this with a sermon.

'A church was built of leafy branches in readiness for Easter Day, on the plan of a city church, though set in a camp on active service. The soldiers paraded still wet from baptism... and all looked for help from heaven.'[9]

Meanwhile, the combined barbarian host was on the march:Their approach was discovered by scouts and, when the Easter solemnities had been celebrated, the army—the greater part of it fresh from the font—began to take up their weapons and prepare for battle and Germanus announced that he would be their general. He chose some light-armed troops and made a tour of the outworks. In the direction from which the enemy were expected he saw a valley enclosed by steep mountains. Here he stationed an army on a new model, under his own command.

By now the savage host of the enemy was close at hand and Germanus rapidly circulated an order that all should repeat in unison the call he would give as a battle-cry. Then, while the enemy were still secure in the belief that their approach was unexpected, the bishops three times chanted the Alleluia. All, as one man, repeated it and the shout they raised rang through the air and was repeated many times in the confined space between the mountains.

The enemy were panic-stricken... They fled in every direction, throwing away their weapons and thankful if they could save at least their skins. Many threw themselves into the river... and were drowned in it.

The booty strewn everywhere was collected... The bishops were elated at the rout of the enemy without bloodshed and a victory gained by faith and not by force.[10]

Since this is a second-hand account by a non-military person of events fifty years earlier we may discount some of what Constantius tells us. It is possible that Germanus was in at least nominal charge of the operations. As stated earlier, he may have had military training before becoming a cleric. But an organized unit of Britons would necessarily have had their own commanders. Further, other particulars only make good sense. The prospect of divine aid for men going into battle certainly builds morale. Likewise, the barbarians' flight at the first shout of 'Alleluia!' is consistent with what we know of such raiders before and since. When confronted by an unexpected show of force, a party interested more in loot than in fighting will normally opt for a quick getaway.

The account may also tell us some interesting things about the British military of this time. We find that these soldiers occupy some sort of camp away from any city. Moreover, this camp seems to guard an important avenue of approach for the barbarians. The Britons possess their own weapons. They muster in formation. They have scouts who warn of the enemy's approach—and who can, moreover, raise the alarm a few days ahead of time. They are able to set up a devastatingly effective ambush. But this begs the question: who were these soldiers?

One thing we can be sure of is that, like practically all soldiers throughout history, most were young. If we imagine an average age of not much over twenty-five, the majority would have been small children or infants at the time when Constantine and Gerontius sailed to Gaul. It is possible they were a mere scratch force thrown together for this battle. But when we remember that among both Romans and barbarians war had been the business of professionals for hundreds of years, this seems doubtful. Far more likely is the suggestion that these young men were in some sense the 'heirs of Gerontius'. They were the sons of the soldiers who had raised the standard of revolt against Rome in 410, many of whom were probably Alans. If we accept this, then the 'Alleluia Victory' becomes comprehensible. On both the Wall and the Saxon Shore, intelligence gathering was important, and men on horseback would have been by far the best gatherers. This explains why the Britons had so much time to prepare. Outriders detected signs of the gathering barbarian army well in advance.[11] Germanus' biographer may credit the saint with the idea of the ambush, but if the steppe influence was still strong in the British army it is precisely this type of tactic that would have been the most effective against a raiding force on foot.

The location of this foray appears to be somewhere in Lowland Britain, probably near London itself (see Map 2). The conclusion is clear. In 429 Britain still possessed a military force of some capability, probably derived in part from the professional army stationed there during Roman times. But the corollary was that this force now faced barbarians able to penetrate to the very heart of Britain.

And at least one of the young men blessed by Germanus on that spring day of 429 went on to much bigger things. Two different sources give us the details. A stone pillar erected by the descendants of Vitalis speaks of his son 'whom Germanus blessed'.[12] The *Historia Brittonum* relates how a certain man of humble birth, Catel Durnluc, *and his sons* were blessed by this same saint.

The hero had been blessed—and blooded.

BATHS

Here we must introduce an important source for this period, and a most entertaining character as well: the Gallo-Roman aristocrat Sidonius Apollinaris. A native of what is now Clermont-Ferrand, he eventually became the bishop of that city. But his life prior to this was far from ascetic. Like most Gallo-Roman nobles, Sidonius led what we might call 'the good life' in what is now southern France. In his letters he speaks of the fine banquets and witty conversation he enjoyed in the last days of imperial rule. In one missive Sidonius describes a journey in which he was 'ambushed' and 'captured' by servants of two local landowners. But this captivity proved far from disagreeable. These 'traps which their kindness had arranged' forced him to spend a pleasant few days eating, riding and conversing in the most elegant style. At times the party engaged in a fifth-century version of *boule*; at others they discussed the merits of Horace, Augustine, and Origen. But for us, the most significant event was when Sidonius' hosts invited him to... take a bath. Sidonius tells us that the two landowners made many apologies for the fact that their brick bath-houses were still 'under construction'. All the same, they managed to provide the future saint with a proper Roman bath. Sidonius describes how a ditch was dug by a river, and how baked stones were used to heat the shallow trench. 'Then while the ditch was heating it was roofed over with a dome constructed of pliant hazel twigs... In addition rugs of hair-cloth were thrown over the roof... Its kindly warmth relaxed us and cleared our clogged digestions.'[14]

We may doubt that the two permanent baths were ever constructed. Times were unsettled in Gaul, and would become more so as the century wore on. But if we also recall Saint Germanus' chapel 'built of leafy branches' there may be more here than just a simple bath in the old Roman style. Instead, we may be observing a phenomenon that was occurring all over the Late Roman world. It has often been pointed out that the archaeological record for fifth-century Britain is very different from that of Roman times. By the 430s—just at the time of Germanus' visit—such items as mass-produced pottery (plentiful in the previous century) were beginning to disappear. The last of the villas had fallen into decay, and so had the baths. Many scholars see this apparent decline in Britain's material culture as proof that there was a radical break with the Roman past. They contend that after 410 Britain was in a kind of 'Year Zero', where practically all aspects of Roman life ceased.[15] Yet the two instances mentioned above—building a chapel and constructing a bath-house—are both activities that are fully Late Roman. The key element, though, is that neither would show up in any archaeological record. The likely alternative to the 'Year Zero' theory is that after 410 many Britons were still living Roman lives, but in ways that have not left any trace in the archaeology. But then the question becomes: why?

The reason is almost certainly the barbarian threat. Gildas acknowledges this when he speaks of his countryman 'lying in mountains, caves and woods' in the 440s.[16] The danger from Saxon, 'Scot' and Pict was so great that many Britons now feared to live in their former communities. But at the same time a threat is not a conquest. We know that most of the land was still worked at this time, implying that the population had not greatly diminished either.[17] Indeed, archaeology confirms that Britons occupied a very large portion of the old diocese until the latter part of the fifth century. But the *threat* of attack may still have changed British behaviour in a number of fundamental ways. The danger from sea barbarians who could kill, rob and enslave meant that every Briton had to be much less conspicuous, and much more willing to react at short notice to a barbarian incursion. The flimsy structures that Sidonius and Germanus encounter are an indicator that by now most Late Romans were unwilling to expend more than minimal effort on the construction of structures that might soon have to be abandoned.[18]

ANGLIA

Constantius' account is also important because it is our first indication that the barbarian threat was beginning to change. One clue to this is the route the Saxons took to the site of the 'Alleluia Victory'. If these pagans had been raiders rowing up the Thames under cover of darkness, they would simply have beached their craft, stormed ashore and taken whatever came across their path. But these raiders act differently. They come from a long way off, evidently many days' march. British scouts discover their presence, and the main British force has time to attend a church service before battle. The engagement is fought in an upland defile, presumably some distance from the Thames Valley itself. It is difficult to see why marauders would disembark from their ships, make a long, difficult march that discloses their presence, and then scurry away at the first sign of trouble. This is puzzling, and there seems only one explanation. The raiders were never in ships in the first place.

But if they were not ship-borne, where did they come from? It is here that archaeology gives us another important clue. We know that the North Sea began to rise during this period. Large numbers of Saxon settlements in what is now the Low Countries were inundated, their fields either under water or too brackish to farm.[19] By mid-century whole villages had been abandoned. Coincidentally, the earliest evidence of Saxon settlements in Britain occurs sometime between about 425 and 450. Moreover, most are located in East Anglia (see Map 2).[20] There is thus a real likelihood that the Saxons whom Germanus encountered came from the northeast, from these newly established settlements. But this begs the question: why East Anglia?

As we shall see, raiding is one thing, but settlement quite another. The naval guerrilla campaign waged by the various enemies of Britain succeeded only because relatively small groups of men could achieve sudden and devastating local superiority over a village or a villa. Barbarian settlements, on the other hand, include vulnerable women and children. In most areas of Britain any erstwhile pagan settlers would have been quickly discovered by the local inhabitants and reported to the nearest military authorities. As Vikings and Elizabethans were to discover in their first encounters with Native Americans, isolated colonial bridgeheads rarely succeed in the face of determined opposition. Settlers need land, supplies, and, above all, peace. Otherwise there will be no crop to sustain them through their first winter. Much of the coast of Britain would thus have been closed to permanent settlement for all but the strongest landing force.

Except in East Anglia. This was a world of fens and sluggish rivers very like the one the Saxons had left behind. Few Romans lived here, and those who did were cut off from each other by the vast marshes. Small groups of Saxon settlers could row up the winding rivers to establish isolated settlements on land less drowned than the rest. Although the Anglian swamps would not seem to us the most salubrious of places, for the Saxons they may have been a kind of paradise. Even if British soldiers were summoned to suppress the invaders, few Roman roads ran here. Elsewhere mounted detachments could make life intolerable for newcomers on foot. But within the Anglian fens well-armed and well-led cavalry could be ambushed and cut to pieces. Centuries later, Norman knights would learn the same hard lesson from Hereward the Wake. We must also remember that this region was the part of Britain most like the Saxons' old homes on the drowning German coast. They would *feel* safest here. And, after a long sea voyage, that may have been the most important factor of all.[21]

WARFARE

That Vitalis' son would be fighting Saxons in and around London may seem quite an analytical leap. Vitalis could easily have originally been one of the 'Men of the Wall', or stationed far to the west. Past writers have placed Arthur in areas as far apart as Cornwall, Wales, and Scotland. Some even have him flourishing in Brittany or Gaul. But if a Saxon presence were growing in the East Anglia of the 420s, eastern Lowland Britain would be the most likely place for a *Dux Bellorum* to emerge. This was the richest part of the diocese, and included its old capital, London. It was the region that contained the largest portion of the landed elite, who both required protection and could pay for a well-equipped force to provide it. Saxon attacks here would galvanize British resistance as in no other part of the diocese. A respected scholar's description of the Proud Tyrant's most likely identity is illuminating. He is described as a military 'overlord' of some of the southern *civitates*.[22] This may be a very good description of Vitalis' son—at one stage in his career.

In 429 the Proud Tyrant—the man we have identified as the best candidate for Arthur—was in no sense a *Dux Bellorum*. He can only have been a junior officer hoping for advancement. But any astute young commander hoping to succeed in battle must understand his enemy. Just what kind of enemy would an ambitious officer have faced in the fens and forests of eastern Britain?

On a psychological level the Saxons would have had a number of real advantages. First of all, Vitalis' son faced a foe both mysterious and more than a little frightening. These 'Angles' maintained many of their old pagan practices, including cremation of the dead on funeral pyres—distasteful to any orthodox Christian. Even the appearance of these barbarians was unnerving. A contemporary describes Saxon warriors as shaving the front part of their scalps to appear more ferocious.[23] While obscure cultural traditions could explain this, the more likely alternative is that it was an early version of Germanic *Schrecklichkeit*. Another custom tends to strengthen this hypothesis. The name for their female priestesses, *Waelcyrge* ('chooser of the slain'), is the Saxon equivalent of 'Valkyrie'. But these Saxon women may have had a much more sinister function than hauling slain heroes off to a Wagnerian *Walhall*.[24] Like other Germans, Saxons believed that after each victory their gods demanded the sacrifice of a portion of the loot. This macabre 'tithe' included human captives, and the 'choosers' of these victims may at times have been these same *Waelcyrge*.[25] With such dubious customs as these, the Saxons would have been a peculiarly terrifying enemy. Not only was their very appearance unsettling; any captured Briton could expect only a grisly death. Like recent executions of hostages in Iraq and Afghanistan, sacrifice at the hands of pagan women may have been a tactic designed to break the British will to fight.

On the level of armaments, however, Britons had something of an edge. By courtesy of the Patrician Constantius, they had the latest versions of Roman armour and weapons—and manuals that explained how to use them. Most soldiers carried spear, sword and shield. At minimum they wore the felt *pilleus*, the flat-crowned service cap that was common to all Late Roman soldiers. If they were lucky they might also wear a ridged helmet with cheek pieces, and perhaps armour of some type. We know that crossbows existed in Britain at this time—an excellent standoff weapon either in the field or on city ramparts. That cavalry were employed is certain, given the excellent reconnaissance Germanus received before his ambush. Such troopers would have wielded the long Roman cavalry sword called the *spatha*. It is also perfectly possible that some still bent the steppe bow used with such devastating effect by Gerontius. In a very real sense these young men were carrying on the traditions of the Late Roman army.

Most Saxons, on the other hand, would have gone into battle with only a shield and a spear. If they carried a sword at all, it was normally the short *seax* knife, little longer than a butcher's knife, and resembling a weapon that men like Jim Bowie would make famous on another continent. But a few of their nobles could present much more of a challenge. They carried long swords similar in shape to the Roman *spatha*. But Saxon smiths had modified these swords into something altogether more deadly. By means of pattern welding—putting an edge of hard, brittle steel around a softer, more flexible iron core—they had created a weapon that could bite through all but the best Roman armour.

Vitalis' son would also have learned that Saxons were a people with few illusions about war. Abstract military ideals like honour and chivalry were unknown to them. Significantly, the one archaic Saxon epic that has come down to us, *Beowulf*, is about a warrior hero from Sweden, not continental Saxony or England. Their mentality is best seen as that of the bandit or guerrilla: a foe who strikes when the enemy is least prepared. If surrounded, they would try to escape, and if that failed they would die fighting with all the desperation of a cornered animal.

These were therefore *not* a people who saw death in battle as their highest ideal. Unlike Goths or Burgundians—or medieval Anglo-Saxons—they would not make hopeless last stands beside their kings. Much of this was due to the fact that they had no kings. There is no record of kingship among continental Saxons before the 700s.[26] Indeed, the Saxon kings who arose in Britain later in this century may actually have been in imitation of British political institutions. In this earlier period they seem to have revelled in an almost anarchic freedom. Observers speak of every member of a ship's company shouting out his own orders.[27] There are also reports of oath breaking, of a willingness to violate treaties without warning.[28] The anarchy and the perfidy went hand in hand. Both in turn stemmed from the fact that Saxons were much less hierarchically differentiated than Goths, Franks or Vandals. Saxons obeyed a leader not because he was a king or noble, but because of his skills in war—or, more precisely, because of his abilities to acquire wealth for the rest of the group.

This anarchic freedom also made Saxons a peculiarly difficult foe to beat. If a Saxon leader made a peace agreement, his followers felt little obligation to follow it. After all, their leader had taken the oath, not they. Far better to follow another lord who could provide more loot. In the end Vitalis' son would have found the Saxons a kind of hydra-headed enemy. The Britons might destroy one settlement, many settlements. But there would always be another encampment where the local warlord was bold enough to go after the *Weala* gold and slaves. It is perfectly possible that from time to time both sides made sincere attempts at peace. But without a strong barbarian leader able to enforce these agreements, such efforts were doomed.[29]

This, then, was the foe Vitalis' son faced in 429. Like any intelligent young officer, he knew that the Saxons were far from invincible. The barbarians had no edge in either weapons or battle tactics. Men like his father had passed on their knowledge of how the Romans had once made war. Gildas' mention of Roman military manuals argues that the young officer had access to the latest Roman military doctrine, and undoubtedly venerable military classics like Caesar's *Gallic Wars* as well. This expertise could make all the difference in defeating a larger but less organized barbarian force.

But Vitalis' son also knew that time was not on the side of the Britons. With each year the Saxons pushed further up the eastern rivers—a malignant cancer spreading through the bloodstream of the diocese. These new settlements were bases: bases from which the raiders could attack the surrounding countryside, drive off the peasantry, and thus deny food to the cities. Purely defensive operations like the 'Alleluia Victory' could never decisively end this kind of threat. The only alternative was attack. As both North American settlers and Native Americans knew centuries later, the best way to defeat such a foe was not to confront him in open battle, but to strike his settlement when least expected.

Vitalis' son knew something else as well. Not all British peasants were leaving the newly seized territories. Some were staying. With whatever Latin words each group held in common a *modus vivendi* was being established.[30] Slowly, surely, beyond the ken of contemporary observers and later archaeologists, a new world was being created in these fens and marshes—and unless decisive measures were taken this new world would eventually become a nation called England.

The 'Alleluia Victory' suggests that by 429 Saxons were marauding in the vicinity of what was probably London. More disturbing, though, is that both archaeology and written sources tell us that within a decade Saxons were moving into another region.

But this time it was not an area inaccessible to British armies. It was on the Thames, and on the *Upper* Thames at that.[31] London had fallen.

7.

'THEY LEFT THEIR CITIES'

FLIGHT

441 AD—The Britons, hitherto troubled by various events and disasters, were subjected to the sway of the Saxons.[1]

The entry seems unequivocal. It comes from a chronicle completed in Gaul only a decade later, in 452. Indeed, this source is commonly called the 'Gallic Chronicle of 452'. It is the account we possess that is closest in time to actual events. However, the statement also happens to be far from true. Archaeology and written testimony agree that most of the island remained in British hands until the end of the fifth century. Welsh nationalists might even claim that *spiritually* the Anglo-Saxons never managed to subdue the 'Cymric' part of Britain at all. So why would a Gallic chronicler bemoan the 'loss' of Britain in 441 when it never occurred? This is curious, to say the least.

Archaeology reveals that the earliest evidence for Saxon occupation is in East Anglia and an area centred on Dorchester-on-Thames.[2] Yet these are isolated areas, not a coherent state. Some see the Thames Valley sites as evidence of the arrival of the Proud Tyrant's mercenaries, the *Adventus Saxonum* ('Coming of the Saxons'). They argue that this is where he first settled his barbarian hirelings, and that sometime before 441 they revolted. It is an attractive theory, in particular for those who would like to see an Arthurian figure in the late fifth century—the usual floruit advanced for the *Dux Bellorum*. Unfortunately, any equation of the 441 entry with the Revolt rings false, for several reasons. First of all, the best authority on the archaeology of the Saxon settlements sees the East Anglian and Thames Saxons as *migrants*, not mercenaries.[3] The coast of East Anglia was far less strategically important to Lowland Britain than the mouth of the Thames and the Straits of Dover, yet no Germanic group settled these strategic areas until a quarter of a century later. Secondly, the Thames sites are farther *upriver* than many contemporary British settlements; if the archaeology is any guide, there was a 'Saxon-free' zone around London until the end of the century.[4] How could Britain be 'reduced to Saxon rule' if the capital itself remained in British hands for half a century longer? Thirdly, Bede and the *Anglo Saxon Chronicle* testify that the Proud Tyrant called in his Saxon mercenaries shortly after the year 450. Many scholars believe that the *Anno Domini* dates found in the *Chronicle* were generated far later than the fifth century. As argued in Appendix III, there is very good evidence to the contrary. But the date for the *Adventus* is different. It is no guess. Unlike the other entries, it is keyed on a *Roman* date: that is, the first year of the reign of Valentinian III as senior emperor.[5] This was in 450 AD, a decade after this supposed 'fall of Britain'. But fourthly—and most tellingly—Gildas quotes a British appeal to the Romans for aid dated 446 (the year of Aetius' third consulship), and then places the story of the Proud Tyrant and the Saxon Revolt *later* in his narrative.[6] There seems little doubt. The entry for 441 is not a reflection of the Revolt that Gildas describes.

But if not the Revolt, what is it? What event or series of events could have convinced a chronicler in Gaul that the Saxons had conquered Britain? There is only one event that would be so significant that contemporaries might see it as the

'Death of Britain'. We have already seen something like it in 410, although on a larger scale. If Saxons had *temporarily* captured London, if raiders had penetrated into the Upper Thames and were beginning to settle there, this would be more than enough to justify such an entry. A Gallo-Roman ship captain, perhaps the very skipper who transported Germanus and Lupus on their dangerous voyage, would have reported the capital overrun with barbarians. Word would soon have spread that the eastern coast of Britain was a no-go area for continental Romans. To a chronicler ending his work in the year 452, Britain would indeed have seemed lost forever.

The Saxon advance would not have stopped here, however. The estates of the Thames Valley were a rich prize for barbarians. Once London fell, Saxons could push upriver, pillaging at their leisure. If the raiders stayed over the winter, as Vikings often did two centuries later, the very heart of Lowland Britain would be under barbarian control.

How does Arthur fit into all this? We have seen the first fleeting image of Arthur in the preceding chapter. Now, a decade later, we may actually hear his voice. It is not a gentle voice. It is impatient, even arrogant: the voice of an experienced man who has seen his leaders blunder through caution and stupidity. It is the voice of a military commander who thinks he knows how to save a hopeless situation.

And it has been in Gildas all along.

A very cursory reading of Gildas might lead one to believe that he too gives an account of the Saxon onslaught of 441. Once the Romans leave, he first talks about 'a garrison equally slow to fight and ill adapted to run away'. Then he tells us that the Britons 'left their cities', and that 'the enemy… pursued them with more unrelenting cruelty than before, and butchered our countrymen like sheep, so that their habitations were like those of savage beasts; for they turned their arms upon each other…

Thus foreign calamities were augmented by domestic feuds.'[7] Then, in 446, only five years after the 'Fall of Britain' reported by the Gallic chronicler, Gildas notes a request for foreign intervention: a second British appeal to the Romans more desperate than the first. All of this seems plausible, even eerily familiar, to anyone with knowledge of recent ethnic conflicts in Bosnia and Darfur. However, there is one tiny flaw in all this. For Gildas at least, these foes are not Saxons at all, but Irishmen and Picts. Moreover, he seems to think that all of this is taking place at Hadrian's Wall, far to the north. Perhaps his critics are right: Gildas' story is so garbled that even he is not a reliable witness.

Perhaps. But Gildas also tells us that no Saxons were in Britain at *any* time until the year of the *Adventus*, i.e. in 450, *after* the second request for aid in 446. This is quite simply wrong. Archaeology reveals that Saxons were in East Anglia from the second quarter of the fifth century. It may therefore be worth while asking *why* no Saxons appear in this part of his narrative. The answer cannot be that Gildas wants to protect their reputation. For quite understandable reasons, he considers the Saxons even worse than the Picts and Irish; his description of the Revolt is little short of an apocalypse. The solution to this riddle might be to ask another question, this time in Latin: *cui bono*? To whose advantage would it be to downplay the fact that Saxons were driving Britons from their cities in the 440s? It surely cannot be Ambrosius. He is Gildas' great hero precisely because he wages unremitting war on the Saxons. But a likely candidate, indeed the *only* plausible candidate, is the Proud Tyrant himself, the ruler we have postulated as Arthur. Gildas affirms that Saxons were one of the main props to this ruler's regime. The Proud Tyrant would thus have had every reason to downplay the fact that his allies had once been invaders. Far better to point to victories over Picts and Irish and, if conflicts with the Saxons must be mentioned, keep the ethnicity of the foe well in the background. Of interest, this second appeal to the Romans is for aid not against Saxons... or Irish... or Picts, but against generic 'barbarians'. Further, in the list of Arthur's battles his foes are described simply as 'pagans'. In both cases, we may be seeing a fifth-century version of political correctness.

That the evidence Gildas used for this part of his narrative originally chronicled a Saxon incursion is also strengthened by the one piece of evidence he cites that may plausibly derive from a fifth-century document: this second request for aid, commonly known as the Appeal to Aetius. It appears to be the précis of a letter dispatched to the Patrician Aetius. The date is given as the year of his third consulship. It is important to understand that such consular years were the standard means of Roman timekeeping. Each year a consul was elected in both the eastern and western empires, and from thence forward the year was known by the names of the two persons so honoured. Emperors and important leaders like Aetius were often repeat consuls, and we know that Aetius' third elevation to this post occurred in precisely 446.

What is just as important is the fact that this Appeal is written in a style very different from that of Gildas. He is most likely using a text from an earlier period that was common knowledge to most educated Britons of his time. It is therefore worth quoting, to see what its original purpose may have been.

> To Aetius, now consul for the third time: the groans of the Britons... the barbarians drive us to the sea, and the sea throws us back on the barbarians: thus two modes of death await us, we are either slain or drowned.[8]

We immediately see an anomaly here. Clearly, Irishmen attacking from the west—or Picts swooping down from the Wall—are *not* driving Britons toward the sea. An attack up the Bristol Channel or in northern Wales would in fact be driving Britons *away* from any body of water. Moreover, most British cities of any size were very far from Hadrian's Wall. Why would

Lowland *decuriones* have to abandon their cities because the Wall had been breached? The flight from urban centres that Gildas describes would make sense only if cities like Canterbury, St Albans, *Noviomagus* (Crayford) and London itself were under threat, and their populations fleeing westwards.[9] Gildas does not realize it, but his own narrative is the best confirmation of the Gallic Chronicle. The Appeal is a near-contemporary description of the same event. *Saxons* were the main threat to Britain from 441 to 446.

This also strongly suggests that much of Gildas' narrative may date from the time of the Proud Tyrant's regime. This talk of Pictish and Irish attacks is a *conclusion* drawn by Gildas himself, due to his ignorance that 'East Anglian' *migrants* had preceded the Saxon mercenaries by a quarter of a century.[10] It is based on a logical but false assumption that no Saxons existed in Britain prior to the *Adventus* date of 450. It is a pardonable mistake; indeed, one that the Proud Tyrant would *want* him to make, in order to whitewash the Germanic mercenaries.

More to the point, however, much of what Gildas says may also reflect the frustrations of a seasoned military man *at that time.* The talk of British leaders approaching the Romans 'like timorous chickens' in their first request for aid and the second plaintive request addressed to Aetius place whatever passed for Britain's military and political leadership in an extremely unflattering light. Gildas' characterization of British troops at this time is also extremely illuminating.

> A useless and panic-stricken company, who slumbered away their days and nights on their unprofitable watch. Meanwhile the barbed weapons of their enemies were not idle, and our wretched countrymen were dragged from the wall and dashed to the ground.[11]

Gildas would have no direct knowledge of the fighting qualities of British soldiers serving some eighty or ninety years earlier. He could easily have portrayed theirs as a heroic last stand, or passed the whole issue over in silence. But these unkind words are exactly what any leader of something resembling a Roman field army would say about troops ordered to make a static, piecemeal defence of each individual British city. True, Late Roman military doctrine required that cities be garrisoned and provisioned against barbarian sieges. But this was only so that the enemy would be deprived of supplies, and thus easier for the mobile troops to destroy. This devastating criticism is directed at leaders who refuse to confront the enemy in open battle.

It is also doubtful that this 'useless and panic-stricken company' is defending Hadrian's Wall, where we find a sharp population decline at just this time. Instead, these are the soldiers of Lowland Britain, parcelled out to each walled city by men of the *decurio* class. In protecting themselves and their own families, the landed elite have allowed the barbarians to run rampant through eastern Britain. Gildas' text is a very loud 'I told you so.'

Clearly, Gildas in 520 is using British history to show that all their troubles are a divine punishment for the Britons' moral failings. But the actual *data* that he presents tell a rather different tale. First, Britain's military and political leaders are obliged to ask Rome for help in about 418. But even when substantial aid and training are given to the Britons, the barbarian threat continues to grow. Then, instead of concentrating all available forces into something resembling a Late Roman field army, Britain's soldiers are sent to hold scattered fortifications. Disaster ensues, so complete that the Britons must again turn to Rome. It is the step-by-step critique of an experienced commander who has fought the barbarian threat for years.

There is little evidence that Britain's cities were subjected to fire and sword. But this does not argue against the veracity of either the *Gallic Chronicle* or Gildas. Instead it may actually reveal the nature of the barbarian threat. The Saxons were using the same methods they had employed against St Germanus in 429: going after soft targets. Siege warfare was totally beyond them, and would remain so for years to come. But they could raid as easily by land as by sea. Like a fifth-century *Janjaweed*, they could loot farms and carry off captives. They could set fire to crops and slaughter livestock. Their numbers may have been relatively small, but in only a few years such raiding would drive off the rural peasantry and turn Britain's farms into wasteland. Once this happened, the urban population would begin to starve. It is then, and only then, that the Britons would have 'left their cities'. Many nobles may never have actually seen a Saxon. But as they departed in the last convoys for western cities like Bath, Gloucester, and Cirencester, they knew that they had failed. Worse still, they had shown themselves unworthy to lead Britain.

During this time Vitalis' son followed the same road westward. Like Aeneas, he probably took an aging father from a fallen city. By now he also had a wife, as well as a son and daughter. The sights they saw on that trek were surely unsettling, even for folk brought up in a dangerous era. Gildas gives a graphic picture of this time: 'The discomfited people, wandering in the woods, began to feel the effects of a severe famine. For many hunger compelled them without delay to yield themselves up to their cruel persecutors.'[12]

In an age when the UNHCR and other NGOs routinely step in to aid refugees, it is important to remember that nothing like them existed in the fifth century. The abandonment of Britain's eastern cities implies the flight of thousands—probably tens of thousands—of people. Many would have died on the journey. Even after they reached places of safety, it is still doubtful that the majority could have found any real livelihood. Most land in the west was already settled. As Gildas says, the fugitives would have been relegated to the margins of society, 'wandering in the woods'. If their displacement lasted from 441 to 446, many thousands would have been condemned to years of slow starvation.

We may also see here the death knell of what was left of town life in eastern Britain. Significant trade over any distance would have ceased with the beginning of the Saxon raids. Whatever remained of the artisan class would have either sought other means of subsistence, or simply starved to death. Except for the few towns that still survived in the west, Britain had essentially reverted to a rural economy. The *decuriones'* failure meant that much of urban civilization in Britain was gone for ever.

Vitalis' son probably made no effort to hide his contempt for the island's highest leaders. And other Britons were listening. By the year 446 he seemed the one Briton capable of salvaging something from the debacle. True, desperate *decuriones* were sending a delegation to Aetius, the Roman generalissimo in Gaul. They hoped that the greatest soldier of the age might once again send 'cavalry by land and mariners by sea'. But Vitalis' son was a realist, as only an experienced military commander can be. He had followed events on the continent for years and knew exactly what Roman capabilities were. He too thought that Aetius might be their salvation.

But not in the way that the *decuriones* expected.

AETIUS

Aetius, the *Magister Militum*, or Marshal, of the western empire, in a sense personifies the realities of fifth-century Rome. His father, Gaudentius, came from a humble family in the Balkans. After rising to high rank within the army, he married a Roman woman of noble lineage. In this way Gaudentius became an 'insider' at the imperial court. This gave Aetius a good start in life. But the young man's early experiences also set him apart from his other well-connected peers. At an early age he was chosen to live as a hostage among the Huns. Treated with great respect, he was able to study these people at first hand and so understand the intricacies of mounted steppe warfare. He also developed a close personal relationship with a certain Hunnic prince called Attila.

Once released, Aetius chose his father's profession, and was soon singled out as an officer of promise. Eventually he caught the eye of John, the usurper who seized the western throne after Honorius' death. When John was deposed in 425, Aetius quickly switched sides to the legitimate regime of Valentinian III. By 433 the young general felt confident enough to take on Marshal Boniface, the Roman military ruler of North Africa. When the latter died in battle, Aetius became Patrician, and thus the real power behind the weak and vacillating Valentinian III.[13]

Aetius was a gifted commander. A master psychologist, he was able to deal effectively with both his barbarian allies and his Roman supporters. His Classical education gave him easy entrée to the highest circles of Roman society. His early contact with the Huns and Goths enabled him to understand—and thus command—a number of different barbarian peoples. He could recruit ready-made formations of Huns or Alans and use them effectively. He could make—and break—alliances with any of the barbarians then inhabiting Gaul, be they Burgundians, Visigoths, Franks, or Alans. Aetius also seems to have had an uncanny ability to find and promote talented subordinates. Aegidius, Majorian, Ricimer—the list of his protégés is a roll call of the chief Roman actors in the latter part of the century. This rare combination of talents made Aetius one of the most formidable Roman leaders of the age. Little wonder that refugees skulking in cities like Gloucester and Bath saw him as the one man capable of saving Britain.

Once given command of Rome's western armies, Aetius fought ferociously to defeat its enemies. In 436 he destroyed the Burgundian kingdom on the Rhine. In 437 he put down an insurrection by peasant rebels, known by the overall name of

Bacaudae. That same year, despite a subordinate's debacle, he was able to come to a *modus vivendi* with the Visigoths. In 446 he repelled an invasion from across the Rhine by the Ripuarian Franks.[14] The wars show a talented soldier in his prime. But they also give a glimpse of a Late Roman field army in action. It is no accident that many of the recruits within his forces were Huns. They were as skilled at horsemanship as the Alans and, with the expansion of the Hunnic kingdom westward, were in greater supply. Now they would engage in the same kind of mounted warfare that the British marshal Gerontius had practised in 407. One season Aetius' troops might be in the north fighting Burgundians, the next in the south fighting Goths. But this kind of mobility was possible only by means of a still-intact road system. With it, Aetius could surprise and out-manoeuvre formations of barbarians much larger than his own. This often called for unorthodox tactics. In one famous incident a fast-moving cavalry column arrived just in the nick of time to raise a lengthy siege at the city of Narbonne. The troopers then fed the starving citizens from sacks of grain strapped to their saddles.[15]

But just at the time of the Saxon onslaught in Britain, the situation changed dramatically for Aetius. Attila became less of a friend and more of an enemy. The supply of Hunnic recruits dried up. Like previous Roman rulers, Aetius sought other steppe barbarians to fill the gap. And, as so often in the past, he turned to the Alans. But it was no longer possible to recruit individual Alans into Roman units. Like the Goths and Burgundians, the Alans had established an independent state of their own in northeastern Gaul. They even had a king, a wily old steppe warrior called Goar. In 442, the year after London's fall, Aetius made a shrewd proposal to Goar. He invited the Alan ruler to lead his armoured warriors south, to Orleans. There they would establish a new kingdom between the Seine and the Loire. Evidence for this Alanic kingdom has survived to this day: a number of French place names in this area derive from the ethnic name for these people, 'Alan'.[16]

The site for this new kingdom was far from random. The Visigoths, always a danger, lay just across the Loire. Moreover, the region occupied by the Alanic settlements—between the Seine and the Loire—had a significance that any British commander would have immediately understood. By commanding the two main rivers in northern Gaul they limited any possible threat from a shipborne foe. And this was not just a theoretical danger. At this very same time Saxon settlers were moving into enclaves on the northwestern coast of Gaul. Eventually these settlements would stretch from Boulogne to Bayeux. Not surprisingly, the Saxons chose areas very like East Anglia. The mouth of the Somme, for example, is just the sort of flat, flooded area that would have attracted families fleeing the drowned world of the Netherlands and north Germany. We even see similarities in place names on both sides of the Channel. In Britain we find Folkestone, Cambridge and Buckingham; in Gaul we find Faquethun, Cambrique and Bouquenghen. Even the town of Sangatte (Sandgate) has associations with unwelcome immigrants far earlier than the twentieth century.[17] By placing the Alans where he did, Aetius protected the cities of central Gaul, above all Paris. It was an intelligent strategy, and it might be replicated outside Gaul.

APPEAL

Now, in 446, a delegation of Britons meekly trooped into Aetius' office. Dressed in their most splendid garments, they began their presentation. They pointed out that controlling the Gallican Straits would protect both Britain and the empire. The Saxons were a greater threat than in former times. If they were not neutralized the whole Gallic coast was at risk. Grinning weakly, they asked how the Patrician could afford *not* to intervene. As they fell silent, they knew they had made a logical, even a compelling argument.

7. 'They Left Their Cities'

But Aetius refused point blank. He had little interest in naval affairs, and this talk of 'choke points' and aquatic ambushes ignored his real concern. The main danger to Rome did not come from a few sea barbarians. It came from Attila and his hordes. Aetius made a cold but rational decision: no aid could or would be sent. Britain was quite simply expendable.

The delegation was crushed at this decision—and so were the fugitive *decuriones* back in Britain. Only a few walled places—cities like Gloucester, Cirencester, and Bath—lay between the Saxons and the Bristol Channel. One more push and Britain would be cut in two. The wayward diocese would die like a snake severed at its middle. Saxons would rule Britain in the same way that Goths and Vandals reigned in imperial territories, with the Irish and Picts gobbling up the leavings. Every Briton, high or low, could feel only black despair.

One man felt something else, however. A bitter satisfaction—that was understandable. But also the inner calm of someone utterly convinced that only he can save a hopeless situation. Vitalis' son had followed Aetius' career for some time. Ships like the one that had taken the envoys to Gaul had been bringing back news of the Patrician's victories for years. A modern Roman field army had been defeating barbarian armies many times its size. The same could be done in Britain.

Vitalis' son also saw things that others had overlooked. The pagans had stolen away thousands of captives. But more than a million souls remained in the diocese: souls who could feed an army; souls who could learn the *armatura* and take their place in a line of battle. The barbarians had devastated much of the island, but fine Roman roads still existed. The Britons had lost untold quantities of gold and silver, but their iron remained. And with it they could forge the swords and spears that would hew the way to victory. Only one more thing was needed.

A leader: a *Dux Bellorum*.

8.

'THEY OVERTHREW THEIR ENEMIES'

BATTLES

Then Arthur fought against them in those days, together with the
kings of the British; but he was their leader in battle [*Dux Bellorum*].
The first battle was at the mouth of the river called Glein. The
second, the third, the fourth and the fifth were on another river,
called the Douglas, which is in the country of Lindsey. The sixth
battle was on the river called Bassas. The seventh battle was in
Celyddon Forest, that is, the Battle of Celyddon Coed. The eighth
battle was in Guinnion fort, and in it Arthur carried the image of the
holy Mary, the everlasting Virgin, on his [shield], and the heathen
were put to flight on that day, and there was a great slaughter upon
them, through the power of Our Lord Jesus Christ and the power of
the holy Virgin Mary, his mother. The ninth battle was fought in the
city of the Legion [Chester]. The tenth battle was fought on the bank
of the river called Tryfrwyd [*Traeth Tribruit*]. The eleventh battle
was on the hill called Agned. The twelfth battle was on Badon Hill
and in it nine hundred and sixty men fell in one day, from a single
charge of Arthur's, and no one laid them low save he alone; and he
was victorious in all his campaigns.[1]

The above quotation is usually termed Arthur's Battle List.
At first glance it seems to be a simple, straightforward
document: the sort of report a successful general might send
from the front. We see no poetic flourishes here; no metaphors

106

Plate I

Aeneas dining with Dido off what Sidonius Apollinaris calls an '*orbis*'—a circular or 'round' table. Compare the longhaired and clean-shaven servants with the *protectores* in Plate VI. Detail from folio100v of the *Vergilius Romanus*, cod. lat. 3867 (Courtesy Vatican Library)

Plate II

A Late Roman dragon standard from the Museum of Koblenz. One of these would have flown over every Post-Roman British cohort (or *cosgord*—the later Welsh word for war band) (Courtesy Generaldirektion Kulterelles Erbe, Direktion Archäologie, Koblenz)

Plate III

The emperor Constantine the Great wearing a *pilleus*—the flat-crowned Late Roman Army 'service cap.' (Courtesy Beast Coins)

Plate IV

Long-haired, clean-shaven *protectores* (bodyguards) of a Late Roman emperor, with civilian officials on the right. Note the 'Cross of Constantine' on
the shields—the same design associated with a later military strongman from
Britain—Arthur. (Courtesy Elafius)

Plate V

A modern reconstruction of the Sutton Hoo Saxon *cyul*. Note the sail and high prow. The largest of these could carry sixty warriors to Britain. (Courtesy Edwin and Joyce Gifford)

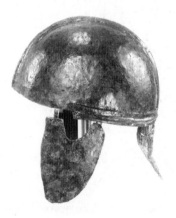

Plate VI

A 'ridged helmet' from the Museum of Worms. The sort that a fully-equipped Post-Roman British soldier would have worn in his battles with the Saxons of eastern Britain.
(Courtesy Stadtarkhiv, Institut für Stadtgeschichte, Worms)

Plates

Plate VII

The Post –Roman maritime citadel of Tintagel--as psychologically intimidating to Arthur's sea-borne enemies as the earlier Saxon Shore forts. (Courtesy Cornwall County Council)

The Regnal Year 423

Plate VIII

A coin with the portrait of the eastern emperor Theodosius II. His accession as senior emperor in 423 was to be a crucial benchmark in Late Roman—and British—timekeeping.
(Courtesy Forum Ancient Coins)

Plate IX

Senior and Junior. The reverse of the same coin, showing the western emperor Valentinian III standing in a subordinate position beside his senior colleague, Theodosius II.
(Courtesy Forum Ancient Coins)

The Regnal Year 450
'The Year of Badon'

Plate X

Upon the death of Theodosius II, the western emperor Valentinain III (left) became senior emperor, and Marcian (right) became his junior eastern colleague. The beginning of their joint reign in 450 was remembered by subsequent Britons and Saxons as the most important imperial regnal year of all. (Courtesy Forum Ancient Coins)

Plate XI

Portrait of Anthemius, who became western emperor in 467. He and eastern emperor Leo stand side-by-side on the reverse. The failure of Arthur's expedition against the Visigoths was to doom both Anthemius and the western empire.
(Courtesy Forum Ancient Coins)

'Avalon'

Plate XII

An aerial view of the Saxon Shore fort at Richborough. The present dry land to the east marks where the wide - but still fordable - Wantsum Channel once ran. It was here at the 'Ford of Afael' that Arthur fought his last battle. (Courtesy English Heritage and Skyscan) or similes. But whoever had this written down was also far from naïve. Great pains were taken to stress the body count in particular battles, and to credit divine aid at a critical point. On the face of it this appears to be a succinct account of the deeds of an ambitious military leader.

Unfortunately for the credibility of the Battle List, it is found not in Gildas, but in the *Historia Brittonum*, a work from the ninth century. For this reason alone many scholars have dismissed it as simply too remote in time to have any relevance to events three centuries earlier. Moreover, in the *Historia*'s narrative this bit of Arthuriana comes *after* the reigns of both the Proud Tyrant (called 'Vortigern' in the *Historia*) and Ambrosius. These battles would therefore have to take place in either the late fifth century or the early sixth, in a period far later than the Saxon onslaught of the 440s. With this in mind, most 'Arthurians' see the *Dux Bellorum* as a local warlord fighting a last-ditch battle with the Saxons in about 500. It might seem curious that his putative contemporary, Gildas, not only fails to mention Arthur in his narrative, but also makes it very plain that no battles were being fought in his time. Gildas explicitly tells us that the generation that had witnessed the Saxon wars has quite died off. But all the same, 'Arthurians' try to explain away Gildas' testimony by various ingenious means.[2] In the end a very distinct battle line has been drawn with regard to the Battle List. Practically all scholars accept Gildas' negative testimony and see Arthur as little more than a myth. Most 'Arthurians' reject this thinking, arguing that something more than bardic genius must lie behind the account of twelve desperate battles. But could there be a third alternative, one that accepts both of these apparently irreconcilable points of view?

First of all, it is very interesting that the compiler of the *Historia Brittonum* actually gives us no chronological information about Arthur. Chapter 66 of the *Historia* provides a very elaborate timeline for the entire fifth century, to include specific dates for events connected with the Proud Tyrant and Ambrosius. But there is no mention of Arthur anywhere within it. Another curious thing is that the foes in the list are nowhere described as Saxons. Instead, they are given the generic name of 'pagans'. This raises our suspicions that some of these battles may have been fought not against Saxons, but against the Picts and Irish that Gildas claims were ravaging Britain in 446. The resolution of the apparent contradiction between Gildas and the Battle List may lie in the likelihood that the *only* information that the *Historia* compiler possessed about Arthur was this list. The compiler would then have made the very logical assumption that Arthur was a separate, autonomous personality in British history, and so must come after the reigns of the Proud Tyrant and Ambrosius. That Arthur might actually have been either of these last two rulers was something he simply did not consider.

The Appeal to Aetius itself may offer more insight into this question. On the face of it, the Appeal is a most peculiar event. Its whole point is that the Patrician Aetius did *not* send aid to the Britons. It is quite simply a non-event, of no apparent significance to the ultimate fate of Britain. Yet every early source mentions it. The *Anglo-Saxon Chronicle* (*ASC*) recounts only a handful of events between 380 and 450, but very prominent among these is the Appeal. Bede, Gildas, and the *Historia* all mention it as well. What is even stranger is that Gildas, who normally uses every opportunity to chastise the moral failings of his fellow Britons, reports the Appeal without comment. Even he can draw no spiritual lesson from it. Why would an event with no apparent significance be thought so crucial to British history?

Gildas' very next passage answers this question: 'Others of them, however, lying hid in mountains, caves, and woods, continually sallied out from thence to renew the war... And then it was, for the first time, that they overthrew their enemies.'[3]

The significance of the Appeal can only be that it marks a watershed. Before 446 the diocese teetered on the edge of extinction, beset on every side by seaborne enemies. In 446 the Britons requested aid from Aetius, without success. Yet shortly after this Gildas reports that they achieved a victory, and Bede states that after 450 Britain's erstwhile enemies, the Saxons, became her allies. The most likely person to have accomplished this reversal of fortune was the man Gildas says was ruling Britain at this time: a military leader we have identified as both the Proud Tyrant and Arthur. All of this evidence suggests that the Battle List in the *Historia Brittonum* is *not* a record of warfare in AD 500; Gildas gives us rather decisive evidence to the contrary. Instead, the list is an account of how Britons who still retained much of their Late Roman military expertise 'overthrew their enemies' in the mid-fifth century.

Many will object that this is mere speculation. If the Battle List does not belong where the *Historia* places it, it could be the product of any era. After all, one respectable theory equates Arthur with the second-century Roman commander Artorius Castus.[4] Alternatively, it may merely be a legend that became attached to a real person, of no more value than Geoffrey of Monmouth's *History of the Kings of Britain*. One prominent scholar has even argued that the only 'safe' conclusion is that the compiler of the *Historia Brittonum* simply made the whole thing up himself.[5] The sober, scholarly conclusion *must* be that there is no evidence that can tie the Battle List to the world of fifth-century Britain—or to any other time and place.

But, as we shall see, we *do* have the evidence. And once again, it has been in Gildas all along.

LISTS

This Battle List is one of the most analysed (perhaps over-analysed) pieces of Arthuriana ever. Literally hundreds of historians, both professional and amateur, have spent countless hours mulling over these place names, trying to pin down the 'campaigns of Arthur'. Unfortunately, so many conflicting theories have been advanced, largely based on linguistics, that most scholars prefer to ignore the issue. They doubt whether the list can be of any value in understanding fifth-century Britain.

It is certainly true that linguistic analysis alone can never tell us anything certain about the Battle List. Our knowledge of fifth-century British place names is simply too fragmentary. But all the same, some of the locations are certainly real. Most agree that the 'forest of Celyddon" is the Caledonian Forest in southern Scotland (see Map 2). The 'City of the Legions' is almost certainly Chester, near England's present border with northern Wales. 'Linnius' may be in the vicinity of Lincoln, on the marches of East Anglia, northwest of where the earliest concentration of Saxons was located. There also happens to be a River Glen in this same area, feeding into the Wash. The other sites are more controversial. But it is significant that those that can be identified are on the periphery of what was left of Roman Britain. Taken together, they are precisely the areas where we would expect an aggressive *Dux Bellorum* to repel onslaughts by Picts, 'Scots' and Saxons: at the frontiers.

Another striking feature of the Battle List is that the majority of these engagements take place in the vicinity of bodies of water.[6] Indeed, the first six encounters are *all* on rivers. This should actually be no surprise. The Saxon *cyuls* could move men and supplies quickly, facilitating the establishment of base camps on inland rivers—bases that then became full-fledged settlements. Moreover, the best counter to such surprise landings would be fast-moving, hard-hitting cavalry—the descendants of the field armies of Late Roman times. When we remember archaeology has found considerable evidence of early Saxon settlements along many of Britain's eastern rivers, this suggests that the most likely foes in these first six battles were Saxons. They were the only people settling the interior of the diocese at this time. They could use their flat-bottomed *cyuls* to carry large numbers of warriors deep into Britain's hinterland.

The compiler of the *Historia Brittonum* was writing in a time remote from the fifth century, and would have us believe that all twelve of these battles were against the Saxons. But the last six battles differ markedly in location, type and emphasis. Only one of them is by a body of water, and it is described not as a river, but as a shore or strand (*traeth*). This implies a location on or not far from the sea. Another, the seventh, is in the Caledonian Forest, far to the north and near the present border with Scotland. As for the last four, at least two are in western Britain: Chester and Bath/Badon. This is very far from any Saxon settlement of the time, suggesting that one or more of these last four struggles may actually have involved some other foe. What the Battle List *may* be telling us is that the first eight battles were fought in eastern and northern Britain, while the last four were fought in the west.

A perceptive critic will now say, 'But what about Gildas? He says nothing about these battles. Surely they were concocted at a much later date than the fifth century.' But is this really true? Or have we simply not read Gildas with enough care? It is important to recall what he says immediately after the year 446:

> And then it was, for the first time, that they [the Britons] overthrew their enemies, who had for so many years been living in their country; for their trust was not in man, but in God... the boldness of the enemy was for a while checked.[7]

The *reason* he gives for why the Britons 'overthrew their enemies' is of more than a little interest. According to Gildas they won because 'their trust was not in man, but in God.' Curiously, the Battle List attributes Arthur's victory in his eighth encounter at Guinnion not to Arthur's own prowess but to Christ and the Virgin Mary. This might seem like a mere coincidence—until we read something else Gildas says only a few lines down, this time about the Picts: 'the Picts in the far end of the island kept quiet from now on.'[8]

The only conceivable reason that hitherto successful Pictish raiders would suddenly cease their attacks is because of British military force. And this precisely coincides with what we are told about Arthur's seventh victory in the Caledonian Forest. A successful British campaign in southern Scotland would indeed be pushing hostile Picts toward 'the far end of the island'. Gildas may not realize it, but his statements about God-given British victories and a sudden Pictish quiescence are our best indication that the first eight encounters of the Battle List actually occurred. Gildas and the *Historia Brittonum* are merely giving two very different versions of the same series of events.

Gildas tells us that the Britons went on the offensive shortly after 446. The Battle List gives us important clues as to where these battles were fought. Any depiction of these first eight encounters must be tentative in the extreme, for there is much that we do not know. But there is enough to suggest that a new commander was leading the army of Britain into battle. Just how well he performed would decide the fate of a million souls.

BATTLES

By the end of 446 *Londinium* had been under Saxon control for five years. Important towns like *Verulamium* (St Albans), *Calleva* (Silchester), and *Ratae* (Leicester) either were under constant attack or had fallen to the invaders. British refugees, often men of high birth, were filling the western towns of *Corinium* (Cirencester), *Glevum* (Gloucester), and Bath. To the British magnates of the west the choice was stark: either share the fate of their unfortunate colleagues, or place the country under military control. Now their most successful commander was offering a plan of nation-wide resistance. No longer would the Britons keep most of their troops inside the cities. A genuine mobile field army would be created, similar to the one used by

Marshal Aetius in Gaul. It would move about the country, destroying the enclaves of Saxon, Pict and 'Scot'. But to do so, every part of the country must support it. Every Briton must obey its leader without question. It was a hard bargain, but the *decuriones* knew they had no alternative.

The leader of this force bore the old Roman title of *Dux*. This *Dux* now outlined his high-risk strategy. The Saxon threat was on a wide front, from south of the Thames to the area of Lincoln. Enclaves of Pictish raiders existed farther north. An effective strike force of mobile cavalry and infantry could liquidate all of these. But to create this force he would need to gather soldiers from every part of what was left of Roman Britain. Cities like Cirencester and Gloucester, Bath and Chester would be denuded of troops, left vulnerable to Saxon attack. Many *decuriones* were horrified when they heard this. Only a few walled cities now stood between the Saxons and the Bristol Channel. A new Saxon onslaught would cut Britain in two, drive her citizens into the sea. But any formal complaints came far too late. The *Dux* was already on the march.

His first gambit was to lead a mobile force up the straight Roman road that ran from *Corinium* (Cirencester) through *Ratae* (Leicester), then north to the area of Lincoln. Cohorts[9] of elite cavalry and picked infantry marched quickly over the well-used highway, a bright windsock coiling above each unit. British communities along the way provided food and shelter to the force: that is, once the troopers began thumbing their bright steel weapons beneath the noses of the local *decuriones*. But as the force moved further north it passed wretched refugee settlements, then deserted villages. The Saxons were very close.

Now the real work of the *Dux* began. His tactics very much resembled those seen on the American frontier of the nineteenth century, or in any number of guerrilla wars in the twentieth. He sent forward cavalry scouts, or *exploratores*, to reconnoitre the country ahead. These moved upriver, sniffing out the Saxon bases. His main forces followed behind, ready to launch a surprise attack when the barbarians were located. Very soon a rider returned with intelligence. A pagan enclave lay just ahead. The *Dux* called his commanders together. They would assault the next day.

What followed was a variation on tactics we have seen in countless irregular wars from Bosnia to Darfur. Only the weapons were different. Just as the sun rose, a line of shouting, screaming riders galloped toward the settlement. Above their heads streamed a gilded dragon banner, its mouth devouring the cold morning air. Surprise was total. Groggy Saxons awoke inside their huts, stumbled out into the chill dawn. As they exited they were cut down one by one—or burned alive inside. Others, more cunning, took refuge behind beached ships. But this did them little good. The horsemen of the *Dux* were everywhere, driving the Saxons toward a solid wall of infantry advancing from the opposite direction. In the end, all but a lucky few died from sword, spear, or arrow. British captives were freed, and given an escort back to a place of safety. Those Saxon women and children not slain in the fighting were bound and sold as slaves. Valuables stripped from the dead—cloaks, brooches, swords, belt fittings—were divided among the soldiers. After forty years of trial, StPatrick's kinsmen were taking a sweet revenge.

The campaign continued. More settlements were found. More Saxons were slain. Now, however, the alarm had been raised. The barbarians were fleeing before the British onslaught. The *Dux* followed, never slackening his pace. Finally, probably near the mouth of the Glen River, his *exploratores* sent word that a Saxon force was drawn up, ready for a last stand. A pitched battle followed. Once again the gilded dragon triumphed. But this pitched battle was really only incidental to the *Dux Bellorum*'s overall strategy. With each mile he was winning back the fruitful land of Britain…

The Battle List reports more battles along rivers. Four may have occurred in the area that is now Lincolnshire. The fact that Picts are often reported working with both Saxons and Irish suggests that this was an area that Saxons *and* Picts were settling. That it was necessary to fight four battles at all indicates that this was a critical region. Once secured, it would drive a permanent wedge between the two peoples. A vast amount of British territory would also be freed from the barbarian threat. The sixth battle was located on an unknown river called *Bassas*, and probably had the same overall goal. But the next, the seventh, is different. In the original it is called *Coit Celidon*, and is almost certainly the Caledonian Forest in southern Scotland.

CELIDON

We might think that this is evidence that the *Dux* led his entire field army far to the north. After all, this is what the Battle List *seems* to say. But it is important to note that nowhere are we told that Arthur was present at all twelve encounters. In fact, his presence is explicitly cited in only two battles: *Guinnion* and *Badon*. Moreover, it would have been very unwise for any leader to move his entire force so far from what can only have been the main threat to Britain at this time: the Saxons. Just what, then, was the significance of this 'northern battle' at *Coit Celidon*?

Something earlier in the Battle List may resolve this puzzle, and it is worth quoting again to see what may really have occurred: 'Arthur along with the kings of Britain fought against them in those days, but Arthur himself was the military commander [*Dux Bellorum*].'[10] It is a curious phrase, and is often taken to mean that Arthur was a mercenary commander. In modern terms, he would have been some sort of military contractor hired by the petty kings of his day to fight their wars. But if so, it is curious that there are so many 'chiefs' and only one 'Indian'. Nor is it clear why the List praises Arthur, but is silent about his supposed superiors. The fact that he, and he alone, is the *Dux Bellorum* may have another significance entirely. This title argues not that Arthur was a mercenary leader, but that he was the *commander-in-chief* of all British forces. These 'kings' were not his superiors; they were his *subordinates*, subordinates who were winning their own individual battles under his overall direction.[11] They resemble Napoleon's marshals—a number of whom also became kings in their own right. Remarkably, in the earliest Welsh literature about Arthur this is precisely the relationship he has with two of his closest companions, Cai and Bedwyr. In one of the earliest Welsh poems mentioning Arthur, the *Pa Gur*, we find Cai fighting in *Mynydd Eiddyn*, i.e. 'the mountain of Eiddyn'. This is actually Edinburgh, whose original name was Eiddyn.[12] This appears to be telling us that it was Cai, not Arthur, who was the hero of this 'northern expedition'. The best explanation is that he is one of the 'kings' who were aiding Arthur in his battles. The Battle List is not simply a Dark Age warlord's boast about his personal triumphs. Instead, it is the record of a carefully thought-out campaign of manoeuvre that eventually defeated all of Britain's foes.

The names of Arthur's two legendary lieutenants may also tell us something very important about the make-up of British leadership at the time. The name Cai is probably Roman in origin. The most likely time that a child would be christened with such a name is at the beginning of the fifth century, when the Roman army was composed of men with names like Constantine, Marcus and Gerontius. Like the *Dux Bellorum* himself, Cai is best seen as the son of a Roman soldier stationed in Britain.[13]

The name Bedwyr is of even more interest. It does not appear to be either Latin or Celtic. Instead, it may indicate just how diverse Britain's Late Roman society really was. We have already met a martial steppe people called the Alans. Their language was related to Persian, and a form of it is still spoken among the Os, or Ossetians, of the Caucasus to this day. Of interest, in the epic literature of the latter people we encounter a hero named 'Batraz'. This, however, is not simply a name. A very similar word, *Batyr*, is found in the epic literature of many other Caucasian and Central Asian peoples to this day. It means 'hero', and the best explanation for the name Batraz is that it was originally *Batyr-Os* (literally 'hero of the Os', i.e. the Ossetians).[14] Bedwyr may simply be a variation on the steppe title of *Batyr*. In other words, it is very possible that one of Arthur's trusted lieutenants was christened with a name from the steppes of what is now Ukraine, reflecting the diverse make-up of the Late Roman army.

But still, where *was* Cai's chief during this far-flung northern campaign? The answer can only be—far to the south, fighting the eighth battle at *Guinnion*. Again, a careful examination of what the Battle List says about this eighth encounter can give us a valuable insight into Britain in the late 440s. *Badon* is the most famous of the twelve battles, and since Gildas' time has been seen as Arthur's greatest and most decisive victory. The list tells us that it was here that Arthur slew 960 foes with his own hand. All the same, it is curious that even more 'reporting space' is devoted to the eighth battle, the one at *Guinnion*. For some reason this entry gives us the most details. It mentions a great slaughter of the 'pagans'. Arthur carries an image of the Virgin Mary on his 'shoulders'. He credits the victory not to his own prowess but to the aid of Christ and the Virgin Mary. This raises a question, however: why is so much emphasis placed on this eighth battle, so that it threatens to overshadow even Arthur's greatest victory at *Badon*? The answer can only be that *both Guinnion* and *Badon* were decisive battles. But they were battles that defeated different enemies, and in different parts of the country.

So, where was this stronghold of *Guinnion*? There have been many candidates advanced for *Guinnion*, all too often based on purely linguistic considerations. Perhaps a better method might be to look at other information. One important clue may be that *Guinnion* is explicitly called a *castellum*, or castle. This is almost certainly a walled fort, but not so large as a city. Interestingly, the amphitheatre at the modern city of Cirencester was converted into a *castellum* at just this period. The last half of its present name, Cirencester, is the Saxon form of the Latin *castrum*, or fort. Moreover, of all the cities recorded as existing in post-Roman times *Corinium* is linguistically closest to *Guinnion*. Except for the easily dropped 'r', all of the consonants in each name are merely variants of the same basic sounds. Of much more importance, however, *Corinium* stood at the nexus of five Roman roads. Altogether, they provided effective control over much of western Britain. One of these roads also just happens to lead to the northeast, through what is now Leicester to Lincoln—the probable venue for five of the river battles. Most crucially, however, *Corinium* stood in the direct path of the Saxons who had swept up the Thames Valley in 441. By 446 it was *the* forward bastion of what was left of Lowland Britain. This was a critical defensive position, the most important in all of Britain. This points to but one conclusion: the most likely location for *Guinnion* is the town of *Corinium*, the present Cirencester.

And, in a curious way, this report of divine aid in both Gildas and the Battle List may contain a grain of truth. Victory at *Guinnion* may have come not through the prowess of Arthur, but from forces beyond the control of any mortal.

GUINNION

In smoky halls all over the newly conquered Thames Valley the talk was the same. Saxon warriors spoke of *Weala* attacks in the north—and not just minor raids, but campaigns of extermination. Kinsmen who had dreamt of carving out kingdoms in the north were drifting back to their old settlements. Now they were broken men, bewailing the loss of comrades, wives and children. They claimed that the *Weala* had a new leader. He and his army were unbeatable.

The chief men among the Saxons debated the matter over brimming cups of mead. After many days and many cups, some claimed that they saw a solution. It was the *herpaths*,[15] the *Weala* roads, that were the problem. These allowed the horse warriors to move with lightning speed to every corner of the island, attacking where they willed. It was by one of these roads that the new *Weala* leader had brought death to the north. This road began at one of their strongest forts. It was this place that was the source of all their woes. If it were taken the *Weala* would be nothing. This *Dux* would be nothing.

Soon the idea caught fire. Messengers went from settlement to settlement. A great army would gather in the spring, so large that no *Weala* force dared oppose it. Once this *castrum* fell, they would march down the *herpath* to the sea, take the other walled places that still held out. Men boasted that they would found even greater kingdoms than before.

Only a few of the elders laughed at this talk. They recalled the grim jest of a Gothic chieftain many years before. After failing to take a great *Weala* city he had sworn a might oath: from that day forward, he would have no more quarrels with walls…

The attack on the *castellum* of *Guinnion* was unlike anything the Saxons had attempted before. Up to this time their depredations had been focused *outside* walled cities. By simply burning crops and destroying livestock they could force the Britons to abandon their homes and flee to the west. But a *castellum* was something different. Much smaller than a city, and filled only with soldiers, it could be a very big problem. It would have far fewer mouths to feed, and, if provisioned in the old Roman style, it might hold out for months. In the meantime this *Dux* could play all sorts of tricks.

We do not know the particulars of this campaign. But keeping in mind the nature of both forces, we can guess how it played out. In the spring thousands of Saxons began straggling along the pot-holed *herpath* that led to *Corinium*, while others rowed *cyuls* filled with supplies up the Thames. Within days *Corinium* became the fifth-century equivalent of an open city. The population had fled long before. The only *Weala* remaining were cooped up in a fat round tower converted from the old Roman amphitheatre. Men who had strode triumphantly through the gates of the great *castrum* of *Londinium* laughed. This little place would fall in no time.

In the coming days a few may have tried to scale the high walls—only to plummet back to earth, leg or back broken beyond repair. Even those who watched from a distance were not safe. Every day saw men twitching in their death agonies, transfixed by crossbow bolts. The wiser knew they must simply wait. Let hunger destroy the *Weala*, just as it always had before. Days passed. Weeks passed. Still the gate of the *castellum* remained firmly shut. A month came and went.

But now it was not the *Weala* who felt hunger, it was the Saxons. All the surrounding farms were empty, and game had disappeared from the forest. The rains came. Swords became pitted. Linden-wood shields warped. Men in iron byrnies grew ruddy from rust. The crude shelters they constructed kept them neither warm nor dry. Everywhere there was the stench of dung and offal. On occasion *ceorls* arrived with food from the ships far away. But it was only to feed their own masters. Those without cursed the lucky few. At times open conflict broke out. And after the first month came the worst of all: plague. Men began to weaken. Soon dozens were dying each day. The *Weala* gods had cursed them.

8. 'They Overthrew their Enemies'

Their leaders met. They came to a hard decision. Starvation and plague were foes that swords could not defeat. Camp was broken. At dawn thousands of emaciated Saxons were marching back down the *herpath*. Food had run out long before, so they had little to carry. But soon even their few remaining possessions weighed them down. Warriors began to straggle badly. Some fell out, too sick to go on.

And then the *Weala* riders appeared. Men heard sounds of combat ahead. They passed bodies lying on the road, bloody gashes on heads and shoulders from the long *Weala* swords. Hours passed. And with each hour they came across more bodies; more bracken stained with blood. But now the Saxons barely noticed.

In late afternoon the famished warriors heard new shouts to their front. But this time these were followed by something else. There was a loud drumming sound, the noise of iron striking linden wood. Minutes later a torrent of men rushed past. Some were wounded. All were panic-stricken. As they tried to form a line of battle, the Saxons finally saw it, glinting fitfully through the green leaves.

A gilded dragon's head...

The above description may seem fanciful, but every part of it reflects either Late Roman military doctrine or the actual battle space in which *Guinnion* was most likely fought. Roman commanders of this period avoided head-on encounters whenever possible, preferring to let starvation defeat an enemy horde. Once again Vegetius expresses it most succinctly: 'For armies are more often destroyed by starvation than battle, and hunger is more savage than the sword.'[16] We see practically every successful Late Roman commander employing it, from the Patrician Constantius in the fifth century to Belisarius in the sixth.

Of course, in an age and among a people where personal and public hygiene were at a low level, the almost inevitable companion to hunger would have been disease. And if these two maladies had inflicted the majority of losses on the Saxons, any contemporary writer would have been fully justified in attributing the victory not to human might but to heavenly intervention. As in the Old Testament, the 'pagans' had been struck down by the wrath of the Divine Itself.

KINGS

If we are to believe the Battle List, *Guinnion* was in some ways Arthur's most decisive battle. It had quite simply saved the diocese from destruction. And not simply saved it, but restored it. The loss of so many Saxon warriors would have ended any barbarian threat from the east. Gildas' next lines only confirm this. 'No sooner were the ravages of the enemy checked than the island was deluged with a most extraordinary plenty of all things, greater than was before known.'[17] Britain is an agriculturally rich country, and given peace can recover quickly. What Gildas says next places Britain's newfound prosperity in a very sinister light, but it may also tell us just how much this victory changed what was left of Roman Britain:

> Kings were anointed, not according to God's ordinance, but such as showed themselves more cruel than the rest, and soon after they were put to death by those who had elected them, without any inquiry into their merits but because others still more cruel were chosen to succeed them.[18]

Just who were these kings, and why were they being 'elected' at this time? We know from archaeology that the area around London was Saxon-free until the sixth century. This talk of kings being anointed suggests that not only had the Saxons been turned back, but the *Dux* had gone on the offensive.[19] Soon he moved eastward, destroying the barbarian settlements that had been established along the Thames Valley since 441. It was nothing less than a reconquest of all that had been lost. In the end he reached *Londinium*. It was doubtless far different from the city that St Germanus had known. It may even have been largely deserted. But it still had great symbolic value. London was the capital of the diocese, the seat from which its old Roman governor, the *vicarius*, had ruled the island. Possession of both it and the army made him *de facto* ruler of Britain. But very soon the *Dux* went further. It was here that the man his followers called Arthur—the 'Bear-Man'—was probably anointed as king of Britain. We have no way of knowing whether his soldiers raised him on a shield, as armies had done with earlier emperors. But just as usurpers on the continent gained legitimacy by capturing Rome, so too could a British *Dux* gain the same status by entering *Londinium*.

Gildas does not tell us who these 'kings' were, nor who selected them. But they can only have been the kings mentioned in the Battle List, chosen by the man who had led them to victory. And what these kings ruled was most likely each of the *civitates*, the Roman districts based on the old British tribes. The kings were to be this new ruler's governors, to act as his loyal deputies. Gildas later explicitly tells us that the Proud Tyrant had a council, and the only plausible candidates for this body are the kings whom the good cleric mentions. But here we may also begin to see the ruthless side of Arthur's character. As the son of a relatively humble man he had no inherent right to rule Britain. In a new regime with little real legitimacy, one or more of these appointees had good reason to believe that his claim to rule Britain was as good or better than the Proud Tyrant's. As we shall see, there is evidence for at least one insurrection, or *discordia*, some years later. Such a situation was inevitable in a new regime possessing few (if any) political institutions.

Gildas does not say who chose these kings, but his talk of kings still more cruel than the originals can only be an indictment of the man who had chosen them in the first place, the Proud Tyrant. This shows a subtle shift in Gildas' narrative. Until now the Britons have been simply misguided and cowardly. Suddenly we hear talk of deliberate cruelty—and just who ultimately exercises this cruelty is in no doubt. The best explanation for this criticism is that Gildas is the authentic voice of what was left of the old *decurio* class. Significantly, in Roman times they had been responsible for the prompt delivery of local taxes to the *vicarius* in *Londinium*. If they failed in that task they could legally forfeit their own wealth. Now a military strongman ruled, a strongman whose main support came from Britain's military establishment. This establishment required funding, and the *decuriones* were expected to provide it. They may have had hopes that peace would bring back the genteel life of the fourth century. But instead of building new villas, they found that each year a large portion of their income was confiscated to support the *Dux Bellorum*'s wars.

Arthur had won an astonishing victory. He had reconquered vast areas from the barbarians. But his triumph also made enemies—enemies who would outlive him and write their own versions of history.

HISTORY

It is only when we examine Gildas side by side with the Battle List that we begin to see Arthur's influence on how all subsequent generations would view fifth-century Britain. From Maximus' usurpation onwards, Gildas gives the most negative view of the sons of *Britannia*. No Briton except Ambrosius does anything of worth. The best explanation for this is not that Gildas is simply manufacturing incidents and phrases that parallel Old Testament narratives. Instead, it is much more likely that an account he had heard since childhood forced him to come to the very logical conclusion that Britain's history was a sorry tale indeed. When combined with his subsequent knowledge of Holy Scripture, he had no choice but to conclude that the Britons were on the same disastrous path that the Children of Israel had followed.

Any historical narrative is, however, only one version of the truth, and the one Gildas relates up to the time of the British counter-attack benefits but one person: the Proud Tyrant. Further, once we realize the good cleric is actually giving us a version of the Battle List, we discover not a story of tragic folly, but of epic triumph. First Maximus denudes Britain of her troops, forcing the Britons to request aid from the Romans to counter the Picts and Irish. The Romans remove the threat and leave. But the barbarians return, requiring another Roman expedition in 418. The imperials once again banish the enemy, even teaching the Britons how to defend themselves. But afterwards the islanders cower in their cities, too afraid to employ the bold methods the Romans have taught them. Disaster ensues, engulfing Britain's eastern cities and threatening to divide the island in two. In 446 a frantic appeal is sent to the greatest soldier of the age. But even Aetius cannot help. Then, miraculously, a Christian champion in the mould of Constantine appears. Aided by Jesus and Mary, he halts the barbarian incursions, sending them reeling back to the north and east. Cities are redeemed. Peace and prosperity are restored. Finally, in a liberated London, 'kings' are anointed. It is an almost perfect drama, confidently asserting that only the *Dux Bellorum* can protect Britain from her foes.

But again, this is only *one* version of history. Not all of Arthur's battles would have been equally successful. And talented subordinates were indispensable to his success. What is also revealing is that Gildas' narrative completely omits the one event in which Arthur's father may well have participated: Constantine III's usurpation of 407. British folly that might have placed the new king in a bad light was best forgotten. Far better to blame Maximus for any failed foreign adventures.

Doubtless a Tacitus or even an Ammianus would have given a more balanced view. But even with all its obvious faults, this 'Arthurian' version of history gets us closer to events in fifth-century Britain than ever before. Moreover, that it has survived at all can only be due to Arthur. Once he became Britain's ruler, he would have made every effort to spread his version of events far and wide. It was probably disseminated in various forms, both oral and written: so much so that two different versions of it—the Battle List and Gildas' account—survived the ravages of time.

The specification of a particular consular date, Aetius' third, also suggests that the Proud Tyrant meant the year 446 to mark a watershed in the British calendar. For Britons it was a kind of 'Year One'. Interestingly, the earliest British chronicle, the *Annales Cambriae*, or *Welsh Annals*, begins in almost precisely this year. Moreover, we have two citations in the *Historia* that are specifically 'keyed' on Vortigern's (that is, Arthur's) accession date. These are powerful political declarations, indicating that the beginning of this campaign against the pagans was also the year of Britain's salvation. The *Dux* had been transformed into a king of kings, in the mould of David and Solomon.

RUMOUR

In the midst of all this prosperity and king-making Gildas suddenly reports a new danger, greater than any yet seen. Not all of the barbarians have been defeated. On the contrary, they are planning a counter-attack in even larger numbers. To the leader of a state still recovering from barbarian ravages this can only have been disheartening. Years of struggle might all be in vain.

Gildas' report is interesting both for what it says and what it does not say: 'A vague rumour', he tells us, 'suddenly as if on wings reaches the ears of all, that their inveterate foes were rapidly approaching to destroy the whole country, and to take possession of it as of old, from one end to the other.'[20]

This extract says nothing about the ethnicity of these foes, although Gildas can only mean that these are Picts and Irish. We might venture to correct him and say that these are counter-attacking Saxons, save for two very critical pieces of evidence. First, Gildas' next report is that the Proud Tyrant invites in the Saxons. It is doubtful that any sane leader would invite in his own enemies to defend him. Secondly, Arthur's ninth battle is described as being fought at the 'City of the Legions'. This can only be Chester. In the past this has been used to cast doubt on the Battle List's authenticity. From archaeology we know that it would be extremely unlikely that a Saxon army would have been campaigning this far west in the fifth or early sixth century. But if these were actually raiders coming from Ireland, Chester would be one of their prime targets. In this case Gildas seems to be correct about who these new foes are. Indeed, if Picts and 'Scots' were Arthur's enemies in his last four battles, it would go a long way towards explaining why Gildas assumes that they were the enemies in earlier encounters.

It is at precisely this point that Gildas tells us that the Proud Tyrant hired his federates. There is of course nothing implausible in hiring Saxon mercenaries. Many other Late Roman rulers employed Germanic federates, with varying degrees of success.

However, in turning to the story of the Saxons Gildas leaves one very important thread hanging—or rather, he leaves an entire invasion force hanging, about to strike Britain a mortal blow. After all, precisely what *did* happen to all those Picts and 'Scots'? Did they attack and then suffer a defeat? Did news of the Saxon alliance frighten them into abandoning their expedition? Gildas is entirely silent on this, and many of his contemporaries may have been as well. For, if we remember that most Lowland Britons remembered the Proud Tyrant with horror and disdain, what happened next may have been something they preferred to gloss over.

Behind Gildas' few disjointed sentences may lie one of the most extraordinary campaigns in British history.

9.

'A PROTECTION TO THEIR COUNTRY'

TRIBRUIT

That the Britons were engaged in battles ranging from *Corinium* to southern Scotland could only have come as good news to seasoned raiders in Ireland and northwestern Scotland. They had earned a good living from past marauding. That this new British strongman was embroiled in the east would once again give them a free hand in the west. Very soon the call went out to assemble ships and warriors. As with the first eight battles, the best explanation for these last four encounters is that they are a campaign by Arthur to repel a foe ultimately arising from the sea.[1]

Such a fleet would have seemed to modern eyes more like a small-boat regatta than an armada. Curraghs and galleys were light craft, propelled by a single bank of oars and a sail. But it is important to remember that over a thousand years later Henry Morgan would use a similar fleet of small, nimble vessels to sack Portobello and Maracaibo.[2] This was a dangerous force. The threat Britain faced in 450 was not appreciably less than the one posed by a later armada in 1588.

These 'pagans' would have begun their voyage in late spring or early summer. Hugging the Welsh coast, they followed a route well known to past marauders. They may have stopped to plunder towns in what is now Gwynedd. But their chief goal was to sack a western city still untouched by the Saxon advance. The Battle List tells us exactly what happened next. The first major town of Lowland Britain they targeted was Chester, the 'City of the Legions' (see Map 2). Gildas' mention of a 'rumour' tells us that the attack was expected, and this makes sense. It is doubtful that word about such a large expedition could have been concealed over so many months. When we also remember that Patrick was carrying out his mission at just this time, it is even possible that this intelligence came from an ecclesiastical source in Ireland. Before the first sightings off the British coast, Arthur had laid his plans.

The obvious route to Chester for a seaborne force is up the River Dee. It is somewhere along these banks that the invaders beached their craft and moved inland. But instead of slaves and gold, they soon encountered *spatha*-wielding horsemen. The more adventurous died where they stood. The rest retreated to their ships. How many casualties the Irish and Picts sustained in this reverse is impossible to say. But now their leaders were faced with a hard decision. It is likely that there was much wrangling in a force motivated largely by fear and greed. Some argued for sailing westward and home. But there were veteran warriors among them, men who understood that the indirect approach was often the best path to victory. Chester was a walled city defended by a well-trained and well-led force of Britons. It was not worth the lives it would take to capture it. Better to strike at a time and place unexpected by the Britons. Once they reached the island of Anglesey, they set a course not for the west, but the south.

The Battle List again tells us where the next blow fell. By mid-century the least plundered parts of Britain were in the west, in what are now Somerset and Gloucestershire. A fleet of marauders sailing up the Bristol Channel could easily land in Somerset and follow the fine Roman road that led to the still intact cities of Bath, Gloucester and Cirencester. Any of these would be as rich a prize as Chester. Further, many of the old hands knew the terrain. Past Celtic buccaneers had plundered farms and villas in this area for years. If they were lucky, they might capture more than one city before Arthur intervened.

The Battle List tells us that the tenth battle was fought on the banks of a certain River Tribruit (*Traeth Tribruit*). As with the other engagements, the list of possible candidates is long. There are a number of rivers in this area, the Avon being the most prominent. But another, the Brue, has an even better claim to our attention. The name itself is by far the most likely evolution of the original *Tribruit*. Moreover, at this time the mouth of the Brue was much wider than at present: more a shallow estuary than a river.[3] A long, narrow finger of land (now the Polden Hills) formed its southern bank (see Map 3). It would be the perfect spot to anchor a fleet of shallow-draft vessels.[4] Once disembarked, the barbarians then had only a short distance to travel before they reached the main Roman road leading to the north—the Fosse Way. And on that road lay the city of Bath.

An ancient Welsh poem called the 'Pa Gur' may give some insight as to what happened next. In it we read the following:

By the hundred there they fell,
There they fell by the hundred,
Before the accomplished Bedwyr.
On the strands of Trywruid,
Contending with Garwlwyd,
Brave was his disposition.[5]

This 'Trywruid' is really only a Welsh variant of the name *Tribruit*. This suggests that Arthur had divided his forces, leaving perhaps a cohort in the south to protect the Somerset littoral. And the most likely commander of this detachment is the legendary Bedwyr. In keeping with Late Roman military doctrine, a mobile force was presumably in place to support either Somerset or Chester. But even so, help might not come for days. Even on horseback and with plenty of remounts, Arthur's main force would need to make a journey of more than a hundred miles—on top of whatever effort had been required to get to Chester in the first place. For the moment, Bedwyr and his cohort were on their own.

This may well explain why legend would see *Tribruit/ Trywruid* as Bedwyr's signature battle. No decisive victory against the Picts and Irishmen was possible. All that the British leader could do was to try and delay the raiders. And he soon found an opportunity that any competent Roman commander could have exploited. The buccaneers had been at sea for many days. Provisions were low or non-existent. The immediate concern was to scour the countryside for sustenance. It is at this point that a Late Roman commander would have attacked, killing as many of the scattered Picts and 'Scots' as possible. But however many the British commander killed, he could not destroy the whole force, nor could he bar it from reaching the north–south Roman road. He could only watch as the pirate army turned north, marching quickly up the Fosse Way. This is hilly country, and virtually any rise in this area might be the site of the eleventh battle, the 'Hill of *Agned.*' Again, Bedwyr can have achieved no permanent advantage here; only gained time for a decisive encounter later.

Remarkably, it is still possible to follow the track that the barbarians used to reach Bath. The old Roman road is now a public footpath, leading past quiet farms and ploughed fields. Fifteen hundred years ago, however, an army of many thousands passed this way. They were doubtless tired and hungry. Ash filled their nostrils. An experienced leader would have put every field and farmhouse to the torch. Still, these young men from Pictland and Ireland knew that Bath was not far off. There they would find food... and rest... and women.

The road began to climb upward, sapping their strength. Ahead they could see high ground. At the same time there arose the sound of many voices, beginning at the van and spreading backward. The lead detachments fanned out into the sloping fields on either side. Many were pointing to the heights ahead.

And at last they saw them, drawn up in long, orderly ranks on the hills, dragon banners swirling in the summer breeze: Arthur and his host. The battle of *Badon* had begun.

BADON

We can obtain only fleeting glimpses of this most signal battle, as disjointed—and as vivid—as the impressions of its participants. Gildas describes it as an *obsessio*, a siege of *Mons Badonicus*, although he fails to tell us who was the besieger and who the besieged. A later poem speaks of Arthur's 'assault over the wall'.[6] The *Annales Cambriae* relate the strange boast that Arthur himself carried the cross of Christ for three days and nights during this encounter—a clue as to its duration.[7] Finally, we are told that almost a thousand pagans died in an overwhelming charge led by Arthur himself.

All previous attempts to recount the Battle of *Badon* have sought the 'Badonic Hill' either to the north or east of Bath. One favourite candidate is the high ground of Lansdown Hill, where an engagement in the English Civil War took place. Such theories are understandable, even logical, given that Arthur's foes have always been believed to be Saxons. But a far more likely alternative is that this was the last great battle with the western sea barbarians, and was fought *south* of the city. If the Britons triumphed here, every major foe that had harried them for forty years would be pacified. If they failed, even the recent victories over Saxon and Pict would be at risk.

Gildas' description of *Badon* as an *obsessio*, that is, a siege, has the ring of truth. The best place to halt the pagan advance would have been on the high hills that guard the southern road into Bath. But this may not have been an all-around defensive position, but more likely a series of barriers and breastworks over a wide area, utilizing the winding river valley wherever possible. Most crucially, this would allow the Britons to deploy their cavalry when the time was ripe.

The passage in the *Annales Cambriae* that speaks of Arthur carrying a cross for three days is doubtless fifth-century propaganda. But it also suggests that the enemy made determined efforts to breach the defences over a number of days. Masses of Picts and Irishmen would have rushed the barriers, both day and night. We may imagine Arthur's exhausted foot soldiers making desperate efforts to stem a sudden attack. Amid shrieks and war cries, the works are breached. But then a detachment of mounted warriors arrives. They dismount, draw their *spathae*. A melée ensues. Both attackers and defenders fall. In the end the barrier holds. The last of the Irishmen scramble back over the wall and retreat down to the valley below.

The third day arrives. By now the strife between the invaders is almost as intense as between barbarian and Briton. Picts blame 'Scots' for not attacking hard enough. The Irish make the same charge. Leader denounces leader for lost opportunities and cowardice. There is a growing suspicion among the rank and file that the whole enterprise has been doomed from the start.

Still, the chiefs call for one last effort against the British defenders. In the morning mist warriors grasp shield and spear. They give a wild yell, move purposefully up the hill and toward the breastworks. Fighting is as intense as ever: men tossing missiles in high arcs, shoving spears across the barrier. Some scale the bulwark, only to tumble back into the crowded ranks behind them.

Now comes a new sound—and from an unexpected direction. Men turn. In the sunlit haze they see horses moving. The British cavalry has finally sallied from its defences. But there is something else in the mist: long lines of marching infantry, more infantry than the invaders ever thought the

Britons possessed. These lines begin to turn, swinging like two huge gates toward the rear of the sea brigands. Battle chiefs shout out hoarse, contradictory orders. Men turn to face the threat, but too few. Others throw down their weapons and rush toward an ever-narrowing gap. Everywhere they see shields painted with white crosses. From all sides they hear hoarse shouts in a tongue that is neither British nor Latin.

And high above the advancing ranks, they see a golden dragon coiling in the sun...

A careful examination of Gildas shows that he is giving us a version of the Battle List. The massive Pictish and Irish force that is about to descend upon Britain disappears as if by magic. That Gildas is silent on who achieved this miracle is entirely understandable. After the Saxon Revolt any deeds of the Proud Tyrant were buried with him. But all the same, Gildas' narrative leaves no doubt that all three of Britain's maritime foes were defeated sometime between 446 and 450. The only foes he mentions after this are Saxon mercenaries recruited from *outside* Britain, not the East Anglian and Thames groups that archaeology testifies had been in the island for decades.

But an even more crucial point involves the provenance of the Battle List. There is simply no evidence that can place it anywhere but in the years 446–50. The *Historia Brittonum* 'defaults' to sometime after Ambrosius, but gives us no chronological data as to why this should be so. Arguments that the list was fabricated by either an unknown bard or the compiler of the *Historia* himself lack any evidence at all.[8] Their main 'proof' is an unsupported doubt that anyone called Arthur could possibly exist in fifth-century Britain. Gildas gives us the earliest and most complete chronology for British history down to the early sixth century—and his is the *only* hard evidence that can explain the origin of the Battle List.

Gildas tells us that *Badon* was *the* great British victory. The

Historia and the *Annales* testify that the victor in this conflict was Arthur. But there may be more here than a simple British triumph. If we look at the evidence carefully, we may find answers to riddles that have endured for over a millennium.

The first riddle involves that extremely curious passage in the *Annales*: 'The Battle of Badon, in which Arthur carried the cross of our Lord Jesus Christ for three days and three nights on his shoulders, and the Britons were the victors.'[9] This is in one sense propaganda, intended to show Arthur as a Christian conqueror in the mould of Constantine the Great. But this imagery may be telling us that Arthur sought to emulate that emperor in another way. It has been suggested that the Battle List's citation of Arthur carrying an image of the Virgin on his 'shoulder' may actually be an image on his shield, a confusion of the Welsh word for shield (*iscuit*) with the Welsh word for shoulder (*iscuid*).[10] So too, this 'cross' that Arthur carried for three days may well be the same cross that Constantine had his soldiers paint on their shields at the battle of the Milvian Bridge. This would, after all, be useful for Britons to recognize one another on the battlefield—and to recognize any non-British forces allied with them. This may be telling us something about the circumstances of the actual encounter: that the army at *Badon* was so diverse that recognition of friendly forces was particularly critical.

Another hitherto puzzling aspect of the scanty records for this battle is the following statement in the Battle List: 'nine hundred and sixty men fell in one day, from a single charge of Arthur's, and no one laid them low save he alone.'[11] This may appear at first glance to be mere heroic hyperbole. If this were a later Irish or Welsh legend, such an idea would be perfectly acceptable. Cuchulainn and the Arthur of Welsh legend both inhabit worlds where heroes kill dozens at one blow. But we have suggested that a better explanation for this list is that it is not heroic myth, but propaganda for a real battle leader, and propaganda, to be effective, must be plausible. It is highly doubtful that even the most naïve fifth-century British peasant believed that anyone could slay 960 men in a lifetime—let alone in one encounter. A far better alternative is that the passage means that Arthur's own force killed 960 men in the engagement. But this in turn leaves open the possibility that *more* than 960 men were killed in this battle, and by a force not directly under the command of Arthur. However, the list is silent as to this force's identity.

There is another strange anomaly about this battle. *Badon* appears to be a *Saxon* name for Bath. As most modern visitors to the town know, its Roman name was *Aquae Sulis*. This has puzzled scholars for years, and has led to searches for the 'real' *Badon* in a variety of areas. But the explanation could be far simpler. In an often-overlooked passage in the Laud Manuscript of the *ASC* for the year 443 (or, more properly, 446) we read a version of the Appeal to Aetius. But in this same citation we also find that the disappointed Britons then 'sent to the Angles and made the same request to the Princes of the Angles'. In other words, we find Britons requesting aid from Angles up to four years *before* Hengist's arrival in 450, and *at precisely the time that Gildas places the British counter-attack*. Taken together, these apparently disjointed scraps of information may be trying to tell us something very important about this battle. As with *Guinnion*, any explanation of this contest must be tentative in the extreme. But the best alternative is that another force was at *Badon* on that day—a Saxon force.

This would explain the real significance of the 'Coming of the Saxons'.[12] Far from being the anniversary of the arrival of three boatloads of Germanic mercenaries, it marked a crucial turning point in the history of both Saxon and Briton. *Badon* and the *Adventus Saxonum* are really one and the same event, each occurring very near the time of Valentinian III's first year as senior emperor: that is, the year 450. It would only be later that a 'Jutish' leader in Kent would conflate his arrival in Britain with a revolution in the relationship between Briton and Saxon.

The events that occurred in these years resolve many of the anomalies that have long puzzled students of fifth-century British history. They explain how a 'Saxon conquest' of Britain in 441 could lead to an *Adventus Saxonum* a decade later. They explain why the Appeal to Aetius was followed by a signal victory that made a man with the *nom de guerre* of Arthur absolute ruler over Britain. Finally, they explain why this ruler would 'hire' Saxons to defeat 'Scots' and Picts. Once these anomalies are resolved, a consistent picture of fifth-century Britain emerges. *Badon* was no mere military victory. It marked a fundamental shift in the power relations between Britons and their maritime foes. If used wisely, it had the potential to change the course of British history.

Forty years of fear and defeat had vanished away like the morning mists of *Badon*.

10.

'TO FIGHT IN FAVOUR OF THE ISLAND'

FEDERATES

The Angles or Saxons came to Britain at the invitation of King Vortigern in three long-ships... These newcomers were from the three most formidable races of Germany, the Saxons, the Angles and Jutes. From the Jutes are descended the people of Kent and the Isle of Wight. From the Saxons... came the East, South and West Saxons. And from the Angles are descended the East and Middle Angles, the Mercians, all the Northumbrians... and the other English peoples.[1]

So wrote the Venerable Bede some two centuries after the English Conquest. It is a famous statement. In the nineteenth and twentieth centuries generations of English schoolboys accepted it without question. But in the last few decades Bede's testimony that three separate Germanic groups settled Britain has fallen out of favour with most scholars. They point out that in both the fifth and sixth centuries the Saxons were illiterate. Bede's story simply cannot be authentic. A people without writing could never hand down genuine historical information over more than two centuries.

What is perhaps surprising about this view is that Bede's statement is essentially true. Archaeology confirms that several distinct groups *did* settle Britain in the fifth century, and in just those areas that the venerable cleric describes. Scholars reply that this can only be a 'lucky guess' on Bede's part. Naturally, no one *precisely* calls the greatest thinker of his age a liar. But they do assert that he can only be observing conditions in his own day, and then extrapolating backwards. Any authentic records cannot exist and never could.

As we shall see, there is good reason to believe that both the *Anglo-Saxon Chronicle* (*ASC*) and Bede contain perfectly accurate evidence from Late Antiquity. But more to the point, not only did three Germanic groups settle Britain, but their pattern of settlement was far from accidental. Saxon settlements occur in East Anglia, the Upper Thames and Kent for very transparent, very strategic reasons. They were part of a larger design that would change the face of Britain for ever.

Archaeology suggests that the earliest group, the 'Anglians' as Bede terms them, stayed pretty much where they were. Given the difficulty in suppressing resistance in East Anglia, this laissez faire policy was probably a wise move on Arthur's part. But a different fate awaited the Saxons who had careered up the Thames in the 440s. Archaeology gives us the first clue as to just what this was. While much of the lower part of the Thames remained 'Saxon-free' until the next century, there is substantial evidence for a Saxon enclave on the Upper Thames at just this time.[2] Significantly, this is also precisely the area in which Bede's 'Saxons' supposedly settled.

Our second clue comes from something we have already seen: the citation in the Laud manuscript of the *Anglo-Saxon Chronicle* that tells us that sometime after 446 the Britons requested aid from 'the Princes of the Angles'.[3] Now, this *could* be an appeal to the 'East Anglian' group, or even to continental Angles. But the fact that the Saxon invaders of 441 would have been nearest the Britons in 450—and would have been decisively defeated at *Guinnion*—tells us that they are the prime candidates. And the sequel to the above passage was that these particular Saxons became federates, in exchange for land in the Dorchester-on-Thames area. Eventually this enclave would grow into the kingdom of Wessex—the rootstock of the English nation.

In the past these Saxon settlements were seen as evidence of the mercenaries that the Proud Tyrant hired in 450. They were presented as proof that the Britons were simply too weak and cowardly to fight the sea barbarians by themselves. Alternatively, such settlements have been dubbed 'pirate bases' that just happened to coexist with the surrounding Britons.[4] But a far better explanation is that Arthur was employing the Thames Saxons in precisely the same way that Constantius used the Visigoths, and Aetius used the Alans. In both cases the Romans established these federate enclaves from a position of strength. Gildas' accounts of British successes after the Appeal suggest that Arthur too used his victories to cut a deal with his defeated enemies. It is important to note that all this was taking place at the same time as a combined army of Roman soldiers and barbarian federates was defeating Attila on the Catalaunian Plains. In the 450s Aetius' federate policy appeared to be a resounding success. In hiring rather than exterminating barbarian warriors Arthur was taking his cue from the most talented military leader in western Europe. That these various barbarian groups would eventually bring about the end of *Romanitas* on both sides of the Gallican Straits was something neither Arthur nor Aetius could have foreseen.

The reason why Arthur followed this path is plain. Quite simply, these new mercenaries made him the strongest ruler in the British Isles. One glance at the map makes this clear (see Map 2). The Upper Thames settlements posed a grave threat to Britain in the 440s. But in the 450s these same settlements offered significant advantages. First of all, they were in the midst of a road network that could take them to every part of Britain. This had already allowed them to deploy westwards against the Irish. But just as important, they were on a navigable river. Moreover, this was a river that ultimately led to a place called Thanet.

We have already had a glimpse of Thanet. In the fifth century a twisting salt-water channel called the Wantsum separated Thanet from the British mainland. It was on this low-lying island that the Proud Tyrant is supposed to have settled his mercenaries shortly after 450.[5] The *Anglo-Saxon Chronicle* reports that these consisted of three shiploads of mercenaries from northern Germany, led by the legendary brothers Hengest and Horsa, descendants of Wotan himself.[6] Gildas seems to have been well aware of this Saxon version of events, for he explicitly uses the Saxon word *cyul* to describe the arrival of the three barbarian vessels. But it is important to stress that the *ASC* is above all a record of Germanic dynasties. The kings of Kent claimed descent from these two brothers, so it is only natural that they play a central part in the *ASC*'s story. But Kent was settled not just by three boatloads of warriors, but by many other Germanic immigrants. The question is: who were they, and where did they come from?

The Venerable Bede tells us that 'Jutes' settled Kent and the Isle of Wight—and archaeology reveals a significant difference between settlers in these two areas and those in the other early Germanic enclaves. First of all, the 'Jutes' arrive later, in the years 450–75. They probably took no part in either *Guinnion* or *Badon*. Secondly, they very rarely cremated their dead, as many other Germanic immigrants routinely did. Even their grave goods are significantly different.[7] It is true that much of this material more closely resembles ornaments found in Friesland rather than Jutland, and this has raised some doubts about Bede's account. But whatever their ultimate origins, the 'Jutes' appear to be a people different from the earlier 'Anglian' and 'Saxon' groups.

And that is almost certainly why they were hired. They had

few, if any ties to the Germanic groups that had threatened Britain in 446. Indeed, in the anarchic world of fifth-century Germany these newcomers may have been bitter enemies of the 'Angles' and 'Saxons' already in Britain. Arthur had not forgotten that most basic rule of Roman statecraft: *divide et impera.*

This story of 'Jutish' mercenaries also marks the beginning of the great misunderstanding about the Saxon Immigration. Gildas' account of the three *cyuls* is an authentic reflection of how sixth-century Kentish Germans saw their origins. But this story had nothing to do with the earlier East Anglian and Upper Thames groups. Indeed, if the first 'Anglian' immigrants consisted of small groups slowly infiltrating Britain, it is unlikely that they would have had *any* coherent explanation for their origins. Yet it is this notion that the first Germanic settlers in Britain *must* be mercenaries that has distorted the picture of fifth-century events down to our own time. It forced the compiler of the *Historia Brittonum* to calculate a date for the Saxon Revolt that was a full generation earlier that the landing of the first genuine mercenaries. Otherwise it would have been impossible for St Germanus to meet Vortigern in 429. Even Bede was not immune. He almost certainly places his account of St Germanus' mission *after* the *Adventus Saxonum* because he believed that no Saxons existed in Britain before 450.[8] Otherwise perceptive modern observers use the idea that the original Saxons *must* be mercenaries to construct dubious theories about post-Roman political structures. In the end this notion has acted like a computer virus, masking the very complex origins of Britain's Germanic settlers—and leading almost all observers to seek the victor of *Badon* forty years too late.

HENGEST

The *Anglo-Saxon Chronicle* tells us that the leader of this third group of Germanic settlers was called Hengest. In the nineteenth century Hengest and his brother Horsa were seen as historical figures, the founders of the English nation. But unfortunately for the historicity of this pair, both names also signify 'horse'. The prevalent opinion among contemporary scholars is that Hengest and Horsa were twin horse-gods, brought over from Germany by the 'Jutes' who founded the Kentish kingdom.[9] Strangely, there is no evidence that either Hengest or Horsa were gods. Nor is there is a shred of evidence that a 'twin-horse-god' cult existed anywhere in the Northern World. But all the same, scholars find the two 'horse' names simply too 'suspicious' to be anything other than some sort of cultic artifact.

This is a peculiar notion, in particular because one of the most famous scholars of the Northern World has a very different explanation for Hengest. J. R. R. Tolkien did extensive research on an obscure Anglo-Saxon saga called *The Finnesburgh Fight*. One of its main characters just happens to be named Hengest. Significantly, *this* Hengest is portrayed as an ordinary mortal, and his 'equine' brother is nowhere in sight.

The saga is fragmentary in the extreme. But it seems to concern a state visit by a Danish king called Hnaef to a Frisian king called Finn. Through a chain of unfortunate events the Danes fall out with their hosts, and the affair ends in a desperate battle inside Finn's great hall. The Danish ruler is killed, and one of the few survivors, a Jutish lieutenant of his called Hengest, is forced to swear loyalty to Finn in order to end the bloodshed. For a season Hengest appears to keep the bargain. But all the while he remains secretly loyal to his slain Danish lord. When the spring comes, Hengest helps a vengeful Danish raiding party slay Hnaef's betrayers, including Finn. The Frisian kingdom is destroyed. Hengest then presumably goes on to new adventures elsewhere.

This is a typical northern saga, depicting as it does a battle in the great hall—normally a place of peace and fellowship. But Tolkien argues that there is more to it than this. The name Hengest is very rare anywhere in the North, and the best explanation is that the Hengest of the saga is meant to be identical to the Hengest found in Bede and the *ASC*. Tolkien also points out that Hengest's activity among the Frisians helps to explain why much of the archaeology in Kent might be of Frisian manufacture, and why English is more closely related to Frisian than to any other Germanic language. The *king* of Kent was a Jute, but many of his *followers* may well have been Frisian.[10]

Tolkien's work demonstrates that Hengest was remembered in the Northern World as a mortal man. Far from being a god, he took part in real fifth-century events. But the *way* he is depicted in this saga may be most significant. Loyalty to a lord was the basis of all Germanic warbands, so it is no surprise that Hengest should try and take revenge for Hnaef's death. But what is unusual is that he should do so in the context of a subsequent oath sworn to another lord. It shows that Hengest was loyal—but just where that loyalty ultimately lay depended very much on the situation.

NAVY

What was Hengest's mission? A second glance at the map makes it plain that his force had a function very different from that of the Upper Thames group. The Isle of Thanet is near the Saxon Shore fort of Richborough, while the Isle of Wight is in the same area as the great Saxon Shore citadel of Portchester. Together, these two islands control the maritime approaches to the eastern and southern coasts of Britain, most notably the mouth of the Thames. Hengest's 'Jutes' were therefore not merely good foot soldiers. They had been hired to perform the same task that Roman 'mariners' had accomplished half a century earlier. This 'Jutish' alliance had given Arthur something entirely new.

At one stroke he had acquired a navy.

It is important to remember that this in no way contradicts what Gildas tells us. According to him the last and greatest threat to Britain came from Picts and Irishmen. That was why the 'Jutes' had been hired. But Hengest's mission involved more than the defence of Britain's coasts. These 'Jutes' were the children of a marauding culture—and just now this was precisely what Arthur required. Gildas recounts how the Picts withdrew to 'the far end of the island'. But he adds that 'they occasionally carried out devastating raids of plunder'.[11] These attacks ultimately came from Pictish coastal settlements. These were bases, and bases that were vulnerable to attack from the sea. Remarkably, the *Historia Brittonum* gives us an account of what happened next. It describes how Hengest's two sons Octha and Ebusa 'arrived with forty ships. In these they sailed around the country of the Picts, laid waste the Orkneys, and took possession of many regions, even to the Pictish confines.'[12]

As with the Battle List of Arthur, this could be seen as legendary material, written down no earlier than the ninth century. Many contemporary historians would dismiss it out of hand as evidence. However, the main objection to the veracity of the *Historia* has always been that, far from being a compilation of fifth-century British information, it is in fact a carefully crafted bit of propaganda for Merfyn, a ninth-century king of Gwynedd.[13] Even if one concedes that this could be true for other parts of the *Historia*, it is difficult to see how the fabrication of a fictitious seaborne expedition by a fifth-century 'Jute' would add to the prestige of a ninth-century Welsh ruler. Another piece of 'revisionist' history actually strengthens the likelihood of the Pictish expedition. Significant material in the

Historia is said to utilize Anglo-Saxon sources—the same sources used by Bede.[14] This description of Octha's Pictish expedition *could* be an account by pre-ninth-century Saxons of what they thought Hengest had done in the fifth century. We do, after all, have the parallel example of genuine tenth-century Norse expeditions to Greenland and the New World appearing in thirteenth-century written Icelandic sagas. But, as we shall see with regard to the *Anglo-Saxon Chronicle*, it is much more likely that these accounts of seaborne raids date back to the time of the British-Saxon alliance.

Perhaps the crucial element in all this is that Octha's raids are precisely the strategy that would have worked under the circumstances. Essentially the Picts were waging a naval guerrilla war, similar to the one carried out by the Vikings centuries later. But, as Mao Ze Dong observed, guerrilla operations are impossible without bases. If Octha's 'Jutes' were let loose on Pictish coastal settlements, both Briton and barbarian would achieve their objectives. The 'Jutes' would have acquired loot and slaves, while the Britons would have received the glad tidings that the settlements of the hated Picts had been destroyed.[15]

This strategy of naval counter-raiding is not mere hypothesis. It is an approach used countless times in conflicts both earlier and later. The Roman general Theodosius the Elder did precisely the same thing in his expeditions against the Orkneys and Ireland. The use of buccaneers by the English and French in the seventeenth century to break Spanish sea power in the New World exactly duplicates the relationship between Arthur and his 'Jutish' protégés. If he could not afford a professional navy, he could still unleash his new allies on the Picts. Very soon the raiding would have stopped dead in its tracks.

We also find indirect evidence of a fundamental change in Saxon attitudes, and it is by no means legendary. On the other side of the Channel we see the same rapprochement between Saxon and *Weala* as we do in Britain. As early as 451 we find Saxons fighting with Aetius against Attila.[16] Even more telling is a statement by Sidonius Apollinaris only four years later, in 455. He notes how a Gallo-Roman general by the name of Avitus was able to use diplomacy to make peace with the Visigoths. But this was not the end of his success. Sidonius, ever the panegyrist, also notes that 'No sooner had he taken up the burden of the office thrust upon him than... the Saxon raiding abated.'[17] Since no Saxon victories are recorded for Avitus, the likeliest source of this success was another diplomatic triumph, with the threat of force in the background. In other words, between 450 and 455 Saxons on *both* sides of the Channel were finding it prudent to make peace with the *Weala*. There is one final piece of evidence. In the same year as Avitus' diplomatic triumph, the Church promulgated a change in the way Easter was calculated. Now, we know that later in the century a second change in these calculations was *not* adopted by the British Church, almost certainly because communications had broken down between Britain and the continent. But the change in 455 *was* adopted. The likeliest reason? Arthur's Saxon ships had established peace on both sides of the Channel, permitting normal communications once more.[18]

The traditional image of the Proud Tyrant's mercenaries is thus quite wrong. The Upper Thames and Thanet Saxons were not camps of ignorant barbarians hired by Britons too cowardly to fight. They were military garrisons, strategically placed to serve an expanding state.

Finally, it may be mere coincidence, but the traditional date for the death of that legendary Pictish chief Drust son of Erp is in 458. As we have seen, this is at exactly the same time as the Saxon-British alliance.[19] Drust—like Niall of the Nine Hostages before him—may well have been one more victim of Late Roman naval strategy.

SECURITY

The three Saxon groups were useful to Arthur in another way. He was essentially a Roman military strongman. His recent campaigns are likely to have been expensive. Taxes would have been heavy, and the granting of federate status to the Saxons would have done nothing to make them any lighter. Once peace was established, many Britons may have resented his heavy hand. Saxons loyal to Arthur—and with no ties to the Britons— would have been a useful internal security force. They could both defend *and* overawe the population of Lowland Britain.

This does not mean, however, that the Proud Tyrant was in any way the fool whom Gildas presents. The Saxons were only one of a number of props to his regime. A British army still existed, one that had proved its worth against the invaders on twelve occasions. The fact that Saxons appear in enclaves spread across Britain, instead of in one compact area, also suggests that the sort of rebellion Gildas describes would have been impossible in the early 450s. Non-Germanic belt fittings in Cirencester (*Corinium*) and Gloucester are only one example of native British contingents that counterbalanced the new Saxon allies.[20] As we shall see, Arthur was quite adept at playing one ethnic group off against another. Indeed, this was the 'glue' that held his demesne together.

The use of Saxons as an internal security force may be our first evidence for something else as well. It may indicate a real split between the new military rulers and the old villa aristocracy. It would be unsurprising if the great British landowners looked upon the 'heirs of Gerontius' as upstarts and usurpers. The latter spoke a vulgar form of camp Latin, if they spoke Latin at all. They forced *decuriones* to provide food and shelter to pagan warriors. The soldierly vices and virtues of Arthur's companions would have found little favour with either Pelagians or orthodox Catholics. Gildas' vituperation against the kings of his day may be a distant echo of a cultural dispute begun almost a century earlier.

Still, no Briton could deny that Arthur had brought security to the island. The Picts had been cowed, the Irish defeated, and now the Saxons were allies. This might seem the apotheosis of his regime. But Arthur was not satisfied. He had a far grander design—and in concept and execution it was entirely Late Roman.

11.

'KINGS WERE ANOINTED'

COROTICUS

The 450s. Eastern Ireland. Patrick is angry. The messengers he sent to the pirates have returned empty-handed. The brigands will neither give back the booty they have stolen, nor return the kidnapped Christians. Furious, he begins to write a letter to the chief villain, Coroticus. It is an open letter that will condemn the marauders in the eyes of Christians everywhere.

> With my own hand I have written and composed these words, to be given... to the soldiers of Coroticus; I do not say, to my fellow citizens, nor to fellow-citizens of the holy Romans, but to fellow-citizens of the demons... Like the enemy, they live in death, as allies of Irish and of Picts and apostates. These blood-thirsty men are bloody with the blood of innocent Christians.

He then makes plain the reason for his fury: 'I sent a letter with a holy priest whom I had taught from early childhood... the letter requested that they should grant us some of the booty, and baptized prisoners that they had captured... They roared with laughter at them.' Then Patrick makes an accusation against Coroticus that has a very modern ring to it:

You commit the members of Christ as though to a brothel. What hope do you have in God, or indeed anyone who agrees with you, or converses with you in words of flattery? God will judge...

Coroticus and his villains, these rebels against Christ, where will they see themselves, they who allot poor baptised women as prizes...[1]

Coroticus and his soldiers undoubtedly saw themselves as daring buccaneers. But they also betray an uncanny resemblance to the very unheroic human traffickers we have seen operating in the Balkans and eastern Europe.

It might seem naïve of Patrick to think that a single letter would force ruthless corsairs to give up their captives. This could even be put down to senility, for it is certainly true that the evangelist was growing old. The fact that Patrick had trained his priest up from childhood shows that the incident most likely took place in the 450s, some two decades after the beginning of his mission to Ireland.[2] Yet there is much more to this incident than meets the eye. It may actually give us a window into some of the radical changes that were occurring in western Britain at this time.

If we take a step back and consider the broad sweep of British history in the fifth and sixth centuries, we see a series of transformations that ultimately lead to the formation of medieval Wales and Cornwall. Roman civitates morph into kingdoms, often with entirely new names. Royal dynasties appear out of nowhere, claiming legitimacy from obscure ancestors. Gildas tells us that by the sixth century half a dozen kingdoms were warring among themselves in the west. This has led most scholars to view the fifth century in much the same light. Post-Roman Britain is seen as a cockpit where numerous petty rulers contended against one another. Many observers argue that this chaotic struggle weakened the British, making them vulnerable to a number of outside foes.

But Patrick's letter indicates something entirely different. For Coroticus just happens to be British, and his victims are Irish. His name is entirely Brythonic, while Patrick tells us the 'baptized women' were Christian converts stolen away from their homes in Ireland. This shows a complete reversal in the roles of these two peoples.

To Patrick this can only have been a bitter irony. His fellow Britons were now engaged in the same sad trade that had first brought him to Ireland. Worse still, his newly converted Irish were being oppressed by fellow Christians.

> 'I earnestly beg', he concludes, 'that whichever servant of God is ready and willing should be the bearer of this letter, so that it may not be suppressed or hidden on any account by anyone, but rather be read out in front of all the people and in the presence of Coroticus himself.'[3]

How could Britons—Britons almost overwhelmed by the Irish only a few years before—suddenly be raiding Ireland? Is Coroticus an anomaly? Or could he be a symptom of some radical change in the fortunes of western Britain? Patrick's letter may be our first clue that the new polities that arose in the fifth century were the result not of blind natural selection, but of deliberate design. As we shall see, the best explanation for all the evidence is that a powerful ruler brought about a fundamental political transformation in Wales and Cornwall, a transformation that in some ways has lasted down to our own day.

CADBURY

Arthur's victory at *Badon* had thrown back the invaders, and saved western towns like Bath and Gloucester from sack. But the threat from Irish and Pictish buccaneers still existed. Another look at the map gives a clearer idea of the problem (see Map 4). Arthur's twelve battles had been fought to bring peace to Lowland Britain, a region ranging from Kent in the east to Somerset in the west. In strategic terms this was the logical thing to do at the time. The economic heart of Britain was here; the rich farms in these areas were the main support for Arthur's regime. But until the 450s little effort could be spared for operations in either Dumnonia (the modern Devon and Cornwall) or Wales. Roman influence had never been strong in these areas. Archaeology shows that many elite members of these societies continued to live in the same hill forts as their Iron Age ancestors. In 450 both Dumnonia and Wales were almost certainly beyond Arthur's effective control—and this meant that Somerset and Gloucestershire were still in danger. Even after *Badon*, nothing could prevent Irish corsairs from sailing up the Bristol Channel and making the same hit-and-run raids that had carried St Patrick across the sea to Ireland. The Bristol Channel and the waters off other parts of Britain's western coasts were of vital strategic importance. It was here that the naval ambushes that Vegetius describes could best be carried out. These critical waters had to be made no-go areas for the raiders. But dominating them meant dominating the Dumnonian and Welsh coasts.

Dumnonia was the easier of the two objectives to attain. We do not know the particulars of this struggle, but indirect evidence can help us see the outlines of Arthur's design. We know that South Cadbury became an important British elite site later in the century. Most observers in the past have seen it as the stronghold of an important local chieftain, perhaps even a sixth-century 'King Arthur'.[4] Some see it as a reassertion of 'Britishness', the reoccupation of a site with links to the pre-Roman Iron Age. But whatever the analysis, the stronghold has universally been seen as facing east, serving as a last bastion against the ever-encroaching Saxons that Arthur is supposed to halt.

But could South Cadbury originally have had a different function? After all, it sits astride a very important road. This road connects the old Roman town of *Calleva* with what is now Salisbury. Perhaps not coincidentally, it also offers the most direct route from the Upper Thames into Dumnonia. In short, this Iron Age hill site may not have been reoccupied by sub-Roman Britons anxious to get in touch with their Celtic roots. Rather, Cadbury's strategic position suggests that it was carefully chosen to serve as a base of operations: operations facing not east, but west. Like the Saxon Shore forts and the strongholds along the Wall, its most likely original function was as a headquarters and supply base for Arthur's re-occupation of Dumnonia—a recognizably Roman thing to do.

The result of such an operation would have been a foregone conclusion. Even if Irishmen or hostile Britons existed in this part of Dumnonia, they could have put up no effective opposition. Supported by his new Saxon navy, Arthur's mobile cavalry and infantry would have moved with overwhelming force down the Roman road into the peninsula. Resistance, if any, would have been weak and short-lived. But occupation was only the first stage. Of far more significance was the use Arthur would make of Dumnonia. But to understand this, we must understand the significance of a very special place.

TINTAGEL

Mystery has always surrounded Tintagel. Legend holds that Uther Pendragon captured it in order to wed Ygraine of Cornwall. King Arthur was supposedly born here. Medieval bards claimed that Tristan and Isolde acted out their fatal love story on this same spot. But for most of the last century sober scholarship saw Tintagel in a different light. This promontory could only be a monastic settlement, with little political or military significance. Recent excavations, however, suggest it was something quite different. Scholars now see it as a 'high status' site, perhaps the stronghold of a powerful king.[5]

There are problems with this interpretation, however. Tintagel is what is called a 'promontory fort': that is, a fortified peninsula that juts out into the sea. But it is also more than just a fort. It is one of the strongest defensive works in this quarter of Britain. For this reason it is sometimes seen as a royal residence, perhaps the seat of the kings of Dumnonia. Yet if this were so, Tintagel seems a puzzling place to put a capital. The harsh winters make it uninhabitable for part of the year. More importantly, it faces *away* from the trade coming from Gaul. A far more salubrious place for a royal seat would be on the south coast, at Lostwithiel, say. This would be farther away from the Irish raiders and much nearer to ships coming from the continent.

But some powerful person did use this area, and used it well. No other site in Cornwall has yielded so much archaeology, or, indeed, is associated with so much myth. Only one conclusion can bring together all these contradictions: this powerful person was none other than Arthur—and Tintagel was originally not a political, but a military centre. In plain terms, it was a naval base in the same mould as the Saxon Shore forts. Virtually impregnable to lightly armed Irish and Picts, it would have been the cornerstone of maritime defence for this part of Britain. It could be used as a lookout station to give early warning of Irish ships in western Cornwall. It could re-supply cavalry detachments, and so deny landfall to Irish sea raiders seeking either re-supply or loot. From nearby harbours ships could sortie out to intercept raiders in the Bristol Channel. Most importantly, like the Saxon Shore forts themselves, its brooding presence was psychologically impressive. This was essentially a western equivalent to the 'Jutish' enclaves on Thanet and the Isle of Wight.

The Bristol Channel is, however, quite a bit larger than the Thames or the Solent. Even a place as strong as Tintagel could not hope to control this entire body of water. Further, independent polities existed to the north, in Wales. Here were lands ravaged earlier in the century by Niall of the Nine Hostages. The Welsh[6] would have been incapable of denying this littoral to the Irish, and perhaps even unwilling to do so. It was also a place difficult to pacify fully. One has only to think of the difficulties Edward I faced in subduing the medieval Welsh to realize that this would have been a more difficult task than the occupation of Dumnonia. A comprehensive solution to the Irish threat could come only through a methodical occupation of the Welsh coast.

PAGUS

Sometime in the fifth century a new state arose on the border between what is now Wales and Lowland Britain. Formerly this area had been known as the *civitas* of the Cornovii, named for a pre-Roman British tribe. Its capital *Viroconium* (the modern Wroxeter) became one of the most important cities in the next century. Today we know this area by its Welsh name, Powys. But despite appearances, Powys is really not a Brythonic word at all. It comes from the Latin *pagus*, and is related to our own word 'pagan'. Both words are associated with the idea of someone or something remote, on the border. The Church called non-Christians pagans because the last centres of this belief were in rural, out-of-the-way places. Similarly, a polity called *Pagus* connotes something at the margins, away from the centre.[7] In effect, it is the name someone from a still Romanized Lowland Britain might give to a border province.

The question then becomes: why?

If we accept that Arthur's main business was war, and that his style of *Romanitas* came from the Late Roman army, the answer is obvious. The old *civitas* of the Cornovii had been reorganized, and for a very specific purpose: to conquer and dominate Wales. Further, the *civitas* capital of *Viroconium* was perfectly suited to perform the same sort of mission as South Cadbury. Some of its Roman structures may still have been standing, available for defensive and storage purposes. Its location is midway on the vital north–south Roman road that skirts the eastern boundary of Wales, allowing quick communication with any force preparing to move westward. As with South Cadbury, it would have served as both headquarters and quartermaster for Arthur's forces. With it, the Lowland soldiers had a decisive advantage over any local opposition.

Marching through the cold, wet Welsh valleys, Arthur's troops may not have been as sanguine about their advantages as the above implies. But they would have been fed most of the time, unlike their opponents. They would have been able to deal quickly with any local resistance; both Saxon and Briton had been fighting under Arthur's dragon banner for a number of years. Any 'Scots' or hostile Welsh would have been unable to mount land operations for any length of time, faced as they were by sudden attacks from both land and sea. We do not know how long these campaigns took, or even whether they were opposed. But the outcome is not in doubt. Gildas, if we read him correctly, only confirms this. After the Proud Tyrant hires his Saxons, the eternal Irish and Pictish menace abruptly vanishes from the cleric's narrative.

Really, though, what was being done in Dumnonia and Wales was what Roman armies had been doing for centuries. Even after the break with the empire, a certain type of *Romanitas* was alive and well in Britain. However, it was the *Romanitas* of Constantine the Great and Vegetius, of the *castrum* and the *annona*. Virgil and Cicero were not quite dead, but they had certainly moved to the background.

That Tintagel, South Cadbury, and Wroxeter were originally bases for Arthur also goes a long way towards explaining their subsequent importance. In the fifth century these were administrative and supply centres, drawing in much of the annual harvest from the surrounding countryside. Later, when Britain fragmented into the kingdoms Gildas describes, they became centres for the petty dynasts of the west. The taxes that had originally gone to maintain Arthur's military establishment were used to rebuild and fortify each royal centre. Part of these taxes also went to pay for the luxury goods that began flowing into Britain, thanks to Justinian's penetration of the western Mediterranean. But the Dark Age opulence that is suggested by the finds at Wroxeter, South Cadbury, and Tintagel was made possible by networks of taxation and administration laid down during the time of Arthur.

The name change to *Pagus* may also give us a clue as to the identity of Arthur's garrison in Dumnonia. During Roman times, one particular army unit is known to have borne a British name. It was called the *Cornovii.* This suggests that the *civitas* was an important recruiting ground during Roman times: perfectly logical when it is considered that these were tough hill people, but still within the Roman orbit. Perhaps not coincidentally, a variation of this tribal name, *Kernau,* was later used to describe the western part of Dumnonia. Eventually this would become the name we know as Cornwall. The name *Kernau* occurs only several centuries after Arthur. But with the paucity of sources that we possess, it is perfectly possible that in the fifth century this became an alternate name for western Dumnonia following its pacification. If so, it suggests that, like *Pagus,* western Dumnonia became a militarized province. Its new rulers were military men from the *civitas* of the Cornovii. This is entirely in keeping with Arthur's military and ethnic policies—as well as with Late Roman statecraft. In a sense, the Cornovian soldiers had become federates as well.

DEMETIA

There is more evidence that Arthur dominated much of Wales in the 450s. On the southeastern coast we find a kind of 'mirror image' of Tintagel, in what was then known as the *civitates* of Demetia (later Dyfed). The more Romanized part of Demetia had already suffered the same fate as that of Lowland Britannia. Carmarthen and its surrounding villas were all abandoned at about the time of the 'Fall of the Villas'. In their place, however, we find hill forts aplenty, at Brawdy, Coygan Camp, and elsewhere. Lacking walled cities like *Glevum* and *Corinium*, the local elite refortified the strongholds of their Iron Age ancestors. But it is the promontory fort at Gateholm that is of most significance. Like Tintagel, in the fifth century Gateholm was an easily defended peninsula jutting into the sea. Archaeology has revealed the remains of buildings and high status goods, as was found at the Cornish site.[8] This suggests that Gateholm's original function was identical to that of Tintagel.

Moreover, Tintagel and Gateholm may not have been simply naval bases concerned with their own stretch of the British coastline. An island called Lundy lies at the broad mouth of the Bristol Channel. Interestingly, it is visible from both Tintagel and Caldey, an island offshore of Demetia that is not far from Gateholm. In a word, each of these sites may have been part of a kind of 'early warning' system for the Bristol Channel. Ships from both Gateholm and Tintagel would have patrolled this expanse of water, aided by signal stations on the respective islands. And numbers of these ships were most likely crewed by Saxon federates. The *Dux Bellorum* was making the west secure through a clever combination of Saxons and Saxon Shore expertise.[9]

That it was Arthur who created this system is also suggested by the king lists of the Demetian dynasty. Although scholars are sceptical about the historicity of Welsh regnal lists in general, the Demetian list is different. Its third king, Vortipor, is certainly an historical person. Gildas gives a scathing indictment of him for his sins, particularly his sexual ones. Moreover, the name on a Class-1 stone in southern Wales is almost certainly his as well. Even his title, *Protectoris*, is identical to the one found in the earliest genealogies.[10] We may thus suspect that the two names listed for Vortipor's father and grandfather, Aircol and Triphun, are also genuine. Indeed, they are merely Celtic variations of Latin names (Agricola and Tribunus, respectively).[11] But to be more precise, Tribunus is not really a name, but a title, derived from the Latin word 'tribune'. It strongly suggests that this was one of the titles of Vortipor's grandfather. Of most interest, however, is the fact that Gildas explicitly refers to Vortipor as an old man whose 'head is already whitening'.[12] If we calculate backward from the time Gildas was writing (520–30), Vortipor would have been born in about 460–70. Assigning a twenty-five-year generation to his two ancestors, the likely nativities of his two forebears are as follows:

Agricola	435–45
Tribunus	415–25

This would make 'the Tribune' a younger contemporary of Arthur himself. When we remember that cohorts were commanded by tribunes, the most likely reason this Briton came to rule Demetia was that he was one of Arthur's trusted lieutenants, a man who had fought with distinction at such places as *Guinnion* and *Badon*. Since at least part of Demetia's naval defence may have involved Saxons and their ships, this makes perfect sense. Whatever the identity of the sailors who served here, their commander's first loyalties lay with Arthur.[13]

GLASTONBURY

The conquest of Wales and Dumnonia was complete. Strongholds like Gateholm and Tintagel guarded both coasts from Irish and Pictish occupation, in much the same way as the Saxon Shore forts at Portchester and Pevensey guarded the southern coast of Britain. But the Saxon Shore system had possessed one other defensive feature. The Romans had used the narrows of the Straits of Dover as a 'choke point', where they could ambush and destroy Saxon and Irish raiders. If Arthur were really employing Roman naval doctrine, it is fair to ask whether he created anything like this in the Bristol Channel. The answer is: very likely. Moreover, his new defensive system may have incorporated one of the most famous 'Arthurian' sites of all. Glastonbury.

Like Tintagel, Glastonbury is rich in legend. It was here that Joseph of Arimathea was reputed to have brought Christ's communion cup to Britain. Later, in Plantagenet times, King Arthur's grave would be 'found' here, complete with a carefully inscribed marker. These stories are probably no more than myths concocted by local monks. But one thing is undeniable about Glastonbury. It is high ground. Its peak, the Tor, is visible from a long way off. A fire lit on the Tor can be recognized from at least two other significant features. One of these is a place we have already visited. It is South Cadbury, the 'nerve centre' of Arthur's military presence in Dumnonia. The other is in the opposite direction, to the west. It is called Brent Knoll—and just so happens to lie on the coast of the Bristol Channel. Indeed, in this period it would have been an island at the mouth of the large estuary that formed *Traeth Tribruit*. The implication is clear. Whatever cups or graves there may have been at Glastonbury, its most likely original function was as a vital link in a communications chain that linked the most important military site in southwestern Britain with the sea.[14]

The reason for this is obvious—when we realize that a beacon fire on Brent Knoll can be seen from yet another elevated spot. But this spot is on the *opposite* side of the Bristol Channel, in Wales, at a place called Dinas Powys. Like South Cadbury, this was later one of the most important sixth-century sites in Britain. Still more telling is the fact that a considerable number of Anglo-Saxon metal artifacts were found at this site, including shield ornaments, belt fittings and strap ends. Such material has also been found at South Cadbury itself, and at another nearby fifth-century fort within sight of the sea, Cadbury-Congresbury.[15] It is thus highly unlikely that these strongholds owed their origins to some Darwinian struggle among local chieftains and 'sub-kings'. Far more plausible is the notion that they were founded to control this strategic expanse of water. True, the archaeological 'footprint' of Arthur's troops would have been very light—just as 'footprints' of the armies of Aetius and Aegidius on the continent are largely unknown. The British and Saxon garrisons would have consisted of young men with few possessions, and who may have served only on a seasonal basis. Their dwellings would have been as flimsy as St Germanus' chapel. But if we view these sites as components in an integrated military and naval complex analogous to the Saxon Shore, Arthur's grand design is clear. By controlling the Bristol Channel both at its mouth and at its narrowest point, he could ensure that Lowland Britain would never again suffer from Irish and Pictish raiding.

We have already seen how this 'choke point' operated. Gildas tells us that earlier seaborne barbarians were repelled with 'cavalry by land, and mariners by sea'.[16] Vegetius tells us of the ambush tactics used by Late Roman navies. In practice, lookouts further up the Channel would warn of the approach of any strange craft. The message would be relayed by semaphore and signal fire to the commander at South Cadbury, who would then order his subordinates on both sides of the Channel to launch their ships. Finally, Saxon-crewed vessels would intercept and destroy the leather-sided curraghs. As the Saxons divided up their spoils only the wisest of them would have understood—or cared about—what Arthur had accomplished.

The Irish and Pictish raiding was ended. Cities such as *Badon*, *Glevum*, and *Corinium* could return to something resembling normality. And, as an added bonus, many potentially violent young Saxons were isolated from their settlements in the east.

Arthur was creating a new state in western Europe, a state predicated on a meticulous balance between barbarian force and Roman expertise.

VENEDOTIA

There were other parts of the British world that were still under threat, however. We have only to remember the battle at Chester to recall that northern Wales was a favourite destination of Irish rovers. In later times King Edward I dominated this area with a number of well-nigh impregnable castles. But Arthur may have anticipated him by almost a millennium. A site called Deganwy appears to have arisen at the same time as Tintagel and Gateholm. And, like *Pagus*, the *civitas* in which it was located received a new, post-Roman name: Gwynedd, the land of the Venedoti.

The *Historia Brittonum* purports to tell us more about the earliest rulers of this region. In its pages we read: 'Cunedda, with his sons, to the number of eight, had come from the north, from the country called Manaw Gododdin, 146 years before Maelgwn reigned, and expelled the Irish from these countries, with immense slaughter, so that they never again returned to inhabit them.'[17]

Many scholars assert that the story of Cunedda is mere fantasy. They claim that the *Historia*'s main purpose is not to preserve sober history, but to magnify the dynastic lineage of Merfyn, the ninth-century king of Gwynedd.[18] This author would not dispute that the *Historia Brittonum*'s account is flawed in a number of ways. But these flaws are very different from those previously supposed. Indeed, once they are understood, it becomes clear just how completely Arthur dominated western Britain.

First of all, the blood ties of Merfyn to Cunedda and Maelgwn are justifiably suspect. Many ruling families of Europe once claimed King David as their forebear on evidence just as slight. Although more debatable, it might even be granted that Cunedda never existed. But that a major political change occurred in northern Wales is hardly fantasy. Originally this region was the *civitas* of a British tribe called the Ordovices. But just as *Pagus*/Powys acquired a new name, so too did the *civitas* of the Ordovices become known as the land of the Venedoti. Yet unlike *Pagus* or Demetia, this new name is not derived from any known Latin or Brythonic word. The only alternative is that the name comes from somewhere outside the Romano-British world, and is probably descriptive of the new rulers of the *civitas*.[19]

There is one objection to this argument, however. What the *Historia* says about Cunedda also seems to place him completely outside our period. Gildas, writing in the 530s, portrays Maelgwn as a powerful ruler in the prime of his life.[20] If Cunedda arrived 146 years before the *beginning* of Maelgwn's reign, this would make the patriarch active when Britain was still a Roman diocese, most likely in the time of Maximus' usurpation. This might appear to settle the matter. Even if Cunedda and his eight sons existed, they would have been federates invited in to defend northern Wales from the Irish *before* the break with Rome.

The *Historia Brittonum* gives us an additional piece of information, however, and it is very much at odds with this chronology. We are told that Cunedda and his sons 'expelled the Irish from these countries, with immense slaughter, so that they never again returned to inhabit them'. This is not the story that Gildas tells. For him, the Irish menace lasts right up to the time that the Proud Tyrant hires his Saxons. Even if we might reject

450 as the date for this, *no one* has suggested that the Proud Tyrant ruled Britain during Roman times. If this statement is true, the other statement about Cunedda in the *Historia* is describing events in mid-fifth century, when the Irish threat was finally neutralized. So, which part of the *Historia* ought we to believe?

Another piece of evidence may hold the key. As in Demetia-Dyfed, we also have an early list of dynastic rulers for Gwynedd. In it Maelgwn, or Mailcun as he is termed in the list, has a father called 'Catgolan Lauhir'. Maelgwn's grandfather is a certain 'Eniaun Girt', and his great-grandfather is called... 'Cuneda'.[21] This directly contradicts the *Historia* account, where Cunedda is called Maelgwn's *great*-great-grandfather. Further, Gildas, writing in about 530, presents Maelgwn as one of the most canny and experienced rulers in western Britain. A good guess for his age at that time would be about 40. If we calculate backward that would give him a nativity in about 490. If we assign a generational average of twenty-five years for Maelgwn's antecedents, their respective birth dates would be as follows:

Catgolan Lauhir	465
Eniaun Girt	440
Cunedda	415

This would place Cunedda not in Roman times, but in our period.[22] Indeed, a respected scholar has argued that this dynastic list would give Cunedda a floruit of 450—at exactly the time when Arthur was establishing his control over western Britain.[23] In other words this 'Venedotian' appears to have belonged to the roughly same generational cohort as Arthur and 'the Tribune'. But the probable birth date listed above for Cunedda also does not take into account that Eniaun was a seventh son, nor that the patriarch arrived in Wales with a *grandson* in tow. It would thus be more probable that Cunedda was born earlier, perhaps even before the time of Constantine III's usurpation in 406. The *Historia* also indicates that it was Cunedda *and his sons* who expelled the Irish once and for all. From the point of view of the dynastic list, this makes sense only if the Venedoti received their demesne in the 450s. Eniaun Girt's likely birth date would then make him a young man quite capable of bearing arms at that time. Again, the fact that he was Cunedda's seventh son further suggests that most of his siblings would have been ready and able to defeat the Irish at exactly the time that Gildas says they were defeated.[24] Both the dynastic list and the whole logic of the account argue that the Venedoti were 'planted' in north Wales in the same way as the Saxons had been planted in Thanet, and the Cornovii in Cornwall.

But where did the Venedoti come from? The *Historia Brittonum* argues that they came from the 'Manau of Gododdin', that is, the area north of what is now Edinburgh. Now, it is important to remember that the name 'Gododdin' comes from the old tribal name of the 'Votadini' who inhabited that region. It may be that the *Historia*'s author is engaging in amateur linguistics here, equating Venedoti with Votadini. If so, his linguistics are as flawed as his chronology. Still, this northern origin myth may be true in another sense. When we consider that shortly after attaining their federate status Octha's 'Jutes' harried the Picts all the way to the Orkneys, a tantalizing possibility arises. If Arthur was using Germanic federates in the Bristol Channel, might he not want to 'plant' another, non-Germanic group in northern Wales? An unemployed Pictish or Northern British buccaneer would have been a perfect choice to rule this vital part of the British coast.[25] It would have been entirely in keeping with the divide and rule strategy we have seen Arthur employ in other areas.

But there is more to the Venedoti saga than this. It so happens that the Welsh dynastic lists tell us that one of Cunedda's other sons was called Ceretic. Perhaps not coincidentally, we find that a kingdom called *Ceredigion* (the modern Cardigan) arose at precisely the same time as Gwynedd/Venedotia. Even more interesting is the fact that *Ceredigion* guards the middle portion of the western coast of Wales. With Demetia to the south and Gwynedd to the north, these new polities would have transformed the entire western littoral of Wales into a ring of steel. The best explanation is that all three 'kingdoms' formed a defensive bulwark in the west that exactly paralleled the 'Jutish' enclaves in the east.

But the parallels with the 'Jutes' may go deeper. It is only a short voyage from *Ceredigion* across the Irish Sea to where Patrick's baptized women were captured. This is an exploit that exactly parallels Octha's raid on the Orkneys. Moreover, it is actually doubtful that Ceretic was Cunedda's son. It is far more likely that his dynasty subsequently claimed this in order to increase its prestige.[26] Also significant is the fact that Ceretic is only a variation on the name Coroticus. Together, this evidence suggests that Ceretic is none other than Coroticus himself—and reveals the true purpose of these western enclaves. Coroticus' raid was no isolated incident, but part of a coordinated campaign to intimidate the Irish. That the innocent should suffer as a result of Coroticus' 'aggressive defence' was of no concern to either him or his overlord.

Still, Patrick played the one card that he possessed. Arthur's prime concern may have been naval defence, but a regime that claimed its legitimacy through the good offices of Christ and the Virgin Mary could never entirely ignore the denunciations of a respected bishop. Patrick's complaint gives us an important insight into Arthur's grand design—and its human cost.

The new elite centres and *civitates* that arose in western Britain during the fifth century were not just the result of a Darwinian competition between a clutch of petty, independent states. The evidence, if examined with care, shows the application of a sophisticated strategy that combined barbarian seafaring skill with Late Roman naval defensive expertise. The elite centres that arose at this time are best explained as links in a chain of maritime defence, analogous to the Saxon Shore forts of Roman times. The Bristol Channel and the Welsh coast provided numerous areas where the type of naval ambush that Vegetius describes would have been possible. Both archaeology and dynastic evidence indicate that Saxons, west Britons, north Britons, and perhaps even Picts, were carefully placed to carry out both defensive *and* offensive naval operations. And the man who created all this was Arthur. Like a great architect, he took disparate materials and created a lasting edifice. Using one group of barbarians to counterbalance another, he brought security to all of Britain's coasts.

FOIRTCHERN

Arthur had provided security. The Bristol Channel was no longer a haven for Irish raiders. The western coast of Wales was quiet. But security is not necessarily peace—and is expensive besides. The cost of the Late Roman military establishment had played a large part in weakening the western empire. Even the offensive operations against the Irish risked a counterstroke. Naval strategy could only be one strand in Arthur's grand design. Other means were needed, means less expensive than ships and promontory forts.

One of these was surely the mission of St Patrick, which was now reaching its final flowering. Thousands had been baptized in a faith that was becoming the common possession of both Britain and Ireland. More importantly, these new converts were now *cives*, 'fellow-citizens of the holy Romans', as Patrick phrased it.[27] The knowledge of Holy Scripture—and the Latin in which it was written—was spreading throughout the country. Moreover, a man who had once been a victim of the Irish depredations had gained great influence on the western side of the Irish Sea. Patrick might not resort to Roman naval strategy to halt the raiding. But he could—and did—denounce the raids. Having an ally in the enemy's camp who had once been a victim of the seaborne predators was an intangible, but very real asset.

There is evidence that Arthur took other steps to make peace with the Irish. Oddly enough, the evidence centres on a lacklustre Irish cleric who lived half a century later. He was heir to an abbey jointly left to him by his father and St Patrick, an impressive enough legacy by any standard. But after initially accepting the bequest, in a fit of pique he gave it away three days later. This would not merit our attention, except for two things. The first is that this cleric's name was Foirtchern, an Irish equivalent of the Proud Tyrant's name in later centuries: Vortigern. This in itself is intriguing. We might still think it a coincidence, until we find that his mother is described as the daughter of a 'British king'. What is more, Foirtchern's mother was the wife of a son of Laeghaire, the High King of Ireland in the mid-fifth century.[28] The probable identity of this 'British king' is self-evident, as is Laeghaire's incentive for such a union. He, of all people, had good reason to respect Roman naval defences: in 405 his father Niall had been a victim of the Saxon Shore. Arthur's offensives had caused significant losses to Irish buccaneers, and now threatened Laeghaire's own territory in Ireland. This, combined with Patrick's growing influence, made peace seem a wiser course. We find a substantial Irish presence in Wales after this, and Arthur's peace may well have facilitated a later *Adventus* of Irish federates into western Britain. Many sixth-century Demetian standing stones are inscribed in both Latin and the Irish ogam script. Also, a small Irish kingdom called Brycheiniog later came into being in the tri-border area between Demetia, Powys and Gwent.[29] When we recall the means by which Arthur pacified the Saxons, the reason we see the Irish integrating into Welsh society becomes clear. Like the Saxons and North Britons, they too eventually entered into a *foedus* with the diocese.

NATIONS

If we are to understand the political context of Arthur's reign, we must now examine the situation on the continent. Most significant for our story is that in 451 the very opposite of peace prevailed across the Channel. In that fateful year Aetius confronted the nemesis he had so long hoped to avoid. His boyhood friend, Attila, moved west. All of Gaul was thrown into confusion as a vast army of Heruls, Huns, Ostrogoths, Alans and Gepids thundered through the Champagne country. Aetius, his own forces dwarfed by this horde, desperately threw together a coalition of barbarians and Romans to halt the onslaught. The Hunnish tide swept forward. New immigrants like the Alans debated whether to support Attila or the empire. Saint Genevieve offered up fervent prayers that Paris might be spared. In the end two mighty armies clashed on the Catalaunian Plains. In a contest more reminiscent of the slaughterhouses of World War I than the conflicts of the fifth century, Attila was turned back.[30]

The western empire was saved. But the sequel to the events of 451 was tawdry. The emperor Valentinian III, fearful of his powerful generalissimo, had Aetius assassinated. A subordinate of the marshal avenged the murder by slaying the emperor himself in 455. Rome was thrown into chaos.

It is here that we once again meet Geiseric the Vandal, the lame stripling who had crossed the Rhine with his fellow barbarians some fifty years earlier. He and his tribe had travelled far since then. Battling their way down the length of Gaul and Spain, they had crossed over into North Africa. Here they had established a kingdom of their own, and the cunning Geiseric wound up as its ruler. By 455 this new Vandal king had created a powerful fleet, and, upon news of the emperor's assassination, he sent it sailing across the Mediterranean and up the Tiber. The result was a repeat of the events of 410. Rome was again systematically looted and humiliated.[31]

This second sacking of Rome shook the whole edifice of the western empire. It was now clear that the debacle of 410 was no fluke. It was an event that might occur at any time in the future. This second 'fall' of Rome was not the end, but certainly the beginning of the end. Western Europe now broke up into half a dozen warring polities, some barbarian, some Roman. Although technically still part of the empire, they were already behaving like separate kingdoms. One of Aetius' protégés, Aegidius, took power in northern Gaul. Much like Aetius, he was able to deal effectively with the barbarians, particularly the Franks. For eight years he was even king of that people.[32] Another Gallo-Roman officer, Avitus, ascended even higher. Proclaimed emperor by the Gallo-Roman nobles and supported by the Goths, in 455 he was crowned with the imperial diadem in Rome. Also of interest, a certain young Gallo-Roman nobleman accompanied him to Rome—the future bishop Sidonius Apollinaris. Dreaming of imperial glory, the young man confected a panegyric poem of some 600 lines to honour the new Caesar. As was typical of the times, Sidonius' approach was something very far removed from minimalism: 'O Sun-god, now at last in the circle of thy wanderings thou canst see one that thou art able to brook as thine equal; so give thy rays to heaven, for he is sufficient to lighten the earth.' Alluding to Geiseric's late sack of Rome, the young poet also confidently predicted a swift vengeance against the Vandals. Avitus, he affirmed, 'shall restore Libya to a fourth time in chains'.[33] Not to mince words, the Gallo-Roman emperor's reign was to usher in a golden age. Sidonius' verses gave hope to the now-destitute inhabitants of the Eternal City.

But Avitus' 'golden age' was short-lived. In the wake of the Vandal sack Rome was not merely destitute, she faced famine—

and Avitus could not deliver the needed grain. Soon all levels of society were railing against him. Two military protégés of the late Aetius, a barbarian named Ricimer and a Roman called Majorian, took advantage of the unrest and revolted. Avitus was overthrown and died under mysterious circumstances.

In the meantime the Gothic and Burgundian kingdoms continued to grow. While still technically federates, they did very much as they pleased.[34] Sidonius' vision of a Gallo-Roman-dominated empire had proved as empty as his rhetoric. Still worse, the decline of the western empire seemed unstoppable.

In the 450s Britain might have shared such a fate—except for Arthur. He had reunited most of the diocese and made peace with its neighbours. In a time of political and economic disintegration, Britain was headed in the opposite direction. Suddenly she found herself one of the strongest powers in Western Europe.

12.

'A MOST EXTRAORDINARY PLENTY'

LUXURY

The Golden Age. The Age of Arthur. Until now these words have belonged to the realm of fantasy, not to the world of history. Even the most die-hard believer in a reality behind the myth of the 'Once and Future King' has had precious little to prove that Arthur's reign was peaceful, let alone prosperous. But there is documentary evidence for the Age of Arthur, and again, it has been in Gildas all along.

> No sooner were the ravages of the enemy checked, than the island was deluged with a most extraordinary plenty of all things, greater than was before known, and with it grew up every kind of luxury and licentiousness. It grew with so firm a root, that one might truly say of it, such fornication is heard of among you, as never was known the like among the Gentiles.[1]

This of course is not *precisely* how we conceive of the Arthurian Age. But the problem here is our source. It is doubtful if Gildas would have had anything better to say about America in the 1920s or Britain in the 1960s. These were both wealthy periods, and culturally vibrant as well. But we may be sure that Gildas' focus would have been entirely on the 'licentiousness' of each era. Even Golden Ages cannot satisfy all tastes.

This 'boom' may have had its roots in the upheaval that preceded it. Gildas tells us that large numbers of Britons died in the wake of the Saxon advance of the 440s. Then, while the Picto-Irish fleet is gathering, he recounts a fresh misfortune: 'a pestilential disease mortally afflicted the foolish people, which, without the sword, cut off so large a number of persons, that the living were not able to bury them.'[2] Both of these events would certainly have been traumatic to those who lived through them, just as the Black Death was to fourteenth-century Europeans. But, as with that later human catastrophe, the fifth-century afflictions would have placed many of their survivors in a very advantageous position. Like most pre-modern societies, Late Roman Britain was a place where the great majority always teetered on the edge of starvation. But if the loss of life was anywhere near what Gildas claims, the same amount of land was now available to feed far fewer mouths. Suddenly a single farmer might cultivate a larger plot. He could feed a growing family; even raise a surplus. For the majority of Britons who had suffered through the deprivations of former times, the sudden abundance of food must have seemed like a miracle.

What was this world filled 'with a most extraordinary plenty of things' like, exactly? Archaeology reveals evidence for a recovery at just this time. In the middle of the century—long after the end of villa construction—a Roman-style building, complete with plumbing, was raised in St Albans.[3] A hoard unearthed at Patching contained coins dated to the 460s—signalling an at least partial return to a money economy.[4] There is also quite a bit of evidence for mid-century British iron working. But archaeology still testifies that this new age in no way matched the splendour of the 'Age of the Villas'. It seems to have been a world of wood and earth, iron and leather—little of which has survived in the archaeological record. In place of the square-cut stones of city ramparts, we find in Cadbury and Congresbury the remains of wooden palisades erected on dry-stone walls. In place of stone and brick villas we find traces of the lofty timber buildings of Wroxeter.

Indeed, increasingly scholars are seeing the Anglo-Saxon timber halls of later generations as deriving at least in part from British prototypes.[5] The suggestion that the 'dark earth' layers in many urban sites may be evidence for cities crammed with wattle-and-daub buildings further changes our perspective on fifth-century Britain. This was not the world of Constantine or Maximus. But, for the elite at least, it was not a deprived world either.

In no area would this have been truer than in foodstuffs. A peasantry now protected from the ravages of the invader could produce great quantities of mead and beer, cheese and honey. It is true that the archaeological record reflects an absence of the consumer goods that had once flowed across the Channel. But it might be useful to compare this with the situation in Gaul, a culture that was still largely Roman. Sidonius describes a number of feasts in his letters, yet nearly all the foodstuffs that he mentions are locally produced. He rarely, if ever, speaks of foreign wines or delicacies.[6] Yet the banquets he describes are still fully Roman. In the same way, there seems little reason to doubt that the art of Roman dining was alive and well in mid-century Britain. Many a Cotswold snail would have ended its days on Arthur's round banqueting table.

Incredibly, we may also have evidence of literary tastes existing and being satisfied in fifth-century Britain. A codex of the *Aeneid* that now rests in the Vatican Library, the *Vergilius Romanus*, is asserted by some scholars actually to have been produced in Britain. Certainly, the good Latin education that Gildas received after the end of this era indicates that the language of Virgil was well known in the previous century. Just who authorized the production of this particular book is unknown. But patronage of such works was both possible and logical for Britons who wished to reassert their *Romanitas*.[7]

The Church too appears to have been revitalized at this time. Where once clergymen had sailed from Gaul to Britain, now they travelled in the opposite direction. We find a bishop of British origin, Mansuetus, ensconced in an unnamed see in Gaul, and attending a Council at Tours in 461.[8] In almost the same year the great British cleric Faustus became bishop of Riez. His previous position had been as abbot of Lerins, one of the most important centres of learning in western Europe. Faustus appears to have maintained close contacts with his brethren in Britain, sending them copies of his attempts to reconcile philosophy with faith.[9] He was also a tireless foe of the more extreme arguments for predestination, and fell into some disrepute after his death for his semi-Pelagian views. The theology that had originated in Britain was still a cause of controversy.

Forty years of conflict had swept away much of Roman Britain for ever. But the culture, especially the intellectual culture, had not died. Provided Arthur's state remained united, it had the potential to rival—even to outstrip—the fragmenting societies of the western empire.

TWELVE

Because the evidence is so scant, it might seem that this broad-brush sketch is the best description possible of Arthur's realm. But there is one particular theme that recurs again and again in the record. It may give a better insight into this new Britain, and even explain one aspect of the Arthurian legend.

Gildas tells us that 'kings were anointed' after the initial defeat of the barbarians. Then, in the context of the Picto-Irish threat, the Proud Tyrant *and his council* invited the Saxons into Britain. Curiously, the later author of the *Historia Brittonum* also tells us something about these evil councillors. Here they are called wizards. But they just happen to number twelve. This may seem of no particular significance, until we consider other instances from this period when the number twelve also occurs. Examples include:

—Arthur's twelve battles in the *Historia*;
—A boast in the *Anglo-Saxon Chronicle* (*ASC*) about a devastating victory over the Britons in 465, in which twelve British nobles were slain;
—The account by the Gothic writer Jordanes of 12,000 Britons invading Gaul in 469.

Individually these may not seem compelling, but taken together they suggest that twelve was a number with a peculiar significance to fifth-century Britons. This *could* be simply a Late Roman number fetish. Twelve had a special meaning for Christians, who venerated the twelve apostles, as it did for pagans, who used the twelve signs of the zodiac to chart their futures. But there may be another reason as well: a reason that can shed some light on the inner workings of Arthur's realm.

Britain had been divided into seventeen *civitates* during the Roman period, each centred on a particular regional capital. We have seen how large parts of East Anglia and southern Britain had been taken over by Saxons. We have also seen how Wales and Cornwall were reorganized into new polities. This and the talk of 'anointed kings' suggest that a political revolution had taken place not just in the west, but in every corner of Britain. In particular, the loss of such areas as East Anglia may have resulted in a reduction in the number of viable *civitates*. The above evidence suggests that the most likely number of remaining 'city-states' was twelve. Thus, the Anglo-Saxon boast about the death of twelve British nobles may be a shorthand way of saying that the ruler of every *civitas* was killed at the battle of *Wippedsfleot*. The report of 12,000 men in the British invasion force may indicate that every *civitas* was required to maintain a standing force of about a thousand soldiers. Indeed, this may have been one of the chief aims of

Arthur's reorganization of the *civitates*: to create a reliable standing army. The report of the Proud Tyrant's twelve advisers may not be legend at all, but the memory of an assembly made up of the rulers of each of the reorganized *civitates*. As suggested above, these are the most likely 'kings' whom the *Dux Bellorum* commanded in his twelve battles.

The circular Roman table around which Arthur's councillors gathered would have been the nerve centre of this new state. Here they dined off the good things of the land, while hammering out the policies that were making Britain one of the strongest states in western Europe. We may already know some of these men. Cunedda and Triphun ('the Tribune') are likely candidates. Cai and Bedwyr may be as well. Another may be surprising. Coel Hen, or 'Coel the Old', is often described as a 'northern magnate', a legendary ruler who founded many of the dynasties of the Men of the North. He survives in popular imagination in the nursery rhyme 'Old King Cole'. A more substantial proof of his identity is the fact that a descendant of his, Eleuther Cascord Maur ('Eleuther of the Great Cohort'), ruled in the region of York at the same time as the five evil kings whom Gildas so forcefully condemns. Moreover, exactly the same number of generations separate Coel from Eleuther as separate Cunedda from Maelgwn. Assuming Eleuther was a man in the prime of his life in 530, this would give birth dates for him and his ancestors as follows:

—Eleuther Cascord Maur (490)
—Letlum (465)
—Ceneu (440)
—Coel Hen (415)[10]

It is, of course, possible that Coel, like Cunedda and Triphun, was a ruler whom Arthur assigned to the north. But Coel was roughly the same age, and perhaps even older than,

Arthur. Roman commanders had ruled from the *Principia* in York for centuries. Coel is best seen as a local British military commander who arose in the north after the break with Rome. At some point he may even have been a political rival to Arthur. But the victories that culminated in *Badon* relegated Coel to the role of a regional player. The above information is sketchy, but it is fully in keeping with the policy of an astute ruler carefully structuring his realm for defence. In areas recently reconquered, Arthur introduced foreign military rulers without ties to the local populace. But in those regions already controlled by a powerful warlord he adopted a laissez faire policy. The fact that Arthur now had at least twelve separate rulers under his sway also made it more difficult for one, or even a combination of more than one, to challenge his power.

The number twelve is of interest for another reason. We have seen how the Late Roman dining table is often depicted as circular, and is the best explanation for the Round Table.[11] But another traditional feature of this legendary artifact is that it has twelve seats. In short, this council of the Proud Tyrant's *may* be the prototype for the Knights of the Round Table.[12]

CERDIC

What of the Saxon component in this new culture? The *Anglo Saxon Chronicle* would have us believe that the newcomers owed almost nothing to the original inhabitants. The *Chronicle* glories in the violent deeds of its warlords. They wade ashore and kill thousands of Britons at a time. Populations flee before the invaders as if from fire. And in the *Chronicle*'s catalogue of mayhem no ruler is more ferocious than Cerdic. Indeed, the later kings of Wessex claimed him as their ancestor. Alfred and Edmund Ironsides were his putative heirs—as is the present Queen of England. But there is one odd thing about this savage Saxon. His name is not Germanic at all. It is British. Indeed, it is a variation on a name we have already encountered.

Cerdic is most likely only another form of the British name 'Coroticus'.[13] But why would a Saxon king bear the name of one of the rulers of western Britain?

We have seen the Saxon enclaves that Arthur left in East Anglia, Kent, and the Upper Thames. Kent in particular shows significant interaction between the newcomers and the Britons. The Anglo-Saxon city of Dover is only a variation of *Dubris*, the old Roman name for the town. Likewise, Richborough derives from the ancient name *Rutupiae*. Elsewhere, archaeologists are increasingly finding evidence for Saxon and British communities coexisting side by side.[14] The mystery of Cerdic's origins may similarly be explained by this mingling of the two peoples. Cerdic is first noted as active in about 495, with a son in tow already capable of bearing arms. This would place him at least in his forties, but since he is also said to have died in 534, probably not yet in his fifties.[15] His birth date would thus probably lie between 450 and 460—precisely the time when the *foedus* with the Saxons was in effect. The most likely scenario is that, here again, Arthur was engaging in matrimonial politics. Shortly after 450, a highborn Saxon father and a highborn British mother were wed to cement ties between their two peoples. The father almost certainly would have become at least a nominal Christian, and his child would have received a British name. And 'Coroticus' would have exactly suited the mood of a society proud to proclaim that it no longer needed Romans like Aetius. One tantalizing possibility is that Cerdic was named for the very Coroticus that Patrick so roundly condemns.

This has important implications for the social structure of fifth-century Britain. During Roman times the island's elite had consisted of over a thousand villa-owning families. But the new society was likely to have been much more restrictive in the way that the good things in life were distributed. After half a century of conflict, the man skilled in arms was dominant. Status came to those who could contribute to Britain's war-making capability: the sort of commanders who could lead the Demetian and Venedotian levies into battle. Further, if Saxon ships carried most goods bound for Britain, Arthur may have had some control as to how these were distributed.[16] One possible analogy is Russian society during the Soviet years, where one of the perks of high civilian and military rank was access to scarce consumer goods.

DECURIONES

The boom that Gildas reports appears to have resembled the one that followed the medieval Black Death. And for this very reason fifth-century *decuriones*, like fourteenth-century *seigneurs*, may have found prosperity a mixed blessing. In Roman times, the *decuriones* had been ultimately responsible for the prompt payment of taxes. If this remained true during Arthur's reign, their situation may actually have worsened. The Romano-British world had been turned upside down. Records had been destroyed and multitudes had been displaced. Each *civitas* had been restructured, perhaps radically, to accommodate Arthur's new kings. Even if the *ordines* still existed, the *decuriones* would have ceded much of their former power to military rulers like Cunedda and 'the Tribune'. The most likely reason for the vituperation Gildas hurls at the kings of his day is that he speaks for people like himself—members of the old Latin-educated gentry displaced by this new elite. The rulers 'more cruel than the rest' were expropriating much of the island's wealth to finance their mobile detachments. Like Gildas, the *decuriones* would have used all their skill in Roman rhetoric to oppose Arthur and his new kings.

It has often been surmised that there were 'pro-Roman' and 'anti-Roman' factions in Britain, with the Proud Tyrant representing the latter. There is no evidence, however, that any Roman ruler ever contemplated a reconquest of Britain after 421. On the contrary, the location of Aetius' Alans in the 440s suggests that Rome could not control its own coastline, much less conquer Britain. The chances of intervention from Gaul were nil. However, if we see Britain in terms of a 'military-*Romanitas*' party versus a 'landowning-*Romanitas*' party, we may be getting closer to the truth. Arthur's propaganda proclaims that not even Aetius could save Britain, while Gildas praises Roman valour and decries British cowardice. Arthur claims to have been aided by Christ and the Virgin Mary, while Gildas excoriates the Proud Tyrant for inviting in pagan Saxons. This was a cultural struggle, and the fact that those who identified themselves with certain aspects of Roman culture hated Arthur is not surprising. A ruler kept in power by a group of pagan Germans and North British pirates could never be popular among men still able to read Cicero and St Augustine.

The fury of the *decuriones* may have been fuelled by another factor. If Arthur adopted the federate system used on the continent, the old landowning class would have been forced to share a considerable part of their harvests not just with Arthur's new kings, but also with the new Saxon 'guests'. The fact that Gildas later uses the Latin words *annona* and *epimenia*, the Late Roman technical terms to describe such payments, indicates this was almost certainly the case.[17] From Arthur's point of view this probably seemed a prudent policy. However, if this were the true situation, the surplus would have been divided among many more high-status persons than in Roman times. Even if the expertise still existed, few landowners could now afford to restore their ruined villas. For most British *decuriones* the lavish lifestyles of their grandfathers had vanished forever.

Another cultural factor may help explain this lapse in things Roman: the tastes of the new rulers themselves. Many were military men not far removed from cultures that spurned cities and even permanent dwellings. A soldier whose great-grandfather had been born on the steppes of Ukraine might care very much about his clothes and personal adornment, but very little about an opulent house that he could enjoy only on those rare occasions when he was not in the saddle. He might care very much about feasting and drinking, but very little about floor mosaics and frescoes. He might have great interest in songs recounting the deeds of Arthur and his kings, but little interest in panegyrics by an insular Sidonius, laced with Classical allusions. The sort of *Romanitas* that he represented was that of the Roman *castrum* and the Roman road. The basilica and the villa held little interest for him.

But there may have been other fissures within this society, fissures that went deeper than just 'old money' discontent. During this 'time of plenty' the only mechanism for limiting Saxon immigration was with ships. But these same ships were crewed by... Saxons. An unintended consequence of peace can only have been a flood of new immigrants into the country. Men like Cerdic's father could join the new military elite with ease. But for other newcomers the options may have been far less appealing. Most land was already under cultivation by British peasants. The Saxon military communities were on a fixed stipend from the local landowners. Unable to till the land, and seeing warfare as their natural calling, a large class of idle, armed men is likely to have grown up in these settlements. As well, considerable fear and loathing must have existed on the British side. Memories of Saxon atrocities were fresh. Arthur's Saxons may no longer have sacrificed captives to Wotan. The fact that Cerdic bears a British name, and that the Kentish group rarely practised pagan cremation, suggests that many may have nominally accepted Christianity. But the Britons knew that the new immigrants had sacrificed captives in the past. This, combined with the inevitable vestiges of paganism, would have created tensions between the two communities. On an individual level trade, friendship, even marriage was possible. But as long as one side remained Roman and Christian and the other

Germanic and semi-pagan, the potential for renewed conflict remained.

TYRANT

We have looked at this new society from a number of different perspectives. But overall, what was life really like for most ordinary Britons during Arthur's reign? Did he merit the name that Gildas gives him, the Proud Tyrant, or is this just sixth-century hyperbole?

Archaeology gives us a glimpse into this 'Romano-Saxon' world—and what it reveals may be more than a little unsettling. Excavations at the fifth-century British settlement at Poundbury have uncovered a world that is both advanced in some ways and primitive in others. On the one hand the material culture of these particular Britons appears to have been very austere, with an almost complete lack of the comforts found in the Roman period. There is little pottery, and most of it is of poor quality. There is no evidence of any metal cooking utensils at all. It is almost as if the inhabitants had regressed into the pre-Roman Iron Age. Yet a large number of corn dryers were also found—evidence for large-scale processing of grain on site. Moreover, some of these grains were improved varieties not known in Roman times. Most interesting, though, were a number of skillfully made knives. These were pattern-welded in a way unknown in Roman times, but which was commonplace among the Saxons.[18]

This evidence seems puzzling; even contradictory. But it may actually give us an important insight into Arthur's vision for Britain. He was first and foremost a military man. The Roman discipline he had imposed on his cohorts had saved Britain in its darkest hour, and extending this discipline to the whole of civilian society would have seemed a logical next step. Diocletian had done something like it in the third century. The evidence from Poundbury suggests that Arthur had created an austere, highly regimented society—a state organized for war. The industrial-scale processing of grain is fully consistent with what Gildas tells us about the *annona* food rations for the Proud Tyrant's mercenaries. The metal objects found at a British site, but manufactured using Saxon metallurgical techniques, are evidence for technology transfer from the barbarians to the Britons. The poverty of consumer goods tells us that every other aspect of life in Arthur's Britain had been subordinated to fulfil two main goals: the feeding and arming of his military forces. Most Britons in the 450s and 460s were probably relatively well fed, but in all other respects they may have been leading impoverished, restricted lives.

In essence Arthur may have been attempting to turn Britain into a 'command economy', with all the distortions that this implies. Instead of allowing manufactures to flourish, he was confiscating any surplus to maintain a small military elite. One very big reason for the poverty of artifacts in this period may be that most Britons had little if any incentive to produce more than the bare minimum. The 'time of plenty' appears to have quickly reached a dead end—and the main culprit may have been Arthur himself. It is doubtful that Gildas was the first to call him the Proud Tyrant.

But Britain in the 450s was still in no way the monolithic ideal that Arthur sought. The *decuriones* yearned for their old power and prestige. Peasants can only have resented the taxes in grain that fed Arthur's soldiers. Just as important, these soldiers comprised an extremely diverse range of ethnic groups, many of whom might be difficult to control. Even a Proud Tyrant could find this a very tricky situation.

FAMILY

These factors alone may have made it difficult to govern a newly pacified Britain. But there is also evidence that the fissures in British society extended into Arthur's inner circle.

The tragedy that unfolded next may have been not merely an ethnic conflict, but a family conflict as well.

First is the matter of Arthur's relations with women. Whether under the guise of Arthur or Vortigern, the Proud Tyrant's relations with women are anything but monogamous. The *Historia Brittonum* asserts that Vortigern married several wives, and even fathered a child on his own daughter. The *Welsh Triads*, which contain some of the earliest legends about Arthur, inform us that he had no less than three Queens called Gwynhwyfar![19] Together these citations give a picture of a man who saw matrimony as politics by other means.

We also have evidence for a number of offspring sired by Arthur—although the exact number is problematical. Both the Pillar of Eliseg and the Harleian dynastic genealogies mention a certain Britu as one of the Proud Tyrant's sons. Another son was called Pascent. We have already mentioned at least one daughter, who married an Irish prince. After this, however, the record becomes cloudy. The *Historia* claims that he had a warlike son called Vortimer, literally 'Highest King'. This Celtic name is interesting in itself, because it is similar to the later name that Arthur was known by—Vortigern—and may have been used in conscious imitation of it. But Vortimer is recorded neither on the Pillar of Eliseg nor in the earliest genealogies. The *Historia* also tells us of yet another son, also known by a Celtic name—Cateyrn, or Cattegirn. Curiously, he too is a warrior in the mould of Vortimer, and dies in a battle between Britons and Saxons in about 468. Again, as with Vortimer, this is a name with strong similarities to 'Vortigern'. Moreover, it literally signifies 'Battle Lord', a meaning almost identical to the Latin *Dux Bellorum*. But, strangely, the earliest known genealogies name the father of Pascent and Britu not as Vortigern but as Cattegirn. For some strange reason the name of Vortigern is nowhere found in the genealogy of his own house.

Arthur may thus have had several wives, and from three to five children—a full house, and one with a potential for trouble. It is therefore important to take a closer look at these wives. Their relationships, and those of their offspring, may have played a crucial role in the drama that eventually led to Arthur's downfall. The Pillar of Eliseg, for example, was raised by a dynasty claiming descent from the Proud Tyrant, and the inscription they put upon it claims Vortigern's wife, Sevira, as a highborn ancestress. 'Sevira' is, of course, a Roman name. Moreover, on the pillar she is styled as the 'daughter of Maximus', almost certainly the usurping emperor who died in 388.[20] We ought not, however, to take the inscription to mean that she was literally the daughter of this rebellious general. Any genuine daughter of Maximus would have been in her sixties or seventies when Arthur came of marriageable age. A much more sensible reading of the inscription would imply that Sevira was a female *descendant* of Maximus. This would have been a good match for Arthur on two counts. Maximus had 'worn the purple', so a marriage with his descendant would have given Arthur an indirect connection with an emperor. But Maximus, a Spaniard by birth, had taken a British wife, presumably from a prestigious local family. So marriage with Sevira may have also cemented ties with the old landowning elite. For a *Dux* with possible barbarian ancestors, a marriage with Sevira would have gained him legitimacy among a large section of powerful Britons.

But would she have been Arthur's first wife? It is exceedingly unlikely that the son of a soldier could have obtained so good a match in his youth. More probable is an initial marriage with a woman as humble as himself, followed by a political marriage when his star had risen. It is certainly possible that Arthur's first wife died before his wedding to Sevira. But when we remember that Gildas castigates the kings of his day for setting aside their wives, it is entirely possible that Arthur may have done the same thing.[21] Either way, if Arthur were maintaining two families, tensions in his household would have been almost inevitable. The son or sons of his first wife would have taken a dim view of their stepmother Sevira; if the latter had offspring of her own from a previous marriage, the ill-feeling would have been returned with interest. Moreover, if Sevira hailed from the old Romano-British villa elite, members of this class would have seen her as a natural ally against Arthur's 'new men'. Any sons of hers would have also been viewed in much the same light. This in turn could only have made Arthur's delicate political balancing act that much more difficult.

Unfortunately, there is strong evidence that only eight years after Arthur's triumph at *Badon*, this feat became not just difficult but impossible. Despite all his efforts, in 458 Arthur's carefully built edifice came crashing down around him.

And much of the blame for this may lie at the door of one very ambitious young man.

13.

'A HUMBLE MAN'

RIVALS

Gildas calls him Ambrosius Aurelianus. The first part of this very Roman name may hark back to St Ambrose, Bishop of Milan and mentor to St Augustine. Gildas characterizes Ambrosius as a *vir modestus*, a 'humble man', and this is almost certainly meant to contrast him with the Proud Tyrant, who invites in the Saxons.[1] Paradoxically, Gildas also informs us that the ancestors of this young man had 'worn the purple'. Ambrosius is presented as both a successor to the Proud Tyrant and a tireless foe of the Saxons. He fights a number of battles against the barbarians, not all of which are successful. But overall the portrait is that of a model warrior and a model Christian, in the mould of the Romans that Gildas so admires.

This short account might seem to be all we possess about this very important figure. Until the ninth century the only other citation about Ambrosius is a curious report in the *Historia Brittonum*:

> And from the reign of Vortigern to the quarrel between Vitalinus and Ambrosius are 12 years, that is Wallop [*Guollopum*], the battle of Wallop.[2]

This *discordia* of 'Wallop' (more properly *Guollop*) has always been something of a mystery. No other source seems to mention it. If we accept the *Historia*'s chronology, that it was fought twelve years after the tyrant Vortigern's accession in 425, it would have occurred in about the year 437. Since this is a full four years before the 'Fall' of Britain recounted in continental sources, the 'default' explanation has always been that it was some sort of civil disturbance, perhaps between Ambrosius and another Briton called Vitalinus. However, we have argued that the Proud Tyrant's accession took place not in 425, but 446. This would place the battle (or *discordia*) of *Guollop* in the year 458. This raises our suspicions that all may have not been well in Arthur's kingdom at this time. But who may have been causing this trouble, and why?

It is here that Hengest once again enters the stage. The *Anglo-Saxon Chronicle* would have us believe that Hengest's three boatloads of warriors were the first Saxons ever to settle in Britain, and that they came in 450, the traditional year of the *Adventus*. Although archaeology shows that Hengest was certainly not the first Saxon in Britain, there is no reason to doubt that he was one of the Germanic federate leaders who settled the island of Thanet at about this time. But the *ASC* also tells us that Hengest soon became a foe of Vortigern, fighting four battles against the Britons between 455 and 473. Its text makes the Saxons the victors in every contest, killing myriads of Britons and taking much spoil. Strangely, the *Historia* also speaks of four battles against the Saxons based in Thanet. But here the barbarians are always depicted as the losers. Three times they are driven from Kent and besieged on the Isle of Thanet. In the final encounter, the *Historia* tells us, they 'fled to their keels and... clambered aboard them like women'. The tyrant Vortigern is still king at this time, but it is his 'son', the mysterious Vortimer mentioned earlier, who leads the British to their final victory at Thanet. Given these conflicting accounts, what are we to make of Hengest? And who is this 'son' of the Proud Tyrant called Vortimer?

Scholars have been sceptical of the *Anglo-Saxon Chronicle*'s value for some time. They pointedly ask how an illiterate people like the Saxons could possibly have maintained accurate records of fifth-century events for well over a hundred years. These barbarians were Christianized very late, in 596, and any earlier information 'must' have been in oral form. Scholars point to various suspiciously regular intervals in the *ASC*'s dates that seem to show that its chronology was laid down at a much later time.[3] While Saxon royal genealogies do purport to give an unbroken timeline back to the fifth century, historians have found various anomalies in their chronology, again suggesting that they are too unreliable for serious scholarly research.[4] Today, one of the most widely accepted views of the *ASC* is that it is derived from Saxon 'sagas'; sagas that later Saxon clerics attempted to fit into a consistent chronology.[5]

These arguments ignore one obvious fact: nearly all the citations in the *ASC* before 450 involve not Saxons, but Romans and Britons. It is difficult to see why Saxons would have had 'sagas' about Maximus or Aetius. What is even more striking is the fact that *not one* of the sagas supposedly used to create the *ASC* has survived. No Saxon 'saga' of Hengest's four battles exists in any early source outside the *ASC* itself. This might not seem decisive—until we realize that we actually do have at least four Saxon 'sagas' that *have* survived. We have already seen the story of Octha's naval expedition to the Orkneys. The second is the *Historia*'s account of the Saxon Revolt, which portrays it as a treacherous attack on Britain's nobles while feasting in a Saxon hall—a typical Germanic tale. The 'Finnesburgh Fight' is yet another. Finally, Procopius gives a rather strange romance that involves relations between Saxons in Britain and those in the 'old country' of northern Germany.[6] Curiously, *not one* of these genuine sagas is cited in any of the various manuscripts that make up the *ASC*, strongly suggesting that the compilers of this corpus included only information tied to real calendrical data. In other words, the 'saga hypothesis' in no way describes the evidence that it is supposed to explain.

Apart from this negative evidence, we also have some compelling positive evidence as to where the illiterate Saxons would have obtained a perfectly accurate chronology for this period. Gildas uses the Saxon term *cyuls* to describe the three ships that bring the first Saxon mercenaries. This can only mean that the story of Hengest was already well known to both peoples in the sixth century. Moreover, the *Historia*'s story of Vortimer's four battles consistently gives a Saxon name first for each battle, and then a Brythonic translation—suggesting that the British compiler obtained it from a Saxon source. But if this is true, then we actually have a *Saxon* source *praising* a British hero. The only possible explanation for this is that one of the early Saxon kingdoms adopted a *British* account of fifth-century events. In other words, from the earliest times both peoples shared a common historical narrative for this period—including an accurate chronology. The illiterate Saxons obtained their chronology from literate Britons quite capable of keeping accurate historical records over many centuries.

Proof as to just how far we can trust the *Anglo-Saxon Chronicle*'s chronology comes from one date in particular. It is a record that predates the Saxon *Adventus*, and indeed ostensibly has nothing to do with Saxons. For the year 443 we read:

> In this year the Britons sent overseas to Rome and asked them for troops against the Picts, but they had none there, because they were at war with Attila, King of the Huns.[7]

This is of course Gildas' Appeal to Aetius, 'thrice-consul of the Romans'. But here the *ASC* places it three years earlier than Gildas' date of 446. We have seen how this has shed new light on the *ASC*'s date for the final Roman withdrawal. The year 418 given in that document is more plausibly seen as 421, the year the would-be emperor Constantius was gathering all available troops for an attack on Constantinople. These two citations strongly suggest that the dates in the *ASC* are entirely genuine, but with a kind of three-year 'lag'. If we keep this in mind, the first entry for the exploits of Hengest is little short of astonishing:

> 455—In this year Hengest and Horsa fought against king Vortigern at a place which is called *Aegelesthrep*...'[8]

If we add three years to 455, this gives us a date of 458— precisely the same year as the new date postulated for the *discordia* of *Guollop*. Indeed, since the name of Vortimer's first battle is not given in the *Historia*, it is best to conclude that *Guollop is Aegelesthrep*.[9]

This has some profound implications for fifth-century British history. The first is that this Vortimer is none other than Ambrosius Aurelianus, an equation that is by no means new.[10] It is important to remember that Emrys is the Welsh variant of Ambrosius, and that the *Historia* lists a 'son' of Arthur called 'Amr'. With this in mind, the likely reason why someone called Ambrosius would choose a Celtic title with the 'imer' element in it becomes self-evident. Vortimer, which means 'Highest King', is the exact parallel to the honorific that was later attached to the Proud Tyrant—Vortigern. The best explanation for the provenance of the name Vortimer is that it is a conscious attempt to create a name possessing some of the lustre that was later connected with one of Arthur's sobriquets.[11]

The second is of even more value. The *Guollop* quotation is hard evidence that the accounts in the *Historia* and the *ASC* are not 'cribs' of one another. Instead, it strongly suggests that there once existed at least *four* separate but related accounts of the wars between Ambrosius and Hengest—now contained in Gildas, Vortimer's 'Battle List', the *Historia*'s passage about the battle of *Guollop*, and the *ASC*. The *ASC*'s citations for events in the fifth century are not fabrications or 'guesses'; they were originally accurate to within a year of the events they describe.[12]

Most crucially, however, this fully explains a curious statement by Gildas about the siege of Mount *Badon*: that it was 'almost the last, not the least, slaughter of the villains'. The fact that he neither calls it the last battle against the Saxons, nor claims Ambrosius as its victor, makes sense only if he had some awareness of both the Arthurian *and* the Ambrosian Battle Lists. From the first he would have known that *Badon* was the great battle that brought 'final' peace to Britain in 450—something that Arthur would claim during his reign. Unlike nearly all the other battles of Arthur, Gildas could still visit *Badon*/Bath. To him it would have been the most tangible evidence of past British glory. But from the second Battle List he would have known that Ambrosius' last battle took place in far-off Thanet, where the Saxons 'fled to their keels and... clambered aboard them like women'. It would have been impossible for Gildas to reconcile reports of *two* 'last battles'. Yet it is still to his credit that he did not distort evidence that was, in different ways, perfectly correct. Instead, he simply tried to 'square the circle' in a remarkably opaque passage.

Thus, evidence existed as early as the beginning of the sixth century for a series of four battles fought between the years 458 and 476. The reported encounters between Ambrosius and Hengest are not fabrications. Rather, they argue for a Saxon Revolt that is far more complex and politically sophisticated than previously imagined. They also reveal a story that is more familiar, more 'Arthurian', than any historian has dared to suggest.

And finally, they reveal one of the great tragedies of British history.

DISCORDIA

In the year 458 the dragons of two armies numbering in their thousands fluttered over the green pastures of Kent (see Map 6). At the head of one force was a high-born young Briton called

Ambrosius Aurelianus. In the ranks of the other army was a seasoned Saxon warrior named Hengest. The two men knew each other by sight, and were probably acquaintances. Indeed, as so often in Britain's history, this would be a battle between men who under other circumstances would have been faithful comrades. And now, at a place called *Aegelesthrep* ('Aegel's Strife'), these two armies were about to clash.

Exactly what Hengest's role was in this first encounter is problematical. The *Historia Brittonum*'s statement that *Guollop/Aegelesthrep* was 'the quarrel between Vitalinus and Ambrosius' may indicate that more than just Saxons were initially involved. It is entirely possible that one of Arthur's subordinate kings tried to seize power, and used Saxons as his allies. Indeed, Hengest may have played only a secondary role in this drama. It would be many years before he would become undisputed ruler in Kent. His leadership in the four battles could merely be a projection back in time by his dynasty.

There is another possibility, however. The *Historia* genealogy for Vortigern—the later name for the Proud Tyrant—mentions a Vitalinus as one of this ruler's ancestors.[13] If Hengest were the main leader of the 'Jutish' mercenaries from the beginning, he may have nominally accepted Christianity—and therefore been christened with a *Weala* name. And bearing the Christian name of one of Arthur's ancestors would have been a most prestigious honour. But whoever the commander was on the Saxon side, this battle would be the start of a rise to power that Hengest had only dreamt of on the day he first set foot on Thanet.

Across the grassy interval that separated the two armies, Hengest could see the enemy commander, Ambrosius. The Briton was mounted on a splendid horse, and the nose guard on his gilded helmet hid most of his youthful face. Another, older warrior dressed in similar armour was riding at Ambrosius' right hand. Hengest thought it might be Cai, or perhaps Bedwyr; he could not be sure. Behind them a long dragon banner whipped in the wind, and on either side of them thousands of infantrymen and ranks of mounted horsemen waited patiently for the signal to attack. Hengest knew he faced at least four cohorts, levies from all over southeastern Britain. His older warriors warned that the horsemen would pose the greatest danger...

On that morning of 458, Hengest knew precisely who Ambrosius was, and why the young Briton was in command of so many thousands of Arthur's troops. But we do not have that information. The *Historia Brittonum* describes Vortimer as a 'son' of Vortigern. But the Pillar of Eliseg does not mention a son of Vortigern with a name anything like Vortimer, or even Ambrosius. Moreover, if Ambrosius really was the offspring of Vortigern, why does Gildas condemn the father, yet praise the son? Are these all merely false reports, or could something else lie behind these contradictory passages: something that might resolve them?

The fact that Ambrosius is virtually the only Briton about whom Gildas has anything good to say suggests that both the cleric and his hero stood for the old landowning, Latin-speaking elite. The name Ambrosius underlines his Christian credentials, alluding to St Ambrose of Milan. The name Aurelianus further emphasizes his *Romanitas*, suggesting he would have patronized the creation of such books as the *Vergilius Romanus*. Given this background, he doubtless saw Arthur's alliance with pagan barbarians as far from being a good thing. He would have been more than happy to lead the fight at *Guollop*. But still, just how did a cultivated Romano-Briton end up as commander of an army that had always been staffed by a wide range of barbarians?

Gildas' statement that Ambrosius' forebears 'wore the purple' may hold the solution to this mystery. It most likely refers to a connection with some usurper from Britain. Constantine III might be one candidate—except that he was only a simple soldier who left Britain as soon as he became emperor. Since he and his son were both executed in Gaul, it is doubtful that he left many progeny—or that they had anything much to brag about. A far more likely connection would be with the usurper Maximus. This general reigned a number of years as *de facto* ruler of Spain, Gaul and Britain—until, that is, Theodosius the Great captured and executed him. Maximus was also married to a British woman, and, since he was already a high-ranking officer when he made his bid for the empire, we may suspect that his wife hailed from a prestigious Romano-British clan. We also know that even after Maximus' death his two daughters were treated with respect by Theodosius.[14] If Ambrosius were a descendant of Maximus, he would have had an inside track in any competition for high office.

The *Historia Brittonum*'s identification of Vortimer as Vortigern's son may indicate that Ambrosius was even better connected than this, however. As previously noted, the Pillar of Eliseg tells us that the tyrant Vortigern's wife Sevira was a 'daughter' of Maximus. If we accept that her marriage to Arthur was primarily political, she, like him, may have had a previous union—and one that had produced offspring. In other words, Ambrosius may have been not Arthur's son but his *stepson*. This would explain much of subsequent events. There would have been tensions within Arthur's family: tensions between father and stepson; tensions between stepbrothers.[15] The landed elite (and perhaps the clergy as well) could only have seen Ambrosius as their champion against the Saxon alliance. Moreover, if we remember that Arthur had already spent a good part of his life in constant warfare, he may not have been able to take so active a role in the field as before. He would have been forced to delegate much of his authority to sons and trusted commanders. In 458 all of these factors came together to place Ambrosius at the head of an army sent to deal with a Saxon uprising.

The motivation for the Saxons in this uprising is simpler to explain. The Thanet Saxons had been campaigning on Arthur's behalf for up to eight years. They had endured long sea voyages and death in distant lands. But they remained cooped up on a small island, gazing across a narrow strait at the riches of Kent. They knew that Roman federates like the Visigoths and Burgundians had attained much more enviable positions. These continental federates played the role of warrior-aristocrats, a role much more to the liking of any German of that age. We cannot know the specific incident that ignited the *discordia*, but Saxon desires for a bigger share of the pie must have played a significant part. Gildas' statement that the barbarians demanded larger *annona* payments only reinforces this view. Sometime in the middle of Arthur's reign, the aspirations of Hengest and the Thanet federates translated into open conflict.

...As the sun rose in the sky above *Guollop*, the horns of the Britons began to sound. Insults in several languages flew through the summer air. Small groups of men from both sides advanced and retreated, seeking to disrupt plans carefully laid down the night before. Dragon banners came alive. On each side soldiers took up the *barritus*, a low rumble of thousands of voices, reaching a crescendo just as the two sides were about to attack. Men clashed weapons and shields together. A single arm rose in the moist summer air. Then it fell. Soon thousands of feet were treading down the tall summer grass...

> 'Vortimer fought vigorously against Hengest and Horsa and their people, and expelled them as far as the... island called Thanet, and there three times shut them up and besieged them, attacking, threatening and terrifying them.'[16]

> '455—Hengest and Horsa fought with Vortigern... on the spot that is called *Aegelesthrep*...'[17]

Taken together, these two quotations reveal much about the outcome of this battle. The fact that the British accounts claim a victory for Ambrosius at *Guollop* should be no surprise. In any head-on confrontation, the army of the Britons probably still retained enough Roman discipline and training to win the day. Moreover, the Upper Thames Saxons may have remained true to their later title of the *gewissei*, the 'trusted ones', and refused to join their fellow Saxons in revolt.[18] Very significant too is the fact that the *Anglo-Saxon Chronicle* makes no boast that *Aegelesthrep* was in any way a victory over the *Weala*, as it does with regard to later battles. The only reported result is the death of Hengest's brother Horsa. *Guollop/Aegelesthrep* was Ambrosius' great victory. That is why the Britons remembered '*Guollop*' in the first place.

The passage that tells us that Ambrosius besieged the Saxons 'three times' on the Isle of Thanet tells us what happened next. The beaten insurgents fled eastward. Ambrosius' fast-moving cavalry cut down any straggling Saxon, whether warrior or civilian. In the end the only safe haven lay on Thanet itself. The rest of the *Historia Brittonum*'s boast, that Ambrosius 'shut them up and besieged them', is also significant. It makes no claim that the insurgents either surrendered or were destroyed. And the reason may once again have to do with Saxon ships. Even crossing the Wantsum, the narrow channel between Thanet and the mainland, would have been a daunting task for Ambrosius if the Saxons had command of the sea. In effect, the Saxons had pulled off a fifth-century Dunkirk.

There may have been ways to cross the Wantsum. Bede mentions two fords that existed in his day, some three centuries later.[19] But in the fifth century these may well have been accessible only at low tide, and on so narrow a front that a crossing appeared suicidal. Ambrosius, unable to secure the island, was faced with a stalemate. Instead of a final grand triumph, he had to settle for a long winter siege, eyeing an enemy he could see but not attack. Horses were set out to graze. Men prepared shelters against the coming cold. Ambrosius may well have established his headquarters at the old fortress of Richborough/*Rutupiae*.

Meanwhile, educated Britons gathered at their round tables. They talked of nothing but this new Aeneas, this new Constantine. Hope was returning. Men of the old Roman stamp need not rely on barbarians, whether Alan or Saxon. They had leaders of their own who could win battles. A legend was growing.

These encomiums also reached Arthur's ears. They reached the ears of his sons. Others in Arthur's inner circle were jealous of the young commander's first success. No one could view his victories with ease. They shook their heads, predicting a bad end for the upstart.

The coming spring would tell who was right.

COUNTER-ATTACK

The next piece of evidence suggests that the Saxons had other uses for their ships besides keeping the Wantsum secure. The *Historia Brittonum* speaks of Hengest inviting more Saxons over from Germany.[20] This may be a memory of a call to Saxons on both sides of the Channel to join in the coming year's campaign. Indeed, such a reinforcement of shipborne Saxons would be the best explanation for what happened next. The *Historia*'s report of this second battle is as terse as the *Anglo-Saxon Chronicle*'s account of the first. It says only that a battle took place on the river Darent, probably the Darent in Kent. But the *Chronicle* gives a much fuller account:

> Hengest and Aesc fought against the Britons at a place which is called *Crecganford*, and there slew four thousand men; and the Britons then forsook Kent, and fled to London in great terror.[21]

This *Crecganford* is most likely the modern Crayford, which is in the vicinity of the venerable Roman town of *Noviomagus*. One scenario for the campaign might have been a Saxon landing on the mainland somewhere near Thanet, then a push toward London. But a far more effective strategy from Hengest's point of view would have been a landing near London itself; more precisely, at the last major city on the road that connected the capital with Thanet: *Noviomagus*. London may have been far less populated than before, but it was still both a stronghold and a symbol. The old capital was in danger.

Ambrosius had to respond. But his men had just suffered through a long winter. Bad food and disease would have taken their toll. Moreover, now he may have been in an unusual position for an army schooled in the Roman tradition. The roles of barbarian and Roman were reversed. His army would have to make a rapid march over terrain already stripped bare by marauding Saxons. His force would arrive at *Noviomagus* tired and hungry, with many mounts unfit for combat. The Saxons, on the other hand, would be rested and well fed. Somewhere outside London the two armies met.

Taken together, the two accounts confirm that 459 was a year of disaster for Britain. Four thousand of Ambrosius' soldiers, or more precisely the better part of four cohorts of Arthur's army, were either killed or forced to flee. Nothing like this had happened for over a decade. Ambrosius was in disgrace, as was any advocate of a 'get tough' policy against the Saxons.

It might be tempting to see this as the final act of the Saxon Revolt. After all, the four battles that both the *Historia* and the *ASC* depict are almost certainly the see-saw struggle that Gildas describes between Hengest and Ambrosius. However, there are a number of problems with this. The *Anglo-Saxon Chronicle* places the next battle, *Wippedsfleot*, a full decade after the battle on the Darent. We also have good evidence that a large British force sailed to Gaul in 469, something that would have been impossible if Briton and Saxon had been at each other's throats even a few years before. Moreover, it is important to note that Gildas tells us that the Saxons demanded *annona* payments *twice*. The first request was granted, and this 'for a long time stopped the dogs' mouths'. It was only the *second* demand for more *annona* that brought on the Saxon Revolt.[22] This *discordia*, or quarrel, thus seems to be aptly named. It was a relatively brief civil conflict, after which peace was restored 'for a long time'. But then the question arises: just how was this accomplished?

The most likely answer by far is that at this point Arthur personally intervened. The *Historia Brittonum* charges him with two fatal errors in his dealings with the Saxons. One is that he married the daughter of the Saxon Hengest. The other is that he ceded Kent to the Saxons. Until now, scholars have considered these accounts to be little more than 'legend'. But in light of the scenario just outlined, these are both quite sensible responses to an unfavourable situation. A long conflict would lead to not just *discordia*, but a return to the ethnic warfare of the 440s. Moreover, this time Hengest might have the Upper Thames Saxons and the 'East Anglians' on his side. The 'King Guoyrancgonus' who was forced to cede his Kentish kingdom to Hengest is probably mere legend.[23] But after the Darent debacle, such concessions could be merely a reflection of current reality. Moreover, it must not be forgotten that Hengest at the time could make only limited demands. The best his still relatively small Saxon community could hope for was a larger share of the pie. That one day his people might conquer and rule most of the island probably never entered his head.

The 'legend' of the Proud Tyrant's marriage to a Saxon princess also makes sense, as a way of creating a personal bond between Arthur and Hengest. The *Historia*'s portrait of a dodderer in thrall to a dazzling young pagan may be a kind of 'tabloid' version of a carefully considered policy that returned

Britain to a state of peace. Arthur had done a similar thing when he wedded his own daughter to the Irish High King's son—and when he himself wedded Sevira. More to the point, it appears to have achieved a measure of success. Arthur's peace lasted for a full decade.

This also explains another hitherto puzzling aspect of the evidence. The *Welsh Triads* tell us that Arthur married *three* queens named Gwenhwyfar. In reality this may reflect the three women that Arthur took to wife: his first spouse, then the high-born Sevira, and finally this Saxon 'princess'.[24] Indeed, the equation of the latter with Gwenhwyfar might offer some insight into the origin of the name. 'White Shadow', its literal meaning in Welsh, is an apt name for a pale young Saxon girl ostracized by a hostile court.

All the same, *Crecganford* can only have increased British hostility to the Saxons. The Church would have been extremely dubious about closer ties with pagans who had just been killing good Christians. Landholders, particularly those in Kent, would have been none too pleased at sharing more of their harvests with Saxons. Kentish peasants would have grumbled about heavier exactions. But for now that was all they could do. The British army had failed, and the young champion of the old order was in disgrace. Some Britons may even have welcomed the new peace. After all, the uprising had been localized to Kent. It would have had little direct affect in either the west or the north. For the next few years any opposition was covert. On the surface the victor of *Badon* remained 'most kingly' of all the Britons.

It is doubtful whether this harmony extended to Arthur's own family, however. If Ambrosius were indeed Sevira's son (or even a close kinsman), he can only have seen Arthur's pagan marriage as deeply offensive. We have no way of knowing whether Sevira was still alive at this time. But if she were set aside for the younger Saxon, the gap between the two men would have been unbridgeable. Ambrosius could have neither forgotten nor forgiven the wrong done to his mother. Moreover, one or more of Arthur's other sons may have reached an age where they could assume some of the kingly burdens of office. This could only have fuelled Ambrosius' resentment. Almost by default, he would have assumed the leadership of the anti-Saxon party. True, as long as peace held, he could do nothing. But now Arthur had a mortal enemy in the highest levels of British society, an enemy whose chief aim was to redeem his defeat at the hands of the pagans.

And it would be Arthur himself who would give Ambrosius his next opportunity.

14.

'MOST KINGLY'

RICIMER

The 450s and 460s were a crucial time for Britain. Even more so, they were a crucial time for the western empire. The events that would set the stage for what is called 'the Fall of Rome' occurred during this period. But the island nation, as has been the case for much of its history, was protected from the full effects of this continental strife. Even more, peace and unity were beginning to give Britain the capability to intervene in the turmoil taking place across the Channel. We can be sure that Arthur followed events on the continent with great interest. So must we.

The fall of the Gallo-Roman emperor Avitus left a power vacuum at the heart of Rome, but only for a time. Ricimer, one of the generals who had ousted Avitus, was of barbarian ancestry, and so could not ascend the imperial throne. But this was no barrier to Majorian,, the Roman half of this conspiratorial pair. In 457 he was proclaimed emperor, complete with a freshly minted panegyric to praise him. It may come as some surprise, however, that the man who composed this praise-poem was none other than Sidonius Apollinaris—the author of the panegyric for the unlucky Avitus. This is surprising not just because the cultivated Sidonius was praising a man complicit in the murder of a fellow Gallo-Roman, but because Sidonius himself had only lately participated in a rebellion against Majorian. This had included, among other things, an attempt to surrender Lyons to the Burgundian barbarians. But Sidonius had been pardoned, and by now both parties were anxious to forget past differences.

Sidonius pulled out all the stops for his new patron. Compared with Majorian, he proclaimed, 'Alexander the Great... is an arrant sluggard.'[1] After 600 more lines of classical allusion and hyperbole, Sidonius then addressed Majorian himself. 'Prostratred though we are by devastation and by fire, thou by thy coming dost restore all things. When thou shalt step into the victor's chariot... thou shalt clothe Rome with spoils.' Sidonius ended by predicting the capture of a certain 'African Boccus'—a contemptuous name for rulers from the southern side of the Mediterranean.[2]

Sidonius caught the mood of the time perfectly. The identity of this particular 'Boccus' was clear to anyone who had lived through Geiseric's sack. The reconquest of North Africa was to be the new regime's number one task. Majorian would destroy Geiseric once and for all. Then, with taxes from the fertile provinces of North Africa flowing once more into imperial coffers, the western empire would be on a sound financial footing. This in turn would create an army strong enough to bring the Visigoths to heel.

Central to Majorian's plan was a great naval expedition, to be launched from Spain. In 458 a large fleet was in the building, to be manned by a complement of Romans and barbarian federates. But the wily Geiseric had a plan of his own—and he struck first. In a Pearl Harbor-style attack a fleet of Vandal ships destroyed the Roman armada at its Spanish anchorage. Majorian was disgraced. After signing a humiliating treaty with the Vandals he was duly murdered by his former ally, Ricimer. The barbarian strongman then raised a puppet emperor named Severus to the throne. Never had the name of Rome sunk so low.[3]

Ricimer is an example of how the line between Roman and barbarian was blurring on both sides of the Channel. Half-Vandal and half-Suevian, he had no more than a thin veneer of Roman culture. But now he had acquired powers that even Aetius had not possessed. Raised to the rank of Patrician, Ricimer was both commander-in-chief of the western imperial armies as well as the sole master of a compliant emperor. But however high he rose, the barbarian had no illusions. Romans of all classes held him in contempt. His only claim to legitimacy was his hold over the nonentity Severus. Still, it is probable that he cared very little about his popularity, and very much about his own personal survival.[4]

The murder of Majorian left the Roman military strongman in northern Gaul, General Aegidius, understandably suspicious of the new Patrician. He refused to accept the legitimacy of Ricimer's puppet. Soon Aegidius was making plans to cross the Alps and become emperor himself. He even found an ally in that arch-enemy of Rome, Geiseric. Ricimer's response was to goad the Visigoths into capturing the southern Gallic city of Narbonne. Legally, it was the work of federates under orders from the emperor. But many Gallo-Romans might have been pardoned for thinking that it was a betrayal of the empire itself.[5]

Aegidius was far from beaten, though. Like Aetius before him, he had been careful to cultivate barbarian allies, in this case the Franks. Not only could Aegidius speak their language, as noted earlier, he actually became their king for eight years. Gregory of Tours gives us the story as it came down to him. The Franks' young king Childeric had seduced a number of high-born Frankish maidens. In deep disgrace, he fled to Thuringia. The Frankish nobles then chose Aegidius to replace him. But eight years later the Franks had a change of heart. Childeric was invited back. In the meantime, however, the scapegrace had managed to seduce the queen of the Thuringians. She followed him to Frankland, and their subsequent marriage would produce the greatest Merovingian ruler of them all: Clovis.[6]

For all his personal failings, however, Childeric was wise enough to maintain the alliance with Aegidius. This was encouraging to anyone who still believed in something resembling *Romanitas*, for the Visigothic tide was rolling forward. In 463 they crossed the Loire. For a time it seemed that most of Gaul might fall into their hands. It was only when a combined force under Aegidius and King Childeric met the Visigoths at Orleans that 'Roman' Gaul was saved (see Map 5). The barbarians re-crossed the Loire in retreat. But with a quasi-traitor in the empire's capital, Gallo-Romans like Sidonius knew they could no longer look to Italy for their salvation.[7]

AEGIDIUS

Aegidius may seem just one more confusing footnote to the chaotic situation in Gaul. But he has a larger significance. If we look closely, we can see how he exemplifies a number of trends that were developing on both sides of the Channel.

It has often been noted that northern Gaul's economic conditions closely paralleled those in Britain before 410.[8] The material culture in both areas shows the same marked decline, a decline much steeper than in southern Gaul. In Britain this is viewed as evidence of a precipitous drop in military and political strength. Once the Romans 'withdrew', it is assumed, almost by default, that Britain broke into the petty kingdoms we see prevailing in the sixth century.

Traditionally, many scholars have seen other 'evidence' for this in the situation prevailing in Noricum, in what is now Austria. Eugippius' *Life of St Severinus* depicts a land where Roman authority is breaking down. The few frontier troops who remain are unpaid and eventually disband themselves. Barbarians roam at will. But this is a false parallel. Noricum was undefined *precisely because it was still part of the empire.* Whenever Rome had a choice between defending Italy and Noricum, Italy would win every time. On the other hand, an independent Britain could devote all its revenues to its own defence. That this is the most plausible scenario is evidenced by the very different fates of Noricum and Britain. After a few decades Rome evacuated most of the Noricans to southern Italy.[9] The conquest of what became 'English' Britain took two centuries.

The situation prevailing in northern Gaul is thus by far the more likely parallel with Britain. Aegidius ruled over a cohesive demesne independent of central Roman control. He had a professional military force that could win significant victories against some of the toughest armies in western Europe. Further, like the Proud Tyrant, he depended heavily on 'barbarian' military support. In the 460s Aegidius was the dominant personality in northern Gaul, and what little evidence we have suggests that Arthur dominated Britain in much the same way. This may seem like mere speculation. Gildas gives us an impression of Britons quite as helpless as the inhabitants of Noricum. But the most heavily documented event in fifth-century Britain tells a different tale.

RIOTHAMUS

If we were to read only Gildas, the next major event in Britain was a disaster greater than any suffered on the other side of the Channel: the Saxon Revolt. Gildas' account of it is straightforward. The Saxons rebel against the Proud Tyrant. A time of war ensues between the two peoples, until Ambrosius Aurelianus manages to restore some semblance of stability. But when exactly did these events occur?

The four battles described in both the *Historia Brittonum* and the *Anglo-Saxon Chronicle* confirm that fighting was renewed between the two races. Some ten years after

Ambrosius' defeat on the Darent, they tell us of a battle between the Britons and Saxons variously called *Wippedsfleot*, or in Welsh, *Rhyd yr Afael*—''the Ford of Afael.'. If this were all our information, we might simply conclude that the simplest explanation is the best: a decade after Arthur granted Kent to the Saxons, they again grew dissatisfied with their *annona* payments and revolted.

Unfortunately, the evidence is not quite so simple. Continental sources in particular tell us something radically different about Britain in the year 469. They depict Britain as an expanding state allied with Rome itself. The ruler of this aggressive realm is described as a king, able to launch distant seaborne expeditions. He leads an army able to confront one of the strongest military powers of the age, the Visigoths. Indeed, his actions have a direct bearing on the end of imperial rule in the western Roman Empire. We might expect that this king of Britain would bear the name Vortigern, or Arthur, or even Ambrosius. But instead, the continental sources give us a name unknown in later British records: Riothamus.

Gregory of Tours provides some garbled information about this Riothamus' expedition to Gaul, probably based on an earlier chronicle. Sidonius goes one better. He gives us a letter he wrote to this same Briton, while the latter was campaigning against the Visigoths on the Loire. But it is the Gothic historian Jordanes, who gives us the fullest account:

> 'Now Euric, King of the Visigoths, perceived the frequent changes of Roman emperors and strove to hold Gaul by his own right. The emperor Anthemius heard of it and asked the Britons for aid. Their king Riotimus came with 12,000 men into the state of the Bituriges by way of Ocean and was received as he disembarked from his ships.'[10]

This is not a trivial event. This is a seaborne expedition larger than that of 1066. Further, it is at the behest of the western emperor. Yet while every British source mentions the Saxon

Revolt in some way, none gives any hint of a king this powerful. How can these two diametrically opposed views of Britain be reconciled?

Once again, the sea may provide the answer. As noted above, the best explanation for why Hengest was hired by Arthur is that the 'Jutes' acted as his navy. It is therefore difficult to avoid the conclusion that after the Revolt, Britannia most definitely did *not* rule the waves. Even links with the continent appear to have been severed rather decisively. In 495 the British Church failed to adopt Rome's change in the calculations for the date of Easter, although they had done so in 455.[11] Moreover, after the Revolt much of the eastern coast of Britain would have been under direct Saxon control. The rest would have been under constant threat from Saxon raids. Post-Revolt Britain was a nation fighting for its life. Even after Ambrosius' successes it was significantly weaker and more isolated than it had been under the Proud Tyrant. Admiral Mahan would have questioned how any British naval capability could have been created under such conditions.

But in 469—two decades after the arrival of Hengest—we are told by several reliable sources that Britain was sufficiently recovered to send a force of 12,000 soldiers to the continent. This is a force almost twice the size of William the Conqueror's. Further, even allowing for exaggeration, these 12,000 Britons were a major component in Rome's imperial strategy; they were meant to take on the full armed might of the Visigothic kingdom. Yet Riothamus appears on the stage for only a single year and then vanishes, along with his 12,000 men.

How can this possibly have happened?

Most 'sober' historians make desperate efforts to explain away the evidence. Riothamus is usually termed a 'refugee' from Britain who carved out a kingdom in Brittany.[12] They assert that coming 'by way of Ocean' is a 'scribal error', or a misstatement by Jordanes himself. But these arguments stretch credulity even further than the ancient historians' bald statements about Riothamus. With Saxon warships infesting the Channel, how could even the bravest adventurer bring a force sufficient to overawe a whole Gallic province, much less set up a state capable of fielding 12,000 warriors? If this proto-Breton state actually existed for any length of time before 469, why are continental historians entirely silent about it? Even the small states ruled by Alans and Saxons get an occasional mention. But the demesne of this 'local warlord' merits not a line. What was the name of this Armorican 'kingdom' anyway? Ys, perhaps? Or Lyonesse? Most telling, one of the greatest historians of any age, Edward Gibbon, saw Riothamus as a British king sailing with his army from Britain.[13]

The conclusion is inescapable. Unless we are to throw out several perfectly valid pieces of continental information, Britain still had command of the sea in 469. Further, the voyage of 12,000 men to Gaul could only have been accomplished in the large Saxon *cyuls*. But the corollary to this is simple.

The Saxon Revolt occurred after 469.[14]

This helps to explain something that has been one of the great mysteries of British History: just how could a few boatloads of Saxon mercenaries overawe a nation of over a million souls, so much so that the indigenous population adopted a new language? The answer is that, in a time of peace, with defence of the coasts in Saxon hands, there would have been no practical means for the Britons to limit Saxon immigration. Once Hengest secured Kent for his people, the high-prowed *cyuls* would have carried ever greater numbers of settlers to Britain. During imperial times these immigrants might have assimilated. After all, even the Vandals and Goths acknowledged the superiority of Rome's *culture*. But that edge had vanished by the time of Arthur. The difference in material culture between Saxon and Briton was almost nil. In the growing Saxon settlements there would have been neither the opportunity nor the incentive to assimilate.[15] Arthur's twenty years of peace had allowed several large Germanic communities to grow within Britain—communities that might cause something far worse than Hengest's *discordia*.

Confirmation of this twenty-year period of peace between Saxon and Briton is found in another source, a source whose real significance has until now been misunderstood. This is the *Annales Cambriae*, a ninth-century Welsh chronicle. It contains two passages that speak of Arthur: 'The Battle of *Badon*, in which Arthur carried the Cross of our Lord Jesus Christ for three days and three nights on his shoulders and the Britons were successful,' and: 'The Battle of *Camlann*, in which Arthur and Medrawt fell, and there was a plague in Britain and Ireland.'[16]

The years given for these two entries appear to be about 516 and 537, respectively. But it is doubtful that these dates have any reality. This is precisely the time when Gildas was writing. A Battle of *Badon* in 516 would place this event well within his lifetime—a lifetime that, he assures us, saw no major British-Saxon conflict. Just why the compiler chose these years for his texts is uncertain.[17] But they still give us some important information. They tell us that *Camlann*, Arthur's last battle, occurred some two decades after his victory at *Badon*. With a date of 450 for *Badon*, this would mean that the 469 expedition to Gaul occurred during the reign of the Proud Tyrant. Another conclusion is then inescapable.

Riothamus *is* the Proud Tyrant... and Arthur.[18]

When we remember what Riothamus actually means in Brythonic, this equation becomes a near-certainty. Riothamus signifies 'Most Kingly.'. As we have seen, a number of kings are reported as subordinate to *both* the *Dux Bellorum* and the Proud Tyrant. What could be more logical than to choose a regnal name of 'Most Kingly' to distinguish Arthur from his sub-ordinate rulers?

Many scholars counter this line of thinking by arguing that Riothamus can only be a name given at birth. They assert that such Brythonic names are typical of the period, and can have no 'royal' significance. This, however, overlooks one crucial factor. Almost all the Brythonic names we have for the fifth and sixth centuries come from *western* Britain, a region that was never as Romanized as the east. Indeed, as we have seen, in the early part of the fifth century *all* the British actors use Latin names such as Marcus, Constantine, and Gerontius.[19] We have postulated a Proud Tyrant, born at about the time of the break with Rome, who spent his entire life defending the most Romanized part of the island. But by the 460s conditions had radically changed. Large areas of the Romanized east were under Saxon control. Much of the Proud Tyrant's power base now lay in heavily Celticized areas to the west. Many of his soldiers were 'Cornovians' and 'Venedotians.' A Latin or even an Alanic name had little cachet here. It was far better to adopt a Brythonic name, a name that proclaimed the precise image that this new 'King of kings' was trying to project.

It is important to stress that this is also entirely Roman in thinking. The founder of the Roman Empire had *adopted* the name Augustus—even today far more recognizable than his birth-name of Octavian. Moreover, by Late Roman times the distinction between names and titles was becoming blurred. Roman emperors could be known as Caesar and Augustus—both of which are simultaneously names and titles. Constantius' career path in the early fifth century closely parallels Arthur's. First he was *Magister Militum*, or Marshal, a close equivalent to *Dux Bellorum.* Then he acquired the title of Patricius (also the personal name of St Patrick), and finally Augustus. The ruler of Britain in 469 was first known as Arthur ('Bear Man'), then *Dux Bellorum*, and finally *chose* a regnal name of 'Most Kingly'.[20] For a military strongman with no hereditary right to rule, these various names and titles acted as props to his regime. Each new honorific asserted a broader right to guide the destiny of the island.

It is also difficult to overstate the importance of the identification of the Proud Tyrant with Riothamus. This is more significant even than the Arthur-Riothamus equation. Indeed, once we see who Riothamus really is, the few historical citations about Arthur become superfluous. Even without the Battle List, Gildas still tells us that the Proud Tyrant's ascent took place in the context of the defeat of Britain's three seaborne foes, and that the decisive battle was at *Badon*. As we shall see, several different sources give us the best explanation for *Camlann*, the battle that took place twenty years later. Like the Bible and the *Iliad*, the Arthurian citations tell us where to dig—and what we unearth is the real history of fifth-century Britain.

Far from being an obscure warlord in a time of anarchy and decline, Arthur was at the centre of events in the fifth century. Not only did he exert a decisive influence on British history, but his actions were part of that larger drama, the fall of the western Roman Empire. Much of this story we will never know. But there are other parts that we can discern quite clearly. Faced with potential rebellion at home, and sensing Roman weakness in Gaul, Arthur resolved on a bold step. Just as the continental writers testify, he was going to take his army to Gaul.

EMPIRE

It was 468, the year of Anthemius' second consulship. The *discordia* of 459 had cast its long shadow over Britain for nearly a decade. Arthur was growing old. His great battles, his ambitious projects were things of the past. Like him, Britain was growing weaker with each day. True, there was no war. But all around him his closest advisers whispered warnings in his ear. Trusted generals, men like Cai and Bedwyr, spoke of a new Saxon danger. The barbarians were growing more numerous. They demanded larger gifts, a greater share in the good things of

Britain. *Decuriones* grumbled at the harvests that disappeared down the gullets of the *furciferi*—the 'gallows thieves'. Churchmen complained that Saxons still clung to their old gods.

Saxons also had their complaints. Each year their young men went out on the dark seas to protect the shores of Britain. Each year they stood watch over lonely beacon fires, scanning the horizon for the odd raider. It was they who had won at *Badon*. It was they who had protected the shores of the diocese for almost two decades. But the Britons repaid them with hatred and contempt. Hengest warned darkly that his young men were not *Weala* bureaucrats and craftsmen. They were bored with guard duty. They had heard tales from their elders of booty captured in past wars with Pict and Scot. To any Saxon warrior peace was a poor thing, a womanish thing.

As Arthur sipped his wine by the fire, he felt a pang of regret. The heroic days were gone. No more did he lead his cohorts into battle, fighting beneath his golden dragon. Many old comrades, men like Cunedda and Coel, were dead or in their dotage. He had created a state organized for war—and there was no war. But strife, yes, there was plenty of that. And intrigue. Britons, even Britons in his own court, plotted to bring back the Christian champion Ambrosius. Saxons in their new settlements plotted fresh insurrections, hoping to take a larger share of the *annona*. Even this young Saxon girl had brought him not comfort, but division. His sons shunned her. Churchmen condemned her as a pagan. This was not peace, but slow decay. Unless something was done, his great creation would collapse. The choice was stark: empire or implosion. And could a son of Constantine choose anything but empire?

A smile crossed his lips. There *was* a solution to the problem. And this time Ocean would not be Britain's curse, but her salvation. The Saxons wanted booty? Fine, let them look for it not in Britain, but across the sea. The Britons hated the Saxons? Fine, let them pay for a fleet to carry the *furciferi* far away, beyond the horizon. Let soldiers from Britain cross the Gallican Straits just as the Great Constantine had done.

But *not* as Maximus or the last Constantine had done. This time it would be different. Britain's soldiers would be crossing Ocean as Rome's friends, not her enemies. A message had come from beyond the Alps, as joyous and unexpected as a miracle. The puppet ruler of Rome, Severus, had died. A new emperor ruled in the west. A grand coalition was forming, one that would defeat the Vandals in North Africa and humble the Visigoths. Just as Constantine had breathed new life into the empire, so too would this new Augustus.

Arthur called for more wine, then drank deeply. Already he was planning his last, greatest campaign. Once again he would harness all Britain's resources. But this time it would not be for mere survival but for empire. He would don his heavy gilded helmet; take to the saddle. The dragon standards would fly above his head once more. The good wine began to course through his blood. His smile grew cunning, self-satisfied. He knew that he had other allies on the continent, allies who would help in this great endeavour.

And he had put some of them there himself.

ODOVACER

The Romans called him 'Adovacrius'. In most modern accounts he is known as Odovacer.[21] But that we even possess his name is in itself strange, for Odovacer seems to be little more than a footnote to history. He is usually presented as the leader of a group of Saxon pirates who, in 464, sailed into the mouth of the Loire and captured the town of Angers. His forces then established fortifications on islands near the mouth of that river. But only a few years later a combined force of Romans and Franks drove Odovacer and his Saxons from their strongholds. When we remember that the names of the Saxon rulers who *successfully* settled the coast of Gaul are almost non-existent, it seems strange that this particular failure would merit a mention. Yet Gregory of Tours presents him as a key player in the events surrounding Riothamus' expedition.

That a Saxon can capture a town, and then be remembered for it may seem unworthy of further notice. But there happens to be another anomaly connected with Odovacer, this time with the name itself. It so happens that in all the literature of the Anglo-Saxons, a name similar to 'Odovacer' occurs not once. It is true that the two halves of the name are sometimes found in various Anglo-Saxon compound names. But it is equally true that they are never found together.[22] It seems odd that the name would occur only once in so many centuries.

This seems particularly strange given the fact that another Germanic leader also bore the name Odovacer at precisely this time. Moreover, he would be a key player—*the* key player—in the final days of the western empire. But this Odovacer was no Saxon, no high seas freebooter. His birthplace was in the east, on the steppes. Edecon, his father, was ruler of the Scirians, a people allied to the Huns. Indeed, Edecon was one of King Attila's most trusted advisers. The Scirian Odovacer thus came to manhood at the centre of the Hunnic power structure. He had received the best military education possible within that milieu. In many ways he was what we might call a barbarian 'insider.'.

The breakup of the Hunnish empire brought about a radical change in Edecon's fortunes. The Scirian king died in a hopeless battle with the Ostrogoths. His tribe abruptly disappeared from history. But his son turned out to be a consummate survivor. For some reason Odovacer left home prior to the Scirian debacle, heading west to seek his fortune. In 461 we find him in rags, wandering alone in Austria. A later hagiography of St Severinus mentions the young Scirian. It describes how the tall barbarian, dressed in tattered buckskins, enters the holy man's tiny cell and humbly asks for advice. Strangely, Severinus greets the barbarian kindly. Even stranger, the saint predicts greatness for the vagabond prince—but only if he journeys to Rome.[23]

Eventually Odovacer followed the saint's advice. He joined the imperial army and quickly attained the rank of general. He was to be the leader in the revolt that toppled the last Roman emperor, Romulus Augustulus. Indeed, this would make him the first king of post-Roman Italy. St Severinus' advice had proved excellent, and we know that the barbarian lavished many gifts on the humble cleric in repayment.

But curiously, nothing is heard about *this* Odovacer between the year 461 and the end of imperial rule in 476. Still stranger, this is precisely the time when we find our 'Saxon' Odovacer occupying Angers. The most likely reason for this lacuna in the 'Italian' Odovacer's career is simple: the two Odovacers are identical. This would also explain why the barbarian occupier of a single town in Gaul might be remembered in the chronicles. Anything a future ruler of Italy did was of no small interest to later historians. Further, the fact that Gregory of Tours includes Odovacer's exploits in the same portion of his narrative as Riothamus' campaign of 469 suggests that Gregory's source saw a connection between the two events. Just how they are connected will shortly be explained.

Why Odovacer came to Gaul is nowhere stated. But a curious series of incidents in the 450s may give us a clue. Spanish sources speak of seaborne raids along the northern Iberian coast by a Germanic people called the Heruls. At first glance this seems counter-intuitive. The Heruls were originally from the Baltic, and later settled for a time on the Black Sea. From here they joined Attila's confederacy, taking part in his invasion of the western empire in 451. But with Attila's death in 454 the Hunnic empire fell apart, scattering people like Odovacer and the Heruls throughout western Europe. Several years later we hear of seven shiploads of these Heruls raiding the Spanish town of Lugo. They then sailed on to ravage the coast of Gascony. Another raid brought them as far south as Andalusia. What other adventures they had before or afterward are unrecorded.[24]

Now, this is a group of warriors far from home, engaged in a risky business. They would have needed some sort of base for their operations, and the most likely venue is one of the Saxon enclaves along the Gallic littoral. But this implies Saxon, and probably also Gallo-Roman, acquiescence to such buccaneering. We have no reports of Saxon raiding in the 450s, at least in northwestern Gaul. But Spain and the coast of southeastern Gaul would have been another matter. These were areas either controlled by the Visigoths, or under no particular authority. Indeed, these Herul raids seem to parallel what Arthur and his naval federates were doing on the other side of the Channel. In both cases barbarian seafarers were granted land in exchange for peace with their hosts—and war with their hosts' enemies. The *modus operandi* for the Heruls appears to have been similar to what was taking place among the Vandals in the Mediterranean. There, North Africans provided the nautical expertise, while Geiseric's warriors supplied the fighting skill. Similarly, in Gaul it is plausible that the Saxons provided the ships and sailing know-how, while the Heruls supplied the muscle. When we remember that many of the Heruls would have been veterans of Attila's wars, this would have been a formidable combination.

It was in the 460s that things began to change. As noted earlier, the battle of Orléans in 463 had been a close-run thing. Aegidius' Franks and Gallo-Romans had just managed to drive back the first Visigothic incursion across the Loire. Ricimer's central government in Rome remained implacably hostile to Aegidius. The rebel general knew that he would need other allies to repel any future attacks from the south.

It is here that the sources suggest that Arthur's interests began to converge with those of continental Romans. There are no more reports of raiding by Herul or Saxon. Instead, islands at the mouth of the Loire suddenly fell into Saxon hands. But these were not merely pirate lairs. They controlled the mouth of the Loire, just as the Thanet settlement controlled the mouth of the Thames. This was only the first stage, however. Armorica was a place controlled by neither Aegidius nor the Visigoths. If a force friendly to Arthur could take it, the Proud Tyrant would have a springboard for other continental adventures. But this required not just islands, but towns.

This is why Odovacer—and probably the Herulian buccaneers as well—were crucial. Odovacer was familiar with the state-of-the-art warfare practiced by Goths, Huns, and Romans. Attila in particular had carried out a number of successful sieges, using various engines to capture well-fortified cities such as Naissus and Aquileia. Odovacer would certainly have known of these operations, and may even have been an eyewitness to them. A Scirian prince with such experience was the perfect choice to lead an assault on Angers.

Angers was taken in 464, and the treatment of its citizens appears to have been far from gentle (Please see Map 5). Odovacer thought it best to take hostages from among the city's elite.[25] This suggests that only a garrison remained in the town, perhaps including the erstwhile Herulian raiders. The bulk of the Saxons seem to have settled on the Loire islands.[26] The end result, however, was exactly what Arthur required. These various fortifications screened Armorica from a dangerous enemy—the Visigoths. They also provided a springboard for further operations deep into Gaul via the Loire. Arthur's surrogates had established a secure base on the continent; one which would facilitate a much larger operation.

If there is any single event that marks the beginning of British penetration of Armorica, it is the fall of Angers in 464. The attendance of the British bishop Mansuetus at a church council in Tours in 461, mentioned earlier, is ambiguous, to say the least. Bishop Faustus of Riez was certainly British-born, but was in no way a Breton. Since Mansuetus' see is nowhere named, his ethnicity cannot be proof for a proto-Breton kingdom. Ironically, the capture of Angers by a group of Germanic warriors appears to have been the first act in a drama that would eventually produce the Breton nation.

Still, the fall of Angers was only the first phase of a much larger, much more complex military undertaking. Arthur's Saxon and Herul henchmen had established a bridgehead. The main operation would follow. That this operation would also remove a large number of potentially rebellious Saxon warriors from Britain did not worry the Proud Tyrant in the least.

ANTHEMIUS

467. Spring. Northern Italy. Sidonius Apollinaris was once again on the road to Rome. The journey had been hard. The danger of open warfare between any number of armed groups was never far away. But all the same, Sidonius had a right to be pleased. He would soon perform what had become his speciality: delivering the panegyric for a newly crowned emperor. Once more he would rummage through his Classical bag of tricks, deploying a deity here and a personified city there—all to praise the latest Christian Caesar.

Sidonius' encomiums for this new emperor were probably genuine. The next Caesar would be no parvenu; no military strongman who had seized power through force of arms. But neither was he Roman, like Majorian, nor Gallo-Roman, like Avitus. Instead he was a Greek, known as Anthemius. He had been handpicked by the eastern emperor to sort things out in the west.

Until 465 the eastern emperors had displayed little interest in the plight of their less fortunate western counterparts. But in that year Geiseric began raiding the coast of Greece. This was different. It threatened to destroy the overseas trade of both empires. Vandal piracy had to be crushed. When Ricimer's puppet emperor died in that year, the eastern emperor Leo saw his opportunity. He demanded that the westerners make one of his own subjects the new Caesar.[27]

Sidonius, social climber that he was, can only have approved of Anthemius. The Greek was a quintessential insider. He came from a noble Byzantine family. His father-in-law had been the emperor Marcian. Profiting by these connections, the young man quickly ascended the eastern empire's ladder of success, becoming first a marshal, then a consul, and finally a patrician. But these were no empty titles. Anthemius had fought and defeated incursions by first Ostrogoths, and then Huns. Now he was about to play a key part in the great offensive that was to crush Geiseric for ever.[28]

Once again Sidonius' oration captured the mood of the time. 'This, my Lords, is the man… to whom our commonwealth, like a ship overcome by tempests and without a pilot, hast committed her broken frame, to be more deftly guided by a worthy steersman, that she may no more fear storm or pirate.'[29] Although the new Caesar had only just arrived in Rome, Sidonius already predicted triumph for him, and for 'the fleet and forces that thou, O Prince, art handling.' The end is vintage Sidonius: 'Forward then, Father of thy country, blest of fortune and with happy omen release old captives, to bind new ones anon.'[30] Sidonius can only have been pleased as the crowd acclaimed the new Caesar. It seemed that another Constantine ruled in the west.

The audience could also take some relief in the length of this panegyric. It amounted to only 548 lines—a model of Sidonian brevity. But beneath the flowery rhetoric, the poem actually dealt with serious issues. The maritime imagery was no accident. Great events were in the offing. Roused by Geiseric, the eastern emperor Leo was determined on nothing less than the complete reconquest of North Africa. While Sidonius delivered his oration a vast fleet of ships was gathering in the east. Manned by 100,000 sailors and soldiers, it was an armada that dwarfed Majorian's unlucky flotilla. Just as Scipio's Romans had done in an earlier age, so now the Byzantines would sail to Carthage and reassert Rome's claim to the Mediterranean. Anthemius' part in the operation was to recapture Sardinia from the Vandals. Once the Mediterranean was secure, a reinvigorated western empire could then make short work of the Visigoths. It was a dazzling plan. It is little wonder that Anthemius was seen as a conquering hero even before he conquered anything.

Anthemius may also have been something of a dreamer. He aspired to nothing less than a return to Rome's past glories. But this turned out to involve glories more ancient than anyone had bargained for. Almost immediately, Anthemius managed to alienate the Church. He permitted the Romans to once again celebrate the ancient pagan festival of Lupercalia. Worse still, he appointed a pagan, Severus (no relation to the recently deceased emperor), to high office. Indeed, a curious document written shortly after this time by the pagan author Damascius argues that the new emperor had more in mind than just nostalgia for the Hellenistic past. The pagan official Severus eventually settled in Alexandria, and, if we are to believe Damascius' report, asserted that Anthemius' ultimate objective had been to revive paganism in the west.[31] Damascius may well have been exaggerating. Christianity's ascendancy was by now irreversible, and Anthemius' sin may have been merely over-fondness for ancient philosophy. But all the same, the Greek appears to have felt that only radical measures could save the west from destruction. That infuriating the Church was not a good way to start seems to have escaped him.

Anthemius may have miscalculated in other ways too. The eastern emperor certainly did not want 'barbarism' to triumph in the west. Anthemius' appointment is proof enough of this. But neither would Leo have been anxious to see a rival to his own power spring up in Rome. In the past the armies of the two empires had clashed with each other almost as much as with barbarians. The situation was not unlike the relations between two ideological allies of the twentieth century. The Soviet Union and Communist China shared similar economic and ideological goals, but in the end these could not outweigh divergent political interests. Similarly, Anthemius would have to restore Rome's power, but only so that it did no harm to the interests of his eastern colleague.[32] It was a difficult balancing act, with potentially fatal results.

Anthemius' task was made infinitely more difficult by Ricimer. The Patrician had been the real power in Italy for the last five years, and it is doubtful that he greeted the arrival of a Greek filled with grand ideas enthusiastically. Ricimer, after all, was the son of barbarians, with only a patina of Roman civilization. Throughout his life he endeavoured to play one party off against another. He would not blink an eye at the murder of a rival, real or potential. Indeed, for Gibbon he is one of the chief villains in the fall of the western empire.[33] Intriguer he may have been, but he perhaps best understood the genuine weakness of the western empire. It is arguable that his policy of cutting Rome's losses north of the Alps—a policy later pursued by Theoderic the Great—was the most realistic course in the long run. The problem was that this directly opposed his new emperor's vision.

No sense of this potential rivalry was detectable in 467, during the first months of Anthemius' reign. The new emperor gave his daughter, Alypia, in marriage to his barbarian Patrician.[34] 'The Greek', as Ricimer termed him, then threw himself into the preparations for the destruction of the Vandals. The next year, in 468, the great naval expedition from the east set sail for Africa. Geiseric's ships avoided battle and the 'invincible armada' found safe anchorage in a bay near Carthage. The Vandals appeared doomed. When Geiseric asked for a truce, it seemed that the aged warrior had finally met his match. The Byzantine commander was delighted, and readily agreed. But all the while Geiseric was preparing a cunning counterblow. Using a tactic that would destroy a later armada, the wily Vandal launched a night attack with fire ships. The Byzantine vessels were closely packed and unable to manouevre. Most of the fleet was destroyed, with great loss of life. Both Romes were humiliated.[35]

This was a heavy blow to Anthemius' prestige, particularly since it exposed the weakness of his eastern patron. Worse still, 'the Greek' now faced a barbarian adversary every bit as dangerous as Geiseric. In the previous year a Visigothic prince named Euric had murdered his royal brother and made himself king. This new barbarian turned out to be much more dangerous than his predecessor. In direct challenge to Anthemius' vision, Euric sought nothing less than domination of the western Roman world. Still worse, he was a fanatical Arian, eager to make life miserable for his Catholic subjects. One of his first edicts decreed that whenever a Roman priest died, his post must be left permanently vacant.[36] Soon Euric was searching for *Weala* victims beyond his realm.

The logical course for Euric to follow would have been to repeat the 463 crossing of the Loire and try to take the rest of Gaul. Aegidius had just died, and neither his successor, Count Paul, nor Childeric was a man of the same stature. But instead Euric moved south, marching against the Suevi in Spain.[37] Indeed, from 463 to 469 we find all quiet on the Loire front. Part of this may have been due to the rapprochement between Anthemius and the Gallo-Romans. But part of it may also have been due to Arthur. Odovacer and his Saxons could not have overawed Euric on their own. But if fresh forces from Britain were beginning to occupy Armorica, they could very well have tipped the balance in favour of the Frankish-Roman axis.

From the first, Ricimer appears to have been hostile to a re-invigorated Britain. One of his main sources for information about conditions north of the Alps appears to have been the Praetorian Prefect of Gaul, one Arvandus. It was perhaps characteristic of these strange times that, while barbarian kings ruled most of Gaul, the old imperial structures were still functioning. By the 460s Arvandus' power was severely limited. But all the same, he was the senior Roman official in Gaul, and understood the political situation as few others might. One thing he would have pointed out to Ricimer, if the Patrician had not already found out for himself, was that the enclave in Armorica had both a defensive and offensive significance. The Loire was an easily navigable river. As later Vikings proved, a fleet of ships could sail from its mouth into the heart of Gaul.[38] Now the mouth of this vital artery was controlled by Arthur's allies, the Saxons. They also occupied the city of Angers. From here a fine Roman road joined up with another highway leading east, paralleling the Loire for many miles.[39] Beyond that thoroughfare lay the strategic city of Lyon—and the passes into Italy. We do not know how well grounded in Roman history Ricimer was, but Arvandus would have helpfully reminded the Patrician of how many usurpers had travelled the road that led from the Channel to Rome. The spectre of a danger greater than Aegidius loomed.

Ricimer may also have inquired about another person: Odovacer. Whether the two barbarians ever met is unknown. But Ricimer would still have been aware that a mercenary out for the main chance was fighting in Arthur's ranks—one with no deep loyalties to either Saxon or Briton. Ricimer had much to think about in the coming months.

COALITION

It was probably not long after Anthemius' coronation that his emissaries approached Arthur, more than likely just as the North African campaign began. Anthemius seems to have proposed a grand coalition, similar to the one that Aetius had cobbled together in 451. Part of it would include Anthemius' imperial levies from Italy. Another would involve a combination of Gallo-Romans and Franks, to be jointly commanded by Count Paul and Childeric. A third element was to consist of Arthur's force of Britons and Saxons. It was a formidable combination, but the key element in the plan was the army from beyond Ocean. Only the Britons possessed the strategic mobility to appear suddenly on the battlefield at a time and place that Euric might not suspect until it was too late. The role of Odovacer and his Saxons was thus critical. They controlled an avenue of approach that would quickly place Arthur's force in the very heart of Gaul. If the Britons could link up with the imperial and Romano-Frankish armies, Euric would be confronted by an unbeatable combination.

What could Arthur gain from this coalition? Most likely, lands currently occupied by the Visigoths. This in turn would allow him to divert large numbers of Saxon federates away from Britain and into Gaul. It could ease the tensions that currently existed between the two peoples, and gain him new sources of revenue.

Arthur and Anthemius had an understanding to which—for a time at least—it was in the interests of both to adhere. Their alliance would cow the barbarians, and allow the resurgence of a civilization of which both were heirs. Anthemius had a right to be pleased. His Greek advisers would have assured him that the neutralization of the Visigothic threat was well within his grasp.

Only Ricimer would have disagreed. He would have pointed out that Britain was one of the strongest powers in the west. Now the emperor was allowing it to occupy lands that were nominally his. Few Gallo-Romans were enthusiastic about their Gothic or Burgundian rulers. Not only were they barbarians; they were also Arian heretics. But a Catholic hero in the mould of Constantine the Great was something else again. Arthur's popularity might lead him to aspire to greater things than possession of one or two Gallic provinces. That Anthemius did not listen to his Patrician is certain, for the enterprise went forward.

That Ricimer thought his new lord a fool is no less certain.

ANNONA

Arthur was now assembling a very large force by the standards of Late Antiquity. His army was making not just a short Channel hop, but a voyage almost as daring as that of the later Spanish Armada. It required ships. It required horses. It required men. And most of all, it required money.

Not money as we think of it, however. Much of the silver and gold coinage of Roman times had disappeared years earlier, or remained in carefully concealed (and often wholly forgotten) caches underground. By this time the British economy was operating largely on the barter system. But taxes could still be collected in the form of grain. With it Arthur could feed the Saxons who built the long ships. He could feed the Britons who made the weapons and armour for his troops. He could lay in the supplies that would nourish 12,000 men and their horses during a campaign of many months.

Arthur would not have had much difficulty in collecting additional taxes. Kings of his own choosing ruled the *civitates*. They had been forcing the *decuriones* to collect taxes in kind for years. The *annona* payments were the foundation on which Arthur's Saxon and British cohorts were based. But these new taxes may well have been an unprecedented burden for both peasant and *decurio* alike. In times past the high cost of maintaining Rome's army had distorted her economy, pauperizing both farmer and noble. Now this was proving true for the Britons. Just as important, even if Arthur's venture were crowned with success, few of the peasantry were likely to benefit from it. If the venture failed, even the well-off would feel the pinch.

14. 'Most Kingly'

More ominous, many now complained that the Saxons were the real masters. Arthur, they whispered, had become a hostage to the barbarians. It was they who forced him to tax the Britons more and more. This new adventure would bring no benefit; it was only a pretence for the *furciferi* to obtain more loot. But who could be surprised at this, when Arthur's own wife was a Saxon?

As the preparations for the expedition progressed, Britons high and low could only curse Arthur's name. For the moment any overt move was unthinkable. But the Saxon warriors who had overawed the country for years were leaving. Arthur himself would soon follow them across Ocean. And no Briton could forget how the hero Ambrosius had chased the Saxon *furciferi* to the edge of that same Ocean.

15.

'BY WAY OF OCEAN'

INVASION

469. *Spring. Richborough.* The ships were assembling. In the shadow of the ancient coastal fortress Britons and Saxons feverishly prepared for a long sea voyage. Workmen carried food and drink aboard the long *cyuls*. Warriors stored away spears, arrows, and swords, each carefully wrapped to protect them against the Channel's salt spray. All along the eastern and southern coasts it was the same story. This was a maximum effort, the fruit of Arthur's military and bureaucratic skill. Twelve thousand strong, the expedition would stir imaginations on both sides of the Channel.

The appointed day arrived. Ships struck for the open sea, sails clouding the horizon. More ships were gathered together than had been seen in a century. After the short Channel voyage the high-prowed Saxon ships turned south (see Map 5). Days later the armada turned west, hugging the Armorican coast. The fleet rounded what is now Finisterre, then doubled back toward the mouth of the Loire. Once there, they sailed past the island strongholds of the Saxons. It was here that the armada underwent its final transformation. Soon a long queue of vessels was snaking up the river, its final destination the area surrounding a city that is now called Bourges.

That Arthur's fleet sailed up the Loire without reported opposition shows the real significance of Odovacer's Saxons: essentially they were the vanguard of Arthur's army. Had they been hostile, the Britons would have had to attack and occupy Angers and the Loire islands. Yet even if Odovacer's followers had been temporarily driven away, his force would have remained an unacceptable threat to Arthur's land and sea communications. The Gothic historian Jordanes also tells us something tantalizing as well. He reports that Riothamus 'was received as he disembarked from his ships.' This indicates that some force was already waiting for him in central Gaul. But it was certainly not Childeric and Count Paul, nor was it Anthemius' Romans. As we shall see, these armies came later. There is no direct evidence that Odovacer took part in Arthur's operation. But we do know that both he and his warriors were away from Angers at just this time. And the most likely explanation for this is that Odovacer's Saxons took an active part in the venture, and may even have been the force entrusted with the initial seizure of Bourges. They had, after all, done the same thing at Angers. This is by far the most probable scenario for the campaign. A 'local Breton warlord' venturing up the Loire with a horde of Saxons between him and his Armorican base makes no military sense at all.[1]

For its day it was a lightning campaign, and initially it seemed that the Visigoths were taken completely by surprise. The expedition travelled deep into Gaul without any reports of combat. As Jordanes puts it: 'King Riotimus came with 12,000 men into the state of the Biturges by way of Ocean, and was received as he disembarked from his ships.' Biturges is the district of Berry, in central Gaul. That so large an expedition could sail so far inland may be surprising. But two centuries later we find Viking fleets accomplishing the identical feat.[2] Indeed, when we compare it to the short Channel hops undertaken by Britain's many usurpers, it was an extremely complex operation, brilliantly executed. A battle-ready force of 12,000 soldiers had appeared as if by magic on the boundary between the Visigothic kingdom and the remaining Roman possessions.

To those Gallo-Romans who still held out against the Visigoths, the appearance of the force would have seemed something akin to a miracle. The small Roman army under Count Paul in the north had been joined by a new host of Catholic Romans. Amazingly, a letter to King Riothamus from Sidonius has come down to us. It makes plain that this king is someone about whom the bishop has heard quite a bit. Sidonius addresses the monarch in amicable terms, as 'Riothamo suo', the term the bishop reserves for his dearest friends. The missive begins with a bit of flattery, a relic of Sidonius' days in the halls of imperial power: 'I am a direct witness of the conscientious-ness which weighs on you so heavily, and which has always been of such delicacy as to make you blush for the wrongdoing of others.' He then goes on to describe Riothamus' army as 'a crowd of noisy, armed and disorderly men who are emboldened at once by their courage, their numbers, and their comradeship.'[3] We then expect a missive on some weighty subject. But instead we are disappointed to find that Sidonius' only purpose in writing the letter is to help a 'humble rustic' recover servants who may or may not have run off with the British army.[4]

This does not seem like the stuff of history. But if a minor landowner was complaining to the bishop of distant Clermont-Ferrand, it suggests that at least some of Riothamus' force was deployed south of the Loire—a sensible precaution with the Visigothic threat coming from this direction. That Sidonius also uses such familiar tones may indicate that he knew something about Riothamus, perhaps derived from the British-born bishop of Riez, Faustus. But one point often overlooked is the fact that the letter has survived at all. It is no secret that Sidonius was proud of his contacts; proud that he corresponded with the very greatest men of his day. In a sense these letters formed his scrapbook, depicting his role in the last days of the western empire. That the letter was preserved at all indicates that its importance lies in its addressee, not in its contents. For Sidonius, Riothamus was much more than a local Breton warlord. He was an important actor in the break-up of the western empire. We have no letters to Count Paul or Aegidius, but we do have one to Riothamus. For Sidonius, even a trivial missive addressed to this 'Most Kingly' ruler was important enough to preserve.

As Arthur disembarked near Bourges he had a right to be pleased. A great army had been brought into the heart of Gaul. Now it waited for Frankish and Gallo-Roman forces from the north, and imperial forces from the east. Once these armies combined, Euric and his Visigoths would be doomed.

But other forces were at work, forces about which Arthur knew nothing. As the *cyuls* were dragged on to the riverbanks near Bourges another letter was being written—and it threatened to destroy everything this 'Most Kingly' ruler had created.

ARVANDUS

He was the Praetorian Prefect of Gaul, and so head of the imperial administration that looked to Rome for guidance. He was in his second term of office, having won some renown in his first five-year stint. Sidonius counted him as a personal friend. But whatever his merits, this Arvandus was also a blustering, bull-headed sort of man—a man whose impulses might get him into trouble. He is also emblematic of how Rome's fortunes had diminished over the decades. He had real power. Roman administration still existed in many parts of Gaul. But his control was greatly circumscribed by the barbarians—and by military strongmen like Aegidius and Count Paul. Further, he cannot have been pleased that a renegade diocese once subordinate to his prefecture was moving into his own backyard. Riothamus might receive a warm welcome from Sidonius; but from Arvandus, never.[5]

The Prefect appears to have heard of the British landing soon after it occurred. Anthemius may have felt that the chief imperial representative in Gaul would need to know about military operations in his own prefecture. But, as we have seen, the essence of Arthur's expedition, indeed of the entire campaign, was secrecy and surprise. Without it, King Euric might defeat the imperial coalition in detail. So Arvandus, with this in mind, immediately sent a letter to... King Euric. He also made several helpful suggestions to the Visigoth, 'dissuading him from peace with the 'Greek Emperor', insisting that the Britons located north of the Loire should be attacked, and declaring that the Gallic provinces ought, according to the law of nations, to be divided up with the Burgundians.'[6]

It is difficult to see this as anything but out-and-out treason—and *lèse-majesté* as well. But even more incredible, when charged with this crime, Arvandus went to Rome of his own free will, fully confident that the Senate would acquit him. The only possible explanation is that he felt that 'the Greek' Anthemius was already a spent force. Moreover, it is difficult to see why he would come to Rome unless he believed he had a powerful protector. This can only have been Ricimer.

The truth was that by now the barbarian-born Patrician had had enough of his new sovereign. Ricimer was planning to destroy Anthemius, just as he had destroyed Majorian.[7] His motives for this were varied. Suspicion of the 'Greek Emperor' played a part. Like many twentieth-century dictators, Ricimer probably had little trust in anyone. There may also have been a genuine fear that Anthemius was upsetting the equilibrium in Gaul. Technically, Euric was still a federate subordinate to Rome. Ricimer may have feared that a fully aroused Visigothic king might simply conquer all of Gaul and throw off any pretence of fealty. After all, Arvandus' suggestion that the

Visigoth share Gaul with the Burgundians does contain a glimmer of *divide et impera*. Also, because of Ricimer's barbarian heritage, he may simply not have seen a greatly expanded Visigothic state as a threat. The Patrician's power base lay in Italy, where he could use Franks and Alamanni to prevent any incursions south of the Alps. In the next century Theoderic the Great's kingdom coexisted for some time with Merovingian Gaul. But whatever Ricimer's reasoning, he had set in motion a series of events that would pit the full might of the Visigothic host against Arthur.

We know that this particular letter of Arvandus never reached the Gothic king.[8] But we have a right to suspect that Ricimer had already found other ways to notify Euric of Arthur's intentions. He may also have found a way to prevent the dispatch of Anthemius' troops to Gaul. At just this time there is a report of a very convenient incursion into Italy by the Alamanni. For the foreseeable future, imperial troops would be fighting on the wrong side of the Alps. Arthur had gone to Gaul convinced that he was part of a grand coalition. Now his army stood alone, awaiting the full fury of Euric's onslaught. Almost certainly the man most responsible for this was Ricimer.

BATTLE

In 469 two armies manoeuvred in the summer heat of central Gaul. There were many veterans among both the Britons and the Saxons. They had fought and won against Picts and Irish on a number of occasions. Arthur's forces included elements of the cavalry that had rolled back every threat to Britain in the past. But this new enemy was different. The Visigoths had access to the best arms in the western empire. They might be called 'barbarians', but Euric's soldiers came from a nation that had been fighting—and defeating—Roman armies for half a century. Their grandfathers had sacked Rome. Their fathers had fought Attila to a standstill. Their nobility acted as a cavalry force no less formidable than that of the Britons.[9] And, as Jordanes affirms, King Euric was coming against Riothamus with an 'innumerable army'.

Arthur did not wait for the enemy to attack, however. He appears to have moved *forward*, from Bourges on the Cher to the southwest. Here he took up position at what is now Bourg-de-Déols on the River Indre. It is possible to see this move as an attempt to surprise the Visigoths, to 'steal a march' and attack them while unprepared. If so, it was a cunning manoeuvre, entirely in keeping with what we know of Arthur's past exploits. It may even have met with some initial success. Despite the odds in favour of the Goths, Jordanes describes a long, desperate battle beneath the two armies' dragon standards.[10] Sidonius gives us a vivid picture of a battle at this same time, and it remains the best depiction of what undoubtedly happened on the Indre:

> 'Now the broidered dragon speeds hither and thither in both armies, his throat swelling as the zephyrs dash against it... counterfeiting a wrathful hunger. Now the trumpet's deep note sounds with terrific blast. A shout greets the clarions, and even the spirit of cowards bursts into frenzy. A shower of steel comes down. A hurtling javelin lays one man in the dust. Another man is sent spinning by the thrust of a pike. One gashed by a harpoon, another by a lance, falls from his horse. Yet another... lies there, the prey of a hand beyond his ken. Some of them, with the thigh sinews severed, live on to envy death...'[11]

According to Jordanes it was a great battle, with many slain. But at the end of the day Arthur was defeated. He had been overcome by numbers—and perhaps by something else. His broken army fell back. Now the Gothic cavalry would have been the deadliest enemy, slaughtering stragglers as desperate men fled the battlefield. Jordanes tells us that a large part of

Riothamus' defeated force was lost, and the remainder set off northward, toward the land of the Burgundians.[12]

It is here we must ask a pertinent question. Why, given that Arthur had come by ship, did he feel the need to *march* what was left of his force towards almost certain internment and exile? The only possible explanation is that he had lost contact with his ships, and therefore with their Saxons crews. The Visigothic cavalry might account for this. If the retreat had turned into a rout, men would tend to cluster around their own comrades and lose contact with other units. But there is another explanation, one that fits well with events both before and after this.

The Saxons, or more precisely some portion of the Saxons, had deserted Arthur.

It is significant that just after this we find Odovacer hurrying back to his base at Angers, in a race with Childeric and Count Paul to reach the city.[13] The traditional view of this incident is that the Saxons had been enemies of the Romans all along. But, as mentioned above, it is highly unlikely that Arthur would have left fortified Saxon settlements behind him, many of which were on extremely defensible islands. Moreover, even if Odovacer were a neutral observer of these events, why would he be away from Angers just at this time? And why had Arthur not simply retreated downriver (whether his sailors were Saxon or British) to his bases in Armorica and Britain? The only sensible answer is that Odovacer and his Saxons were part of Arthur's force—and had abandoned the battle at a critical time. This may have been mere desperation by men fleeing a victorious enemy. Certainly the need to get away in such circumstances probably outweighed any sense of comradeship. But given the intrigue that surrounded the expedition, another possibility is that Odovacer had been suborned, directly or indirectly, by Ricimer to *betray* Arthur. Whether the Scirian acted during or after the battle is impossible to say. But the fact remains that Arthur's direct means of escape had somehow been removed.

Events unfolded with dizzying swiftness. At last we can understand the garbled story that Gregory of Tours gives in his *History of the Franks*. Hard on the heels of this battle came another, unexpected encounter. Count Paul and Childeric suddenly appeared before the Visigothic host. It was too late to save Arthur, but all the same the British army had inflicted terrible wounds on Euric's force. The tardy allies renewed battle with the weakened Visigoths. They were victorious. Euric's army was not destroyed, but Gregory records that the Romans and Franks took much booty. This was not to be the decisive encounter between Frank and Goth. That lay decades in the future. But for the moment Count Paul and Childeric stood as victors.

And Odovacer and his Saxons stood alone.

The first reaction of both continental and British Saxons would have been to retrace their journey back down the Loire. Angers would provide a refuge for Odovacer and his immediate followers, while for the British Saxons, the mouth of the Loire was the gateway to their homes across Ocean. It may have turned into a running battle, for Gregory speaks of the Romans and Franks destroying the Saxons' island settlements, expelling all who lay in their path. Odovacer reached Angers first, but with his foes only a day's march behind. The next morning the joint Romano-Frankish force assaulted the town. It seems to have been a hard struggle. Count Paul himself was killed in the fighting. But, ironically, Odovacer was no more able to hold Angers than Arthur had been able to hold Bourges. The town fell to Childeric.[14]

Thus the year ended with a tactical victory for Anthemius' coalition. But the defeat of Arthur was a strategic success for Euric. In the next year the Goth returned to the fray with more men and more ferocity. Going from strength to strength, by 471 he was knocking on the gates of Arles, the Prefecture's capital. Roused by this impending disaster, Anthemius at last made his move. He sent his son, Anthemiolus, across the Alps to relieve the city. But the campaign was a disaster and three of the army's generals were slain.[15]

Ricimer in the meanwhile had been biding his time in northern Italy. He had dealt with the Alamanni menace by a cunning manoeuvre. In a move completely in keeping with Late Roman practice, he seems to have summoned Childeric, of all people, to help him. Even stranger, Childeric invited Odovacer and some part of his defeated force to join in the campaign.[16] As we shall see, in an eerie twist of fate, St Severinus' prediction that Odovacer would find his fortune in Italy was about to come true. And it may also have come true for those Heruls who had harassed Spain in the 450s.

The Alamanni were defeated. But, of much greater importance, Ricimer had done the seemingly impossible. He had removed the threat posed by Arthur, neutralized the danger from the Goths, and thrown back the Alamanni. The barbarian's guile and deceit had removed all immediate threats to his position.

The end of the Alamanni campaign was only the first stage of Ricimer's bid for supreme power. Next he moved against his discredited emperor. He marched south, shutting Anthemius up in Rome. Abandoned by the eastern emperor, 'the Greek' was doomed. In July of 472 the city fell and he was executed. It was the end of both Anthemius and his dream.

But it was also the end of Ricimer. Six weeks later the Patrician died, arguably from disease engendered by his own siege.[17] And in a curious way, his death at this critical moment was a genuine disaster. For all his faults, he was probably the one person capable of halting Rome's slide toward the abyss. His death signals the final phase in the western empire's demise.

But there is still that little matter of Odovacer's destiny. Now we can understand why the Scirian rewarded St Severinus so munificently—and why the 'Saxon' Odovacer is identical to the Odovacer who ruled Italy. If the fugitive prince had obeyed the saint immediately and gone to Italy, Severinus' advice would have seemed of little consequence. Thousands of barbarian warriors had done the same. Odovacer, however, had ignored the saint's advice and gone to Gaul. There he had found only misfortune. But instead of suffering the usual fate of the vanquished, he had been chosen to lead a contingent of troops into the country where Severinus had foretold his destiny would lie. Odovacer's generous reward to the saint was not just for good advice. It was a superstitious barbarian's payment to a holy man who had predicted his unalterable fate. For Odovacer, the fact that he had gone to Gaul and still found his ultimate destiny in Italy was, quite simply, miraculous.[18]

Four years later, Italy would see the fulfilment of Severinus' prophecy. In 476 the Odovacer of history emerged, the military strongman who would drive the last Roman emperor from his throne—ending 400 years of imperial rule in the west.[19]

And marching behind Odovacer as he approached the imperial palace was a contingent of Heruls.

16.

'THE FIRE OF VENGEANCE'

RUMOURS

475. *Liviana, southern Gaul*. Sidonius is writing a letter. The Gallo-Roman aristocrat's circumstances have changed much since his last visit to Rome. Five years earlier he had taken part in the defence of his native city, Clermont-Ferrand, helping to fend off a besieging army of Goths. In the same year he was also elected as bishop of that place. By all accounts he appears to have taken this new duty as seriously as any of his interminable panegyrics. But King Euric viewed clergymen with independent ideas as dangerous. The Gothic ruler ordered Sidonius to be imprisoned in a fortress near present-day Carcassonne. This was not a pleasant experience. But it gave the Gallo-Roman plenty of time to write letters and, fortunately, many have survived.

This particular epistle is of great interest. It is addressed to a young Gallo-Roman named Namatius. At first Sidonius rambles. He gives us his thoughts on the current state of Latin rhetoric, then random memories of his early youth. These are followed by pronouncements on Namatius' hunting skills. But just when Sidonius' words seem to be no more than the idle mutterings of an old man, his letter changes tone completely. 'But lo and behold,' he writes, 'When I was already hoping to close this letter... a messenger suddenly came from Saintes'.

243

Sidonius finds to his surprise that Namatius has become an officer in the Visigothic navy. Each day the young man is taking part in operations against Saxon raiders, sometimes fighting on land, sometimes at sea.

Soon Sidonius' letter comes to resemble a typical modern 'letter to the front'. He admonishes his friend to be careful. The Saxons are a dangerous, unpredictable race. They sacrifice their captives in the cruellest way. But, like countless correspondents since, Sidonius' missive also attempts to buoy his friend's spirits. He calls Namatius a 'provident man' and so less likely to stumble into trouble. Sidonius also counts the young officer as fortunate because he 'follows the standard of a victorious people'—i.e. the Visigoths of King Euric. But Sidonius shows genuine concern as well. 'I pray you nonetheless to send me good news... and so remove the anxiety that fills my heart on your account.' Finally, again like many home-front writers of later times, he sends Namatius two books to read in his spare time.[1]

It is easy to imagine what Sidonius' preoccupations would have been at this time. King Euric's victories had brought about a tragedy that Catholic Gallo-Romans had feared for decades. The Visigoths had overwhelmed their opponents one by one, capturing a large part of Gaul. By 475 they were the dominant force in western Europe. Farther east, a mere boy sat on the imperial throne, and within a year he would be toppled by Odovacer. Sidonius' world was collapsing around him, and he knew it.

But for our story, the most significant thing is his sudden talk of Saxon raiding. Where only a few years before a whole British army had crossed this same Ocean, now it was infested with sea marauders—the first report of such activity since the 450s. *The Annals of Ulster* even speak of Saxon raids on Ireland at this same time.[2] The only possible explanation is some radical change in the situation in Britain.

An earlier letter from Sidonius may shed even more light on this. The good bishop refers to fighting near his home town of Clermont-Ferrand. Very significantly, however, he makes no mention of the siege of that place in 471, making it likely it was written before then. Indeed, the reported combat may even be connected with Arthur's 469 campaign.

Sidonius' letter is addressed to Faustus, the British-born bishop of Riez. Its tone is jocular. Sidonius gives what he thinks is a very witty description of his encounter with another Briton by the name of Riochatus. Months before, Faustus had sent Riochatus on an unspecified mission to Britain. But travel on the roads was dangerous. Because of the fighting, the Briton was forced to stay almost two months with Sidonius. Once it was safe to travel again Riochatus left for the coast, apparently in some haste. But then his host discovered that he was carrying books written by Faustus himself, 'to his dear Britons'. Among them was a learned discourse on religion and philosophy. Sidonius gives a comic description of his subsequent chase and 'capture' of Riochatus and the writings, depicting himself as a 'brigand' on the prowl for 'spiritual treasure'.[3] He even brought along copyists to take down the most salient points in Faustus' work. But this particular letter probably did not amuse the Riez bishop when he received it. Riochatus may have neglected to mention Faustus' books because the younger man was concerned with something far more important. In short, Faustus *may* have sent Riochatus to Britain not merely to deliver books, but for some other purpose.

The Welsh genealogies give us a clue as to what that purpose may have been. In the Jesus College genealogies we meet with a certain British ruler called Riagath. He is the son of Pascent, and therefore the grandson of Arthur; most likely he is identical to this Riochatus. It would, after all, be unsurprising for a younger member of a royal family to study under one of the most prestigious ecclesiastical figures in the west, one who was a fellow Briton to boot. It would also be unsurprising for a prince to return home when his country is in crisis. Taken together, Sidonius' two letters indicate that something very unusual was taking place across the Channel.

And this 'something' was beyond his imagination.

COUP

The failure of Arthur's campaign left thousands of soldiers stranded in Gaul. But the Saxons were the greatest seafarers of their day. They acted as Arthur's navy. They would have been in the best position by far to return quickly to their homes on the other side of the Channel. Many doubtless assumed that they would resume their old occupations as federates for the Proud Tyrant. But whatever their hopes, the key factor was that in the autumn of 469 many shiploads of hungry, defeated Saxons were sailing across the Channel for Britain. It is doubtful that the Britons gave them a hero's welcome.

Gildas, writing some 60 years after the event, says that the Saxon Revolt came about because the Britons failed to give the Saxons their food rations: their *annona*. On the face of it this appears to be merely a very unwise decision on the part of a few British bureaucrats. But there was much more to it than this. Arthur and most of the British portion of his army were stranded in Gaul. Conditions in Britain would have been unsettled, if not chaotic. The medieval writer Geoffrey of Monmouth, in his *History of the Kings of Britain*, asserts that Arthur's nephew Mordred seized the throne while the king was campaigning in Gaul. This could be dismissed as mere legend, for Geoffrey was writing some 600 years after the event. But all the same, once news of Arthur's defeat reached Britain, it would be only logical for the resentments of many Britons to come to a head. The country had been drained of resources to pay for a huge overseas expedition. News of its defeat meant that no Briton, high or low, would profit from it. Moreover, the expenses of the expedition could well have created food shortages in Britain. It may simply have been impossible to levy enough grain to feed the returning Saxons.

It is here that Ambrosius re-enters the picture. After the young man's initial victory over the Saxons in 458, his subsequent defeat on the Darent had placed him under a cloud. But the *Historia Brittonnum* tells us that Ambrosius' *alter ego*, Vortimer, fought a subsequent battle at Thanet: 'at the ford, in their language called *Eppisford*, though in ours *Rithergabail*.'[4]

The *Anglo-Saxon Chronicle* (*ASC*) adds some very significant details:

> '465— In this year Hengest and Aesc fought against the Welsh near *Wippedsfleot* and there slew twelve Welsh nobles...'[5]

This *Rithergabail* is *Rhyd yr afael* in later Welsh, and has the approximate meaning of the 'Ford of Afael'. This reported date of 465 would actually be 468, compensating for the three-year 'lag' the author has postulated for the early dates in the *Anglo-Saxon Chronicle*. This is suspiciously close to the date of Arthur's expedition to Gaul in 469. When we remember that a number of conflicting calendrical systems existed at this time (whose New Year could begin as late as September), the most likely conclusion is that this next battle between Saxon and Briton took place in the same year as Arthur's expedition, perhaps only a few months after his debacle in Gaul.[6]

Still, just how did Ambrosius come to be leading an army once more? The best explanation is that this part of Geoffrey of Monmouth's account is essentially true. Like Ambrosius' fictional counterpart Mordred, he had seized power in Arthur's absence. Once news of Arthur's defeat reached Britain, many Britons can only have seen this as an opportunity to rid themselves of both the Proud Tyrant and his pagan allies. More to the point, there is every likelihood that one or more of the twelve provincial rulers rallied to Ambrosius' dragon standard.

One tantalizing clue is a curious statement in an early Welsh work, the *Mabinogion*. Here Arthur's legendary lieutenant, Cai, is mentioned as betraying Arthur in his hour of need.[7] In another early Welsh work, the 'Pa Gur', we read: 'Before the chiefs of Emrais I saw Cai in haste.'[8] When we remember that Emrais is only the Welsh alternative for the name Ambrosius, it appears that Cai was remembered by subsequent generations for leading troops against Arthur in his hour of need. These may be only legends, but they provide a plausible explanation of how a coup in Britain could succeed.

We may suspect that one of Ambrosius' first commands would have been to suspend *annona* payments to the Saxons. Most Britons could only have applauded this. Some of the peripheral provinces of Britain may have stayed loyal. But the rich Lowland areas furnished the lion's share of the *annona*, and it is difficult to imagine that their citizens would have done anything save rally to a ruler who promised lower taxes and an end to Saxon domination. A whole generation had grown up with little or no memory of the barbarian threat. After twenty years of external peace the majority of Britons were eager to rid themselves of all Saxon influence.

But what of the Saxon princess, the 'pagan' that the *Historia Brittonnum* testifies the Proud Tyrant married? In the Arthurian legend Queen Guinevere plays a pivotal role in the tragedy. The first medieval treatment of this theme, Geoffrey of Monmouth's *History of the Kings of Britain*, tells us that Queen Guinevere betrayed Arthur by becoming the lover of Mordred, the king's 'nephew'.[9] We may dismiss this as fantasy. In an age of courtly love this would have seemed the most likely way that a queen could harm her king. But the much earlier *Welsh Triads* report something entirely different. Here we read of the 'three harmful blows of the island of Britain'. And the worst of these, the one that is alleged to have brought on the fratricidal battle of *Camlann*, is the blow that Mordred gives Arthur's queen,

Gwenhwyfar.[10] At the very least, this signified a public humiliation; at worst it may have involved her injury or death. But whatever Gwenhwyfar's fate, this can only have made any reconciliation between Arthur and Ambrosius impossible.

What happened next has been obscured for over a millennium and a half. Gildas' account of mercenaries rebelling due to non-payment of wages can explain neither the cause nor the success of the Saxon Revolt. But we have a clue as to what may really have happened. The key is the curious phrase in the *Historia Brittonnum*, which reports that Ambrosius, in his guise as Vortimer, 'expelled them [the Saxons] as far as the island of Thanet, and there three times shut them up and besieged them, attacking, threatening and terrifying them.' As we have seen, the first of these three 'sieges of Thanet' occurred after Ambrosius' battle at *Guollop/Aegelesthrep* in 458. Since that leader's second battle took place near Crayford and resulted in an ignominious flight to London, the best conclusion is that it was only in Ambrosius' third battle at *Wippedsfleot* (in Welsh 'the Ford of Afael') that he again 'expelled them as far as the island of Thanet.'

This tells us that Ambrosius' plans included much more than merely halting the Saxons' food rations. After he took power he ordered his cohorts east, to the Isle of Thanet (see Map 6). He was set on a fateful course. He was not just going to remove all Saxon *influence* from Britain. He was going to remove *all Saxons*.

'LIBERATION'

469. Autumn. Richborough. The final act had begun. The last struggle between Briton and sea barbarian would end where it had begun, near the old Roman fort on the edge of Ocean. This time, though, the roles were reversed. The raiders were British and the victims were Saxon. In the waning days of that momentous year, thousands of Germanic immigrants were streaming eastward along the pot-holed Roman road from Canterbury, bowed down by what little they could carry. All had but one goal: to reach the Wantsum Channel. Once there—provided they could somehow negotiate the fords—they might gain safety on Thanet.[11] After the first day, the oldest and the youngest began to flag, many falling by the wayside, too weak to go on. Soon mounted bands of *Weala* soldiers appeared, driving fugitives from the road into fields and ditches. Some Saxons fought back. Not every warrior had gone with Arthur to Gaul. But there was simply no way that warriors on foot could defend masses of fleeing civilians against a well-armed, mobile foe. The flight would end only when the fugitives reached Thanet—or died. Even in that place of refuge, no one knew whether the isle could hold out against the *Weala* for a second time.

Except for the refugees on the Isle of Thanet, only Britons remained in the old *civitas*. Ambrosius' 'liberation' had been accomplished. But now he faced a barrier that had defeated him ten years before: the Wantsum Channel. This time he must act decisively. The threat had to be extinguished once and for all.

Across the marshes and mudflats of the Wantsum, there was anxiety, even hysteria. Infants and the elderly continued to die. Women and children wept. All knew that very soon food would grow scarce, and after that, the *Weala* would begin their attack. But the situation was far from hopeless. More and more Saxon warriors were returning from Gaul. In all directions vessels large and small lay beached, ready for use. Local Saxons knew every bend of the long, winding channel. They knew the rhythm of the tides—when fords would be usable and when they might be treacherous. Of most significance, the Saxons were desperate, with their backs to the wall. Retreat was impossible. Either they won here, or they fell beneath the steel blades of the *Weala*.

There was one more factor at play, however. Ambrosius had received word that someone else was on Thanet, someone who could threaten all that he had achieved. It was someone who might tip the balance at a critical time, just as he had done so often in the past.

Arthur.

CATTEGIRN

Some may doubt this. After all, no one called Arthur (or Vortigern, or Riothamus) is mentioned in the accounts of this battle. But Arthur *was* at the encounter on the Wantsum. Moreover, the proof that he was there also clinches the argument that Arthur is identical to Gildas' Proud Tyrant. The key lies in Ambrosius' Battle List, found in the *Historia Brittonnum*. There we are told of the presence of Cattegirn (Arthur's mysterious 'fifth child') at *Rhyd yr Afael*, the 'Ford of Afael'. We have noted two curious features associated with this 'son'. The first is that his Brythonic name Cattegirn (or Cateyrn) is identical in meaning to *Dux Bellorum*, the Latin title Arthur bears in *his* Battle List. The second is a strange anomaly in the earliest genealogies for Vortigern's dynasty. In two of the Harleian genealogies the first three names are as follows:

Genealogy XXII	*Genealogy XXIII*
Catel Durnluc	Catell
Cattegirn	Cattegirn
Pascent	Brittu

In all other sources both Pascent and Brittu [also called 'Britu'] are listed as the sons of *Vortigern*. Unless some exceedingly strange activities were taking place within Vortigern's family, this can only mean that Cattegirn is identical to the Proud Tyrant—and to Arthur as well. That Cattegirn is somehow Vortigern's 'son' is only a ninth-century gloss designed to explain the contradictions between two pieces of information: Vortimer's Battle List, where the Proud Tyrant is called by a Brythonic equivalent of *Dux Bellorum* (Cattegirn), and the spurious Life of St Germanus found in the *Historia Brittonnum*, where the Proud Tyrant is called Vortigern. It would have been impossible for the *Historia*'s author to accept that the two were identical. Like Gildas, he is attempting to 'square the circle' when faced with two contradictory stories.[12]

It is also important to emphasize that the above is the earliest, and indeed the *only* hard evidence for the provenance of the story of Arthur and *Camlann*. The alternative explanations rest on dubious assertions that either (a) some unknown bard fabricated both Arthur and *Camlann* at an unspecified date, or (b) that the battle was fought at a time when Gildas tells us that Britain was at peace. Neither of these is impossible, but, in the absence of real evidence, they are highly unlikely.

That the 'Most Kingly' ruler who had been defeated in Gaul made his way to Thanet should really be no surprise. British history is filled with stories of 'kings over the water' who return to claim their thrones. Moreover, the last report of Arthur on the continent shows him to be very much alive, and withdrawing into Burgundian territory. He and his army may have been interned for a time. It is possible that the Burgundians even considered holding him for ransom. But once they learned that a new government ruled in Britain, any incentive to keep him was gone. A country unwilling or unable to feed its own soldiers was unlikely to ransom a defeated ruler.

Once free, Arthur would have easily found a ship to take him back to Britain. But this ship can only have been a *Saxon* ship. It can only have taken him to the nearest place where Saxons still ruled, and where he might find loyal followers—the Isle of Thanet.

To some this may seem something like blasphemy. Arthur is always seen as the great champion who battles *against* Saxon invaders. But really, he would have had no other choice. Ambrosius and the British landowners were destroying a system that had brought peace and stability to Britain for twenty years.

If Arthur did not act—and act decisively—the country would slip into chaos. Ambrosius and his supporters were the traitors, not he.

And if he had heard of the treatment meted out to his wife—or received a description of it from her own lips—anything short of Ambrosius' complete destruction was now unthinkable.

CAMLANN

Arthur cannot have been alone when he reached Thanet. His most loyal followers would have accompanied him on the road to the coast. How many of these were able to take ship to Thanet is impossible to say, but it is important to remember that *Camlann* is portrayed as a fratricidal encounter between Britons, not a battle with Saxons. A number of his *civitas* rulers would have followed him on his expedition. Many of the original men to hold these offices, men like Cunedda and Coel, were probably dead by now. But a new generation was taking power. One early Welsh poem speaks of the grave of Einyawn, the son of Cunedda, and that it was a 'disgrace' that he should have been slain. Another says that 'unmerited was the death of Cai'.[13] It may also be significant that Bedwyr, that other loyal follower of the earliest Welsh Arthur, does *not* seem to betray his master as Cai does. The number of Britons on Thanet may not have been great, but it included Arthur's best and most loyal commanders.

And this would have worried Ambrosius very much. His previous successes had come with ease. Now he faced hard choices. It was autumn. Ambrosius could still remember the disaster at *Noviomagus*/Crayford. The Saxon ships were free to bring in more men from across the Channel, both Saxon and Briton. They could outflank Ambrosius' force by sea. If the usurper waited, his new army would suffer the same fate as the four cohorts on the Darent in 459. Time was not Ambrosius' ally. He must act, and act decisively.

We know that in Roman times the Wantsum was midway between a stream and a marsh, and it can only have silted up even more by 469. Bede says that in his day it was fordable only in two places.[14] In view of this, the various names for this battle give us an insight into what happened next. The *'fleot'* element in *Wippedsfleot* is a Saxon word descriptive of a tidal stream. The place names Eppisford and *Rhyd yr Afael* ('The Ford of Afael') tell us that some sort of ford also played a part. Finally, the name *Camlann* may be highly significant. *Cam* in Welsh means 'crooked,', with an added connotation of 'unjust' or 'evil'. The *'lann'* element is more problematic—until we remember that there is a Welsh word, *'lannw'*, which means 'flood-tide'. Together, they give the idea of a 'treacherous flood-tide'.[15] When we recall that this is one of those occasions when Ambrosius 'besieged them, attacking, threatening and terrifying them', his next move is plain.

Ambrosius was going to cross the Wantsum.

BATTLE

The Welsh bards are unanimous in describing *Camlann* as a horrific encounter. Only seven men are reputed to have been left alive at the end of the day. The battle of *Wippedsfleot* is described as bringing on the death of no less than twelve British nobles, one of the most extravagant Saxon claims in the *Anglo-Saxon Chronicle*. And there are some very good reasons why losses would have been so high. If there were at most two fords, this would have drastically narrowed the frontage that Arthur and his Saxons had to defend. At the later battle of Maldon a handful of English warriors stood off a large Viking force under very similar circumstances.

The tide may also have played a crucial part in this encounter, for it is entirely possible that the fords were negotiable only during an ebb tide. Ambrosius' 'window of opportunity' may have been narrow. Finally, if the timing of the assault were dependent on the tide, this window may have been in the early morning or late evening, or even at night. Whatever the specific conditions, however, this would not be a battle in which British cavalry could play any part. It would be a head-on infantry encounter, with little room for manoeuvre by either side.

469. Autumn. Thanet. The Britons who marched out across this 'Ford of Afael' moved with uncertain steps. Mud clung to their shoes and ankles. At times the brackish water lapped up to their knees. It was cold. The chill autumn tide pricked their legs like wasp stings. Few could see beyond the screen of alders to their front. But already they could hear the Saxon lookouts raising the alarm. The water grew deeper, the mud more treacherous. Stumbling through the slippery muck, they formed a ragged line of battle. Ahead the cries grew louder. Slowly the dark tree line ahead resolved itself into ranks of enemy Saxons and Britons. Ambrosius' men began to make out individual faces—faces of men who had fought beside them; men with whom they had shared good wine in a hall, snug from the winter cold; men whom they had once trusted with their lives. Now, however, as the rain of missiles began, nothing but a deep hatred burned in their breasts. Ambrosius had explained it all the night before: these pagans had betrayed their hosts; had become their allies only to rob them all the better. If they were not defeated, Britain would die.

A fury just as bright burned in the hearts of the Saxon warriors. The *Weala* had turned on the federates in their most vulnerable hour. They had killed women and children, had destroyed the good life the sea peoples had made in Britain. Now the Saxons must win or die. As at Towton, a battle in a later civil conflict, men would fight at this ford with a ferocity more intense than they had ever displayed against foreign enemies.

Ambrosius' men reached the shore. There was no way to outflank the Saxons, and very soon the struggle degenerated into a shoving match. Knots of men moved forward, collided with the shield wall, inflicting deadly blows to head, abdomen and legs. Slowly the Saxon side gave way, step by step, but inflicting wounds just as terrible on the attackers. Men grew exhausted from fighting in the filthy water. The wounded stumbled back, clutching broken heads and sliced stomachs. Those who fell before reaching dry land drowned in only a few feet of water. Gaps appeared in the ranks of both sides. Leaders rushed forward to close them, recklessly exposing themselves to a rain of missiles. A sudden breakthrough could lead first to panic, swiftly followed by disaster.

Time passed. More and more men were wounded. The muddy water took on a brick-red tinge. By now the front-rankers could barely wield their weapons. Some tried to move back to let those behind fill the gaps. Others simply died where they stood. Arthur's line shuddered at each assault, but held. 'Men of the Wall' from both sides sank down in the thick Thanet mud.

More time passed. More men grew exhausted. Now even holding a shield was difficult. Rumours spread of slain leaders, both Saxon and Briton. Many of Ambrosius' men were still stuck in the rear, unable to help, but exposed to a storm of arrows. Those at the front just stood in their ranks, silent. Only the hardiest continued to move forward, crying out incoherent threats and curses as their blades flashed in the morning sun. But soon these shouts turned to cries of alarm. The brackish water was beginning to rise. The tide was turning.

Ambrosius now faced a terrible choice: to try one last push, or to retreat back through the rising flood. Precisely what he decided is impossible to know. But the rearmost men may have made the decision for him. Whatever orders were given, first a trickle, then a torrent of fugitives turned and headed for the mainland. The whole column began to disintegrate. Arthur sounded the advance.

It is here that we begin to understand the reason why *Camlann/Wippedsfleot* was remembered as such a horrific fight. Men who had been battling for many hours found themselves splashing through ever-deepening water. To retreat in such conditions meant that very soon the insurgents lost all cohesion. Retreat turned to rout. Many died from blows as they ran. Others simply drowned, too weak to struggle against the rising waters. By the time Ambrosius' men gained the mainland, they were a rabble in full flight.

Doubtless more than a few of Arthur's men also died in this pursuit. The Roman military writer Vegetius echoes Sun Tzu in decreeing that a defeated force should always be provided with an escape route.[16] Cornered men can turn and fight with unexpected ferocity. And it is somewhere on the mainland side of the Wantsum that the unthinkable happened. Arthur was wounded—and mortally.

This may seem like mere speculation. But the *Historia Brittonnum*'s account of the battle is quite explicit: 'there fell... Vortigern's son Cateyrn.'[17] Not only did the *Dux Bellorum* fight at *Camlann*; he *fell* in this battle. And it is here that history and legend become inextricably intertwined. In pre-modern times the majority of battlefield deaths occurred not outright, but later, when wounds turned septic or vital organs ceased to function. If such were the case with Arthur, conflicting rumours would have spread from the very first evening of the battle. Some spoke of his death. Others stoutly argued that he lived. In the coming days and months, as civil war turned to ethnic genocide, a forlorn hope always remained among the Britons that the man who had once stopped the fratricidal conflict might reappear and bring peace once more. Even the death by heavenly fire of Arthur's *alter ego*, Vortigern, speaks to a mystery surrounding the Proud Tyrant's end. In the decades and centuries to come, as Saxon pressure pushed the Britons ever more to the north and west, this idea was transformed into the myth of the great champion who could not die, who might someday return and restore Britain to its former glory. As an early Welsh poem confidently proclaims: 'a mystery to the world, the grave of Arthur.'[18]

That Arthur did not die outright explains something else as well. The legend that Arthur was carried to the Isle of Avalon for healing by three queens is most likely a conflation of Iron Age and Roman legends about the three Goddesses, and the 'Old God' in exile.[19] But it is also cold, hard logic that at the end of that terrible day the most likely place a badly wounded man would be taken is to the nearest healers—and these can only have been among the Saxon non-combatants evacuated to Thanet. Moreover, this name 'Afael' may not simply signify a path across the Wantsum. *Rhyd yr Afael* may actually mean that it is the ford *to* Afael: that is, that Afael was an alternative name for the Isle of Thanet.[20] Here Arthur would have been taken, and here he most certainly died. Later storytellers would embroider this, transforming it into the mythical voyage found in medieval literature. But the name would remain: the name of an island that literally vanished away. In coming centuries and in different languages it would alter, becoming a name with which we are much more familiar.

Avalon.

REVOLT

Gildas' account of what happened next is apocalyptic—the Britons' reward for decades of vice and impiety.

'For the fire of vengeance, justly kindled by former crimes, spread from sea to sea, fed by the hands of our foes in the east, and did not cease, until... it reached the other side of the island, and dipped its red and savage tongue in the western ocean.'[21]

This rampage was not just the product of British vice and impiety, however. It was the direct result of Ambrosius' actions.

Instead of destroying the Saxons, he had only enraged them. They remembered their destroyed homes and fields. They remembered the women and children who had died while Ambrosius was 'attacking, threatening and terrifying them'. And with Arthur dead or dying, there was nothing to restrain their fury.

Gildas continues his tale of British woe:

> 'Some, therefore, of the miserable remnant, being taken in the mountains, were murdered in great numbers; others, constrained by famine, came and yielded themselves to be slaves forever to their foes, running the risk of being instantly slain, which truly was the greatest favour that could be offered them; some others passed beyond the seas with loud lamentations... Others, committing the safeguard of their lives, which were in continual jeopardy, to the mountains, precipices, thickly wooded forests, and to the rocks of the seas (albeit with trembling hearts), remained still in their country.'[22]

This—finally—explains why Gildas says nothing about British resistance, only of flight or captivity. After *Camlann*, effective resistance would have been impossible, *if most of the British portion of Arthur's army were either dead at* Camlann *or marooned in Gaul*. British civilians who attempted to resist would have been fatally short of training, weapons and organization. The vengeful Saxons would have had an unbeatable advantage. Their well-honed battle skills would have enabled them to brush aside those few Britons (and loyal Saxons) still able to bear arms. The Saxon *cyuls* would have had access via rivers to vast tracts of Lowland Britain, pillaging at will. The spoil must have been enormous.

The Revolt fatally sundered the nation. But the chasm it produced was not just between Saxon and Briton. Gildas tells us that in the coming years conflict *between* Britons was far more prevalent than conflict with the Saxons.[23] The rivalry between

Ambrosius and Arthur inflicted deep wounds on the British psyche, wounds that had not healed after half a century. The abuse that Gildas heaps on the five kings of his day—many of whose grandfathers had been loyal servants of Arthur—shows that the bitter legacy of *Camlann* lived on. To Gildas, and to all the other high-born Britons who had lost their lands to the Saxons, the Proud Tyrant *and his council* were traitors. By allying with the Saxons they had brought ruin to Britain. They were worse than their pagans allies.

But in those areas where the Revolt did not penetrate—in Dyfed, in Ceredigion, among the 'Men of the North'—Arthur remained the great saviour, the *Dux Bellorum* who had won twelve amazing victories. Here the villain was not Arthur, but his younger rival. Under the name of Medrawt he became the great traitor who had brought about the Fall of Britain.[24] The two views could never be reconciled, until Geoffrey of Monmouth combined the story of Arthur and the story of the Proud Tyrant into his 'history' of the kings of Britain.

RESURGENCE

Even after *Camlann*, however, Ambrosius was far from finished. The Saxons could not pillage for ever. Eventually they had to return to their ruined settlements and somehow put things right. This gave the Britons a breathing space. Large areas were now either under direct Saxon control or threatened by Saxon incursions. With Arthur and many of his closest advisers dead, Gildas tells us that the choice to lead this rump state fell to none other than Ambrosius.

Ambrosius seems to have learned something from his debacle, and followed a strategy of reconciliation. He sought to co-opt Arthur's offspring by granting a kingdom to Arthur's son Pascent.[25] Even Ambrosius' Brythonic name, Vortimer, is similar to the one by which later generations would call Arthur: Vortigern. The 'humble man' even produced a Battle List of his own. True, the list contained only four battles, compared with Arthur's twelve, and some were embarrassing failures. But all the same, these initiatives cast him in the same heroic mould as his predecessor. They proclaimed to the British survivors that Ambrosius would be the same protector that Arthur had been.

Reading Gildas in isolation, one might assume that Ambrosius afterward carried on a kind of partisan struggle, *a la* Alfred the Great. But the *Anglo-Saxon Chronicle* suggests that, on the contrary, Ambrosius bided his time. For eight years he quietly husbanded his strength, allowing his ruined country to recover. He may even have enticed Saxons from the Upper Thames and East Anglia to join him.

And in the year 476 he made his move. In the *Historia Brittonnum* we read of his third and last attempt to expel Hengest and his Saxons from Kent. Again we find that he 'besieged them' at Thanet. Again his army almost certainly engaged in the ethnic cleansing now *de rigueur* for both sides. Eventually, we are told, the Saxons 'fled to their keels and were drowned as they clambered aboard them like women.'[26] Whether this is anything more than a description of the usual evacuation to Thanet is impossible to tell. But whatever the extent of this victory, it was too little, and, for Ambrosius, too late. Like the Patrician Ricimer, he died soon afterwards, unable to turn temporary good fortune into lasting advantage. Worse still, no other Briton seems to have had the stature or ability to take his place. Hengest's Saxons returned to the mainland.

This time they would stay for ever.

RIOCHATUS

It is easy to see the fifth-century contest between these two peoples as a zero-sum game. At any given time the Saxons gain a certain expanse of territory, and the Britons lose a corresponding amount. But there is another way to look at it. In a real sense, both sides were the losers in this conflict. The events of 469 brought about not just the fall of Arthur's kingdom, but the end of Late Roman Britain. And no figure brings this home more than Riochatus. Sidonius ends his story about the young cleric just as Riochatus is ready to take ship for Britain. If he is identical to the Riagath of the Jesus College genealogies, he returned home to succeed his father Pascent in one corner of the old diocese. Precisely how Riochatus obtained passage across Ocean is unknown, but it was almost certainly in a Saxon ship. Moreover, like so many travellers before him, he may have landed near Richborough, and so taken the old Roman Road to London.

From the moment Riochatus set foot on British soil, however, he would have realized that his world had quite vanished away. As he travelled down the road to London, Faustus' book clutched tightly to his chest, he would have seen burnt farmsteads and fresh graves—the devastation wrought by two vengeful armies. The only remaining inhabitants were Saxons. The Britons had either fled to the west or been killed. Indeed, at times he may have been in real danger. More than a few Saxons wanted to kill every *Weala* in sight.

Very quickly, too, Riochatus understood the larger implications of this new reality. A wedge had been driven between the two peoples, a wedge far greater than any that separated Roman and barbarian on the continent. In Gaul, Arian and Catholic Christians were divided by doctrinal differences. In Britain the issue was not simply alternative forms of the same religion, but Christianity versus paganism. In Gaul barbarian dynasties ruled over subordinate but protected Roman subjects. In Britain, two ethnic groups sought not simple domination, but wholesale extermination of one another. In Gaul Germans used Latin culture and learning as props to their regimes. In Britain, Saxons rejected anything *Weala*, while the Britons despised all the works of the pagan 'gallows-thieves'. In no other part of the former western empire would the division be so stark, nor the chasm so deep.

And as Riochatus clutched Faustus' book to his breast he would have realized that it too was irrelevant to this new reality. His mentor had attempted to use the subtlest logic and the greatest erudition to synthesize Greek philosophy and Christian dogma. But powerful churchmen in both Gaul and Britain would soon condemn Faustus' work as heresy. Among Saxons it would be regarded as little more than a repository of *Weala* black magic. This book that had taken so much effort to compose and copy, this precious book that Riochatus had guarded with his very life, had no place in the new Britain.

But most of all, Riochatus would have pondered how Britain had been brought to this pass. He recalled tales of the *Dux Bellorum*'s battles, when the fate of Britain had teetered on a knife-edge. He remembered how the diocese had been saved, and how Arthur had made it secure from all enemies. He recalled the friends he had grown up with, both Saxon and Briton, friends with whom he had sworn loyalty at the Roman round tables. He remembered the 'time of plenty', when learning and literature had blossomed again. It had enabled him to pursue a different path from that of his father's generation: a path that had led to quiet study under one of the greatest teachers of the age. Finally, Riochatus recalled the grand, fatal decision to send a British army across Ocean.

Each of these things, both good and bad, had come about because of one man. While the rest of the western empire disintegrated into feuding barbarian kingdoms, Arthur had led the Britons to victory. For the very first time he had united the whole of the diocese under a single native ruler. But this same man had lost control of events, had allowed hatred and suspicion to tear his realm apart. The result was a collapse more total than any in Britain's recorded history. The Britain of Roman times was no more. One age had ended and another had begun. As

Riochatus contemplated the man responsible for all of this, he could feel pride—and infinite loss.

So would every generation that heard this great, tragic tale.

EPILOGUE

In the preceding pages the author has provided what he contends is the best available historical narrative for fifth century Britain. He has demonstrated how all the evidence suggests that a single military ruler dominated Britain for some two decades. Known by such names as the Proud Tyrant and Riothamus, this leader's reorganization of the diocese into subordinate kingdoms had a lasting effect down to our own time. Most crucially, the evidence for this leader has been in our earliest sources all along, but unrecognised by previous observers. That one of this ruler's names happens to have been Arthur helps to round out our picture of him, but is important more for literary than historical purposes.

Scholars will doubtless dispute nearly all of this. And their reasoning is understandable, and, up till now, even praiseworthy. The sources *do* appear to contradict themselves on a number of fundamental points, making it seem likely that some or all of the data is fatally flawed. But the author has demonstrated that none of the earliest sources were either fabricated or irrevocably distorted. Any mistakes their authors committed were made for quite logical reasons, reasons that are completely transparent. *All* of the authentic data can be recovered and fitted into a coherent, consistent chronology—a chronology that provides us with the first narrative history for fifth century Britain.

It is certainly true that sober scholarship has advanced elaborate theories that 'prove' that these early writers were pursuing agendas that had little to do with history as we know it. The author has dealt with these assertions in detail in the notes and appendices. But he must note overall that the methodology used to arrive at such conclusions is often a little puzzling. An elaborate scenario of how a particular author 'could' have fabricated or misread a piece of evidence gives us no confidence that he actually did so. A scenario without hard evidence is quite simply a story. It belongs to the realm of literature, not history. The only certain way to refute bad evidence is with better evidence—and the current rejection of practically all the earliest evidence makes this impossible.

The simple truth is that *any* piece of evidence in isolation can be made to seem unlikely. If we had a similar dearth of knowledge regarding France in the eighteenth and nineteenth centuries, say only a citation of the Terror and of the accession of Charles X, any account of Napoleon's invasion of Russia would seem just as doubtful as Arthur's Battle List. In the same way brief citations about Germany in 1919 and 1951 would force us to relegate reports of 'Operation Barbarossa' to the realm of fantasy. The problem is not that the sources are wrong. It is simply that we do not have enough of them.

It might be thought that this rigorous approach as least protects us from making egregious errors. But it is here that we encounter a very strange phenomenon. The earliest sources are rejected on the basis of hypotheses that incorporate the 'battle sagas' of Hengist and Horsa, unevidenced consular tables, Arthur as a fictional 'clone' of Joshua, and phantom fifth century Breton kingdoms. There is certainly nothing wrong with postulating the possible existence of any of these. But what does seem a little puzzling is that this postulated evidence is so often accepted as incontrovertible proof that sources like the *Historia Brittonum* and the *Anglo-Saxon Chronicle* have no basis in fifth century reality. By some curious alchemy data for which there is no certain proof invalidate citations written down in black and white. Just what part of this conforms to the word 'rigour' is far from clear.

Perhaps most strange in regard to 'rigour' is the way that an observer's 'scepticism' about a piece of evidence is accepted as proof that it is somehow invalid. But scepticism in itself is *not*

266

evidence; it is simply a mental state, and no one's mental state, however erudite they may be, can be taken as proof that something did or did not exist 1500 years ago. Indeed, it is well to remember that the technical term for rejection of *all* evidence is not 'scepticism'. It is something called 'solipsism'. The latter is undeniably the most 'rigorous' of all modes of thought. But its use makes any academic activity impossible.

If there is so little real evidence that the sources are fabricated or fatally flawed, it then becomes necessary to ask why this assertion is advanced so often. It is certainly *not* due to bad faith on the part of any scholar or group of scholars. Indeed, what is most striking is that 'scepticism' of the sources is far from just a scholarly phenomenon. It underpins *every* current hypothesis for fifth century Britain, from the most sceptical to the most 'Arthurian'. The 'rigorous' school requires that the *Historia* and the ASC be 'inadmissible evidence'. Various authors who conflate the continental report of Britain's fall in 441 with the Revolt depend on Gildas being wrong about the date of the Appeal to Aetius. The numerous 'Arthurian' enthusiasts postulating a late fifth century Arthur require that Gildas be wrong about the peace that the wise cleric testifies has lasted for generations. The simple fact is that *every* piece of evidence for this period is unwelcome to some point of view. Moreover, given the choice between saying nothing and choosing to discard some source that seems to contradict better evidence, it is quite understandable that most observers have chosen the latter option. That this has resulted in numerous ingenious efforts to eliminate inconvenient data is something no one can have foreseen.

The author has tried a different approach. Instead of looking for contradictions, he has attempted to find underlying relationships between the earliest sources. At each stage he has used the scientific method to determine the most likely of several alternatives. It is true that at some specific points in his overall hypothesis plausible alternatives exist. But the real test of such alternatives is whether or not they can be put into a larger framework. Can the proposed alternative be combined with other data to give us a coherent picture of this era - or does it just create more contradictions? If the alternative argues that a piece of evidence is flawed, does this give us a plausible, verifiable explanation for the provenance of the entire source - or is it only a clever means of getting rid of inconvenient data? Good hypotheses tell us something about observable reality. Their ultimate goal is to answer important questions about an era, as the author has attempted to do with this data set. In most other disciplines, postulating ingenious reasons not to use evidence is seldom a high priority.

The author has presented a comprehensive explanation for *all* of the earliest sources for fifth century British history. Alternatives to this certainly do exist. But it is important to note that the only fair way to evaluate the author's hypothesis is to compare it with an alternative just as comprehensive. Any comparison with the plethora of piecemeal efforts of the last thirty years will only lead to confusion. Also, any fair evaluation requires that the standard for evidence be a little more substantial than unverifiable hypotheses about the religious or dynastic obsessions of writers who died thirteen centuries ago.

It has been over three decades since most of these sources were declared 'inadmissible', and the time for a careful, dispassionate re-examination of this data set is long overdue. In the author's opinion, the only way forward is to develop comprehensive hypotheses that explain *all* the earliest evidence; in essence to aspire to a 'unified field theory' for fifth century Britain. If this book facilitates this process in any significant way, its author will be more than satisfied.

APPENDIX I

A CHRONOLOGY FOR LATE ANTIQUE BRITAIN

[Non-British events shown in italics]

—383 General Maximus defeats a joint Irish-Pictish raiding force.

Maximus revolts in Britain; *leads usurpation against the emperor Gratian. The latter is slain.*

—388 *Theodosius the Great defeats and kills Maximus;* retakes Britain.
(From this year the *Historia Brittonum* dates its 'forty years of fear'.)

—395 *Death of Theodosius the Great. Beginning of joint reign of Arcadius and Honorius, with neither counted as senior emperor. General Stilicho claims that Theodosius entrusted him with the care of the two young emperors.*

Repulse of seaborne raids by Saxons, Picts, and Irish.

—407 Constantine III's usurpation.

Gaul invaded by Vandals, Alans, and Suebi.

Seaborne raids by Saxons, Picts, and Irish increase. True beginning of 'forty years of fear'.

—408 *Death of Stilicho.*

—410 *Visigoths sack Rome.*
Large seaborne incursion by Saxons.

—411 Death of Constantine III. Britain isolated from Rome.
—418 Constantius reasserts control over both sides of the Straits of Dover. Raids abate.

—421 Constantius withdraws Roman forces in Britain to begin preparations for war with the eastern empire. *Marshal Castinus suffers a military disaster in Spain.*

Saxons begin to occupy what is now East Anglia.

—423 *Theodosius the Younger becomes senior emperor on the death of Honorius—28 years after death of Theodosius the Great.*

—429 Saint Germanus helps repel a raid by Saxons and Picts, probably originating from East Anglia.

—434 *Saxon raid on Ireland.*

—441 Saxon raids from East Anglia force British populations in cities along the Thames to flee westward. London falls. *Gallo-Romans believe Britain has fallen to the Saxons.*

—446 The British elite unsuccessfully petition for aid from Aetius, in the year of his third consulship.

Arthur is chosen as commander-in-chief of British resistance. Some sources later report this as his accession date.

Arthur defeats Saxons at the Battle of *Guinnion*, possibly *Corinium*/Cirencester.

A British expedition to the north defeats Picts near the Caledonian Forest, forcing the Picts to retreat northward.

—449 *Bede's date for the accession of Valentinian III as senior Roman emperor. (Also noted in* Annals of Ulster.)

—450 *Actual date of the accession of Valentinian III as senior Roman emperor.*

Arthur retakes London. He replaces local British leaders with his military subordinates, anointing them as 'kings'. He adopts the regnal name of Riothamus, 'Most Kingly'.

Peace is made with the Saxons. Those who dwell on the Thames agree to assume federate status, and eventually become known as the *Gewissei*. A 'Time of Plenty' begins in areas still controlled by the Britons.

A naval armada made up of Irish and (probably) Picts attacks Chester.

Repulsed, the barbarian force makes a second landing in an estuary, on what is now the Brue River (*Traeth Tribruit*).

Marching up the Fosse Way, the invaders are defeated by a combined British and Saxon force just south of Bath, on 'the Badonic Hill'.

—452 *The second date in the* Annals of Ulster *for the accession of Valentinian III as senior Roman emperor.*

Arthur hires 'Jutish' mercenaries—possible enemies of the Saxons—to guard the Isle of Thanet and the Isle of

Wight—69 years before the consulship of Valerius in 521.

—455 *Vandals sack Rome. Gallo-Roman general Avitus made emperor, then deposed.*

—458 Ambrosius Aurelianus wins a battle against insurgents, made up of Saxons led by Hengest. Ambrosius besieges Thanet.

—459 Hengest defeats Ambrosius near *Noviomagus*, threatening London; Arthur grants Kent to the Saxons, bringing ten more year of peace. Arthur marries a Saxon.

—467 *The Byzantine Anthemius becomes western emperor.*

—468 *Great naval expedition against Vandals in North Africa is defeated.*

—469 Arthur leads a costly joint British-Saxon expedition to Gaul, transported in mostly Saxon ships. The force is defeated by the Visigoths. Most of the British elements are marooned in Gaul.

Saxons return in their ships to a country unwilling or unable to feed its federates. Ambrosius seizes power. He leads the remainder of the British levies against a force on Thanet made up of Saxons and loyal Britons, headed by Arthur. The latter is slain, and the only major professional British military force on the island is effectively destroyed.

The Saxons make an unopposed rampage through much of Lowland Britain, displacing most of the British elite.

—471 Saxon raid on Ireland and British areas bordering 'the

western ocean'.

—476 Ambrosius leads a successful counter-attack that temporarily displaces many Saxons from Kent. He dies soon afterward.
Last Roman emperor deposed. Odovacer becomes ruler of Rome.

Time of general peace between Saxons and Britons ensues.

—494 Birth of Gildas—44 years after the accession of Valentinian III as senior emperor.

—521 Consulship of Valerius—69 years after *Adventus* of Hengest in 452. True date of Cerdic's accession.

—529 Consulship of Decius. True date of Cerdic's victory at *Cerdicesford/Cerdicesseora.*

—535 Worldwide global cooling creates famine in Britain. Composition of *De Excidio* unlikely to be after this date (because no mention by Gildas).

Possible death of King Maglocunus from relapsing fever, or 'Yellow Plague'.

—537 Possible death of Cerdic from the same disease.

—547 Bubonic plague from Byzantine world reaches Britain.

—570 Possible death of Gildas.

APPENDIX II

HAPPY BIRTHDAY, GILDAS!

One of the most enduring bits of Arthuriana is the date Gildas gives for the Battle of *Badon*. With the exception of the quotations about Arthur, no other piece of evidence associated with fifth-century Britain has created so much interest—or so much controversy. This is understandable. Just what Gildas meant in his 'forty-four years' citation (more precisely, forty-three years and one month) is of critical importance to the study of this era. A false explanation can lead only to endless confusion. A correct explanation has the potential to transform our whole image of fifth-century Britain.

A host of ingenious solutions have been advanced to explain what Gildas really meant by the battle of *Badon*, forty-four years, and his birth date. And this is quite understandable, if we look at a literal translation of the Latin text:

> From that time on, now the citizens, now the enemy, were victorious... right up until the year of the siege of Mount *Badon*, almost the last, not the least, slaughter of the villains; and this the forty-fourth year begins (as well I know) with one month already elapsed, which is also of my birth.[1]

This may seem confusing—because it is. The above passage gives some idea of the difficulties scholars have had in unravelling what Gildas really meant in this crucial passage. The most accepted reading would have us believe that *Badon* occurred forty-three years and one month before the writing of

Gildas' *De Excidio*, and that Gildas himself was born in the very same month as the fateful encounter between Briton and barbarian. The great German scholar Mommsen certainly agreed with this rendition, and even inserted words not in the Latin text to show how the 'correct' original would have looked. There are, however, more than a few difficulties in reading it this way. First, why does Gildas mention his own birth date in the first place? Why not simply say 'forty-three years and one month ago', or give a consular date? Indeed, is not the very precision of this date somewhat suspect? In all the rest of Gildas' narrative he gives neither the name nor the date for *any* encounter between Saxon and Briton; yet here he gives not only the name, but the date to within a month. Also, isn't it more than a little suspicious that he is born within a month of the most famous battle in post-Roman Britain? This raises our suspicions that Gildas' '*Badon* birthday' may not be as straightforward as it seems.

Since many talented linguists have studied the wording of this text and failed to come up with a definitive explanation, a better approach might be to examine other early examples of insular timekeeping to see if we can find any parallels. The Venerable Bede, arguably one of the most intelligent scholars ever to investigate this problem, made a different kind of calculation for the date of *Badon*. He asserted that the battle took place some forty-four years after the *Adventus Saxonum*, the coming of his own people to Britain in about the year 450.[2] This would give a date of about 494—a date that most adherents to Gildas '*Badon* nativity' could accept. This, however, does not lend any greater credence to the usual interpretation of Gildas, although it does introduce a piece of information that the good British cleric neglects to provide: a date for when the Saxons actually 'arrived' in Britain.

It might be useful to take a closer look here at what Bede says, not because his is necessarily the true date for *Badon*, but because the *system* he uses to calculate this date is of interest.

Bede uses the *Adventus* as his base year. This is understandable. The Anglo-Saxons could with some logic see the year of their arrival in Britain as a kind of 'Year One'. Calculating a date for *Badon* from such a memorable date makes sense. In fact, we see Bede use the *Adventus* in precisely this way with regard to three other important early insular dates, most prominently the arrival of St Augustine to Britain in 596, 'about' 150 years after the *Adventus*.[3]

But it is important to note that nowhere does Gildas actually say that Badon occurred forty-four years after the *Adventus*. Indeed, Bede himself was actually not certain when this event occurred. In his *History of the English Church and People*, the only firm date he gives is a Late Roman date, the first year that Valentinian III reigned as western emperor with the newly crowned eastern emperor Marcian, i.e. the year 450. Bede then tells us that 'in his [Marcian's] time' the Angles or Saxons came to Britain.[4] But since Marcian reigned until 457, Bede's assertion could place *Badon* anywhere between the years 494 and 501. So what made Bede use such an 'elastic' year as his base date?

There has long been speculation that Bede had other information about *Badon* that has since been lost. This is possible. But the answer may be much simpler. The key lies in this date of 450. This is actually an important date from Late Antiquity, for it is highlighted in a number of chronicles from this period. The reason is simple: it is what is called a 'regnal year', in this case signifying the year when Valentinian III became senior emperor upon the death of his eastern colleague, Theodosius the Younger.[5] It is also important to remember that Bede was well aware of 'regnal years', and Late Roman timekeeping in general. He uses regnal years as the main benchmarks in his *Chronica Majora*. He also correctly guesses that Gildas is using that other means of Late Roman timekeeping, consular dates, when the latter reports about the consul 'Agitius': this is simply Aetius, the consul for the year 446. Moreover, the precision with which Gildas gives his interval can only mean that he is reporting his nativity in terms of *two exact dates* separated by *exactly* forty-three years and one month. His birth date can have nothing to with an *Adventus* date about which even Bede was uncertain. Bede thus is very likely to have seen a man of Late Antiquity as using either the consular system or the regnal system. Since no consul (or even name) is associated with the 'forty-four years', Bede can only have concluded that Gildas was using some regnal year in his timekeeping. So the best explanation for what we see is that Bede believed that Gildas was calculating his 'Year One' not from the *Adventus*, but from an exact Late Roman date that all Romano-Britons would have been well aware of: the year 450, the beginning of Valentinian III's reign as senior emperor. Naturally, for the Anglo-Saxon Bede the *Adventus* was the more important event, and he used it both here and in other calculations to unify his chronology.[6] But the 'Year One' that Bede believed Gildas was using is the very precise regnal date of 450.

Like many others since, Bede then appears to have interpreted Gildas' very convoluted sentence to mean that the wise cleric was born in the 'year of *Badon*'. It is important, however, to note that this is never explicitly stated in the text of the *De Excidio*. The relationship between Gildas' nativity and the forty-three years and one month is ambiguous in the extreme, and countless studies have come to very different, mutually exclusive conclusions.

We might hope that other early sources would resolve this ambiguity. The *Annales Cambriae*, for one, actually gives us a hard and fast date for *Badon*:

> 516—The Battle of *Badon*, in which Arthur carried the cross of our Lord Jesus Christ for three days and three nights on his shoulders, and the Britons were the victors.

537—The Battle of *Camlann*, in which Arthur and Medrawt fell.[7]

Unfortunately, practically no one accepts 516 as the date of *Badon*. Even those who place Arthur at the beginning of the sixth century would consider it as much too late. First of all, it is at odds with Bede's earlier report of a battle of *Badon* in 494–501. Moreover, Gildas was composing the *De Excidio* at the very same time as this alleged battle, and he makes no mention of anyone called Arthur, or even of any battles. At the time of his writing (in the 520s or 530s) the Britons seem to have been at peace with the Saxons for decades.[8] But the two dates are related to each other in some way, and the most likely explanation is that the original source for them indicated that *Camlann* was fought two decades *after* the battle of *Badon*. This has an important implication for the calendrical system used in fifth and sixth-century Britain: in at least one case in early British timekeeping, *Badon* was counted as a kind of 'Year One'.

The above analysis appears to put Gildas, the *Annales*, and Bede's reading of Gildas at loggerheads. The dates seem wildly out of synch, and appear to be using completely different systems of timekeeping. But is this really so? It might be useful to strip away the very ambiguous verbiage in Gildas' baroque passage. If we do, we are left with but three pieces of genuine information: a statement that the battle of *Badon* was fought on some date; an exact *interval* of forty-three years and one month; and the statement that Gildas was born on some date. Moreover, the fact that Gildas emphasizes that he knows this date so well may be very significant. Bede appears to think that Gildas was using the regnal year of 450 in his passage. But the wise cleric may not have been the only Briton to see this date as significant. Indeed, it is very likely that *everyone* in Late Antique Britain was aware of this date, and would have found it convenient to date many other events from it.

We have seen how the *Annales Cambriae* appear to use

Badon as their base date. Bede appears to believe that Gildas' base date for his nativity is the regnal year of 450. The two systems seem contradictory, but they may actually provide the key to the solution. The base dates used by *both* Bede/Gildas and the *Annales Cambriae* may really be different sides of the same coin. In short, the best explanation for what Gildas is saying is simply to read the three pieces of information in order. Thus, (a) the year of the battle of *Badon* was followed by (b) an *interval* of forty-three years and one month, at the end of which occurred (c) Gildas' nativity. In other words, the wise cleric was born in the first month of 494, forty-three years and one month *after 450*, the date all Britons memorialized as the year of the battle of *Badon*. Indeed, *every other person* in Late Antique Britain would have known this date—it was the base date from which they calculated *their own* nativities.

It is important to note, however, that 450 may no more be an exact date for *Badon* than it is for the *Adventus*. This is a citation that has a *calendrical* and not a historical significance. Just as the *Anno Domini* date for our own 'Year One' is not the date of Christ's birth, so 450 may just be the regnal year nearest in time to the date of *Badon*. For Gildas and his contemporaries, the main object was accurate timekeeping—*not* the transmission of accurate historical data to later generations.

This simple calculation resolves most of the anomalies currently found in the chronology for fifth-century Britain. It is the best explanation for why Gildas mentions this, and only this battle. It also tells us why he is so certain of its date. Just as most people in the world today know the traditional date of Christ's birth, so most fifth-century Britons would have known the traditional date of the battle of *Badon*. Further, if Gildas was writing in the 520s or 530s he would have been in at least his mid-twenties. This is a perfectly reasonable age to have acquired the erudition he displays—and the firm opinions he expounds about his world and its relationship to the Divine. His death date of 570 in the *Annales Cambriae* would also give him a lifetime of 'three-score and ten'—a plausible age for a respected ascetic monk to attain.

Finally, this would explain the strange way in which Gildas presents *Badon* in his narrative. He first relates the deeds of Ambrosius Aurelianus, but when he comes to *Badon*, he gives no clear indication as to whether or not Ambrosius had anything to do with this battle.[9] Later writers have seized on this reticence to 'prove' that the real victor of *Badon* was Arthur, and not Ambrosius. If we are talking about the military leader who came to be called the Proud Tyrant, in one sense they are entirely correct. But by Gildas' time such an admission was unthinkable. Also unthinkable in a sixth-century Britain beset by Saxons was the idea that anyone but Germanic invaders had been defeated at this greatest of victories. Still, Gildas and his contemporaries had no firm evidence that Ambrosius was present at *Badon*, or even that it was the last encounter fought against Saxons. Significantly, what sixth-century Britons did *not* do was fabricate a legend that made Ambrosius the victor of the 'last battle'—a rather telling comment on their standards of truth. Some minions of the kings that Gildas so roundly castigates may have known the real story, but for most sixth-century Britons *Badon* remained the great victory without a hero.

APPENDIX III

THE *HISTORIA* AND THE *CHRONICLE*:
THEIR COMMON ORIGIN

What is the relationship between the *Historia Brittonum* and the *Anglo-Saxon Chronicle*? At first glance this may seem an absurd question. These two sources appear to contradict one another on practically every level. Chapter 66 of the *Historia* gives the date for the *Adventus Saxonum* ('Coming of the Saxons') as 428, while both the Laud and Parker Manuscripts of the *ASC* claim that this occurred in the year 449 (more properly 450). This same chapter of the *Historia* also gives the date of Vortigern's accession as 425. Yet the first mention of Vortigern in the *ASC* is only in 450, a full generation later.[1] In the end, these discrepancies have presented most observers with a very stark choice. If one source is true, then the other must necessarily be false. Indeed, one widely held view is that both works, and probably most other purported sources for fifth-century Britain, are little more than the fabrications of later generations.

In this regard chapter 66 of the *Historia* seems to be particularly suspect. Here we find a comprehensive timeline, apparently giving precise dates for events over the course of a century. Yet not only does chapter 66 contradict the Laud and Parker Manuscripts of the *ASC*; it also contradicts practically every other early written source on some point. For example,

281

Constantius' fifth-century *Life of Saint Germanus* has Britons fighting off a Saxon incursion one year *after* these same Saxons are supposedly serving in Vortigern's army.[2] Gildas, writing somewhat later, places the *Adventus* after an Appeal to Aetius in the year 446—again, a full generation later than the *Historia*'s date of 428.[3] The Venerable Bede, writing almost a century earlier than the *Historia*, gives the date of the *Adventus* as 449/450.[4] Moreover, his date is predicated upon a date 'anchored' in Late Roman timekeeping, in this case the accession of Valentinian III as senior emperor in 450. In the face of these anomalies one very tempting alternative for most observers is to note that the *Historia* is a product of the ninth century and therefore unlikely to be a valid source for events some three hundred years earlier. It is, quite simply, 'inadmissible evidence'. Yet even if one were to concede that the passages found in chapter 66 of the *Historia* are not genuine citations from fifth-century Britain, the question remains, just where do they come from? This is the question that we will now address.

THE *HISTORIA BRITTONUM*

One widely accepted explanation for the *Historia*'s origin is that its author generated the data contained in chapter 66 almost exclusively from continental sources. By the use of a now-lost consular table and Prosper's *Chronicle*, the compiler was able to generate a chronology for fifth-century Britain, *although he possessed almost no genuine insular information from this period.*[5]

To test this bold assertion it might be well to examine the first citation in chapter 66 that contains putative insular information:

> From Stilicho to Valentinian, son of Placida [*sic*], and the reign of Vortigern are twenty-eight years.[6]

There are several curious things about this passage. The first is that it is very unclear why Stilicho should be mentioned here at all. The sparse records available to any ninth-century observer would never have led him to see Stilicho as the equal of kings and emperors. But more important, the orthodox date for the 'Stilicho' part of this citation, his first consulship in AD 400, can give us no significant date for either Valentinian or Vortigern that adds up to 28 years. Counting 28 years from AD 400 gives us neither the date of the death of Honorius (423) nor the official date of the accession of Valentinian III to the western throne (425). Quite simply, nothing adds up.

The traditional explanation for this anomaly is that there was 'confusion' in the compiler's mind between the date of Valentinian's accession in 425 and the *Historia*'s date for the coming of the Saxons in 428.[7] If the latter date is seen as genuine, this interval does indeed add up to 28 years. But it is still fair to ask: are there any other dates where a 28-year interval might also work—and prove that the *Historia*'s compiler knew basic arithmetic?

It turns out that there are, and they are two of the most significant dates of this period—the death of Theodosius the Great in 395 and the accession of Theodosius the Younger as senior emperor in 423. It is also important to remember that these two dates have the greatest significance in a fifth-century context. This was a time when the empire was ruled by two different emperors, but was still considered to be a single entity; the date when an emperor's colleague died and he became *senior* ruler was thus considered very important. Such dates, counted in 'regnal years', were crucial benchmarks in Late Roman time-keeping. Among other sources from this period, the chronology of the *Gallic Chronicle of 452* appears to be based primarily on regnal years.[8] Thus the year 423 marked both the death of the western emperor Honorius, and the accession as senior emperor of his eastern colleague, Theodosius the Younger.

And it is this system of Late Roman timekeeping that tells us why Stilicho is included in this passage in chapter 66. It is important to recall that *during his lifetime* Stilicho claimed that the dying Theodosius the Great had entrusted him with the guardianship of the two young orphan-emperors, Honorius and Arcadius. Moreover, in the year 395 *neither* of Theodosius the Great's sons would have been considered senior. But one very logical alternative way to express this situation calendrically was to see the year 395 as marking the accession of the *de facto* ruler of Rome at this time, General Stilicho. Since it is doubtful that any ninth-century observer would have had information this detailed about the political situation in fifth-century imperial Rome, the best explanation for this part of chapter 66 is that it was originally a near-contemporary insular reference to the start-date of Stilicho's time as chief actor in the western empire. It is therefore far more likely to be a product of the fifth century than of the ninth.

It *is* true that Valentinian III formally acceded to the purple in 425, following a tumultuous interregnum. But his dynasty (and contemporary Britons) could only have seen his reign as commencing with the death of his uncle Honorius in October 423, i.e. 28 years after the death of his grandfather, Theodosius the Great. Moreover, the two regnal dates of 395 and 423 are used as crucial benchmarks not only in the *Gallic Chronicle of 452* but also in Bede's later works. So *this* 28 year interval between two important regnal dates adds up.

Still, this citation raises other questions. Why is Galla Placidia mentioned here? Certainly she was Valentinian III's mother and a strong-willed woman. But, as with Stilicho, it is difficult to see why any ninth-century observer would include her in a terse *computus* that spans more than a hundred years. A second question is even more pertinent: just why would the compiler see Vortigern and Valentinian III as acceding at the same time? Our best source for the period, Gildas, has Vortigern appear only after the year 446. The *ASC*'s first mention of him is even later, in 449 (really 450). True, it is possible that the *Historia*'s compiler had information now lost to us. But alternatively, could there actually be some calendrical relationship between Vortigern, Valentinian III and Galla Placidia that is not readily apparent?

It is here that the Late Roman concept of regnal dates may once again offer assistance. It is interesting to note that Valentinian III is associated with not one but two regnal dates. The first is the year 423, when he became *de jure* junior emperor. The second is the year 450, when he became *senior* emperor, at the death of Theodosius the Younger. The latter is a well-known date, since both Bede and the *Anglo-Saxon Chronicle* report the *Adventus*, the "Coming of the Saxons," in terms of this regnal year. As far as Galla Placidia goes, it is possible that she is meant to be associated with the earlier date of 423, when her son was a minor, and she was attempting to restore his dynasty to the western throne. But what may also be significant is that Galla Placidia remained an important political force in the empire right up to 450. Moreover, she just happens to have died in this same year. Indeed, for fifth century observers in Britain (who appear to have seen Vortigern as reigning *after* 446, if Gildas is any guide) the year of Galla Placidia's death and of Valentinian III's first regnal year could reasonably be seen as the beginning of "the reign of Vortigern." Thus, 450 has an important significance for Valentinain III, Vortigern, and perhaps Galla Placidia as well.

But 450 is significant for another reason. It also happens to be 55 years after the postulated "Stilicho date" of 395. Now, if we divide this interval by half, this gives us 27 ½, almost exactly 28 years. Moreover, the mid-point between 395 and 450 is the year 423. If the "reign" of Stilicho and the reign of Theodosius the Younger *shared* the year 423, we would have *two* intervals of about 28 years between 395 and 450. One would run from the death of Theodosius the Great (the date which Stilicho asserted was the beginning of his *de facto* rule of both halves of the empire) to the accession of Theodosius the Younger as senior emperor in October 423. The second interval would run from the latter date to the accession of Valentinian III as senior emperor in 450, which, according to Gildas, Bede and the ASC, was also the approximate beginning of Vortigern's rule in Britain.[9] Note as well that Britons would be much more aware of conditions in the western empire, and could easily conflate the accession of Theodosius the Younger as senior emperor with the simultaneous *de jure* accession of Valentinian III as *junior* emperor. As Valentinain's mother Galla Placidia could reasonably be associated with *either* 423 or 450—perhaps both. Indeed, use of Valentinian's and Galla Placidia's name in the citations for *both* of these regnal dates would go a long way toward explaining the eclipse of the 450 date and the second 28-year interval.

Schematically, the situation we have postulated would look like this:

395	Accession of Stilicho
	(28 years)
423	Joint reign of Theodosius II and Valentinian III begins
	(28 years)
450	Valentinian III senior emperor (death of Galla Placidia and 'reign of Vortigern')

Note that all three of these regnal dates are found in Bede, and two are also found in the *ASC*. In other words, this hypothesis is *verifiable* against a number of other early sources. Indeed, if we accept this interpretation of chapter 66, the *Historia* suddenly agrees with *every* other early source, including Bede, Gildas, Constantius and the *ASC*. For reasons that we will shortly address, the *Historia*'s compiler may have collapsed the two 28-year intervals into one, to coincide with his much earlier *Adventus* date of 428. Overall, this also raises our suspicions that the calendrical discrepancies found in the various sources for this period may arise from attempts to synchronize different systems of timekeeping into a single chronology, in this case regnal dates and insular dates (Vortigern's reign). For now, this can only be a very tentative hypothesis. But it is a hypothesis that we can test against other passages in chapter 66.

The next passage in chapter 66 is even more of a puzzle:

> From the year when the Saxons came to Britain and were welcomed by Vortigern to Decius and Valerian are 69 years.[10]

Quite properly, this passage has been thought to be corrupted in some way. No consuls named Decius and Valerian reigned jointly during the fifth or sixth centuries, and the name Valerian does not even appear on the consular lists for this era. The most widely accepted explanation for this passage is that it is the result of two scribal errors. The argument goes that the interval in the chapter 66 passage originally read *89 years* (*LXXXIX vice LXIX*). Subtracting 89 from 521, the year of the consul *Valerius* (*vice* Valerian), would equate to the consulship for the year 432, when *Aetius* and Valerius jointly ruled (Decius being wrongly copied for Aetius). Of course, these two errors still do not equate to chapter 66's *Adventus* date of 428. But this is explained by the assertion that originally the passage stated that there were four years between the *Adventus* and the joint consulship of Aetius and Valerius. Schematically, the errors would look like this, with the missing or miscopied elements in italics:

428   Adventus
           (4 years)
432   *Aetius* (Decius) *and Valerius*
           (LXXXIX years (LXIX years))
521   *Justinian and Valerius* (Valerian)

The above solution is useful insofar as it provides us with a brace of consuls who actually did reign in the same year: Aetius and Valerius in 432. That the number 89 may have been copied as 69 is, naturally, also not impossible. Nor is it inconceivable that a 4-year interval was somehow deleted. However, there are also some problems here. We have no way of *verifying* that these particular errors were really committed; no extant source highlights these particular intervals between these particular consulships. Moreover, just why did the compiler choose the year 521 as the end point for his computation? The orthodox explanation is that the consulship of Valerius in 521 was the last recorded date in the consular table used by the *Historia*'s compiler. But again, this is unverifiable. No extant consular tables end on this date. It is also a little odd that the consular tables that have survived tell us that a consul called Decius actually *was* elected only a few years after 521, in 529. The best that can be said is that *if* several putative scribal errors were committed in precisely the manner that is asserted, and *if* a now-lost consular table ended in the year 521, then, yes, this could have produced the text that now exists in the *Historia*.

In short, the orthodox alternative offers *a* solution to this anomaly, but not necessarily *the* solution. Moreover, this conclusion was reached more than 30 years ago. Are there any alternatives that may not have been considered at the time, and that may offer a different explanation for chapter 66?

In answering this question it is only fair to point out that implicit in the above argument is the assertion that the name Valerius is a valid alternative for the name Valerian, and that the 'final' Valerius in the traditional solution is none other than the consul for the year 521. But if we simply subtract the 69-year interval found in the *Historia* from the date of *this* Valerius, we obtain a most interesting result:

$$521 - 69 = 452$$

The date of 452 is only two years later than the date from which Bede and the *Anglo-Saxon Chronicle* predicate the *Adventus*: 450, the *correct* regnal year when Valentinian III became senior emperor. Of still more significance, we have seen that a consul called Decius actually did exist in this same period, reigning in 529. Together with the regnal dates above, this would provide an unbroken timeline for well over a century, based on the two standard means of Roman timekeeping for this period. This alternative would look as follows:

395	Accession of Stilicho
	(28 years)
423	Joint reign of Theodosius II and Valentinian III begins
	(28 years)
450	Valentinian III senior emperor (death of Galla Placidia and 'reign of Vortigern')
452	*Adventus*
	(69 Years)
521	Consulship of Valerius
	(8 years)
529	Consulship of Decius

The hypothesis for the last three dates requires a misreading of neither the name Decius, nor the 69-year interval—merely the conflation of two separate consuls into rulers for the same year, and a transposition of the names. There is also no need for a long-lost consular table ending in 521—a table for which no evidence exists. In short, the above is the simpler explanation, requiring no heroic omissions from an original text for which we have no certain evidence.

What is also true is that the above *Adventus* date is not precisely the date given by either Bede or the *ASC*. Their date for the coming of the Saxons is predicated on 450, a regnal date that is two years earlier. This might seem a mere quibble. But it may actually be the key to understanding the full significance of this passage. If this 2-year 'lag' were corrected in the "Decius and Valerius" dates, they would look like this:

450	*Adventus*/Joint rule of Valentinian and Marcian begins
	(69 years)
519	Consulship of Valerius
	(8 years)
527	Consulship of Decius

This may not seem significant—until we consider that these three dates also happen to be the three most important dates in early Saxon history as recorded by the *ASC*: (a) the *Adventus* (449 or, more correctly, 450); (b) Cerdic's accession (519); and (c) his victory at *Cerdicesford/Cerdicesleag* (527).[11] This strongly suggests that at some point the consulships of Valerius and Decius were used to commemorate the deeds of a Saxon king called Cerdic. It may also be very significant that 'Cerdic' appears to derive from the Romano-British name Coroticus. So too may be the fact that Justinian is Valerius' co-consul, and that Decius was an *eastern* consul who reigned solo. Indeed, all of these consuls reigned at the very time when British contacts with the eastern empire were being renewed. This gives us some very plausible reasons why the original author of this citation included these two consuls and these two dates in his chronology. Wessex was a sixth-century Saxon state bordering on what remained of post-Roman Britain, and was the most likely 'barbarian' polity to use Late Antique timekeeping. These dates are also *verifiable*, since the fact that the interval between the first two dates is identical in both the *ASC* and the *Historia* is completely transparent. But more to the point, as with the 'Stilicho' citation, here again we see an attempt to synchronize insular timekeeping (in this case Saxon dates) with continental timekeeping.

Thus, the best explanation for the 'Decius and Valerius' passage is that the compilers of both the *Historia* and the *ASC* drew from a common fund of insular chronological information that dated back to Late Antiquity. The same three original citations—separated by the same original intervals—lie behind both sources. The British compiler of the *Historia* retained the consular names in his chronology, but deleted any mention of Cerdic. The *ASC* compilers, naturally more interested in Saxon affairs, did the opposite. A confusion between the earliest Saxon date for the *Adventus* and the regnal year of 450 then resulted in a two-year error in the calculation found in the *ASC*. As with the 28-year 'Stilicho' passage, the two medieval sources drew on the same basic information. But by the ninth century the compilers of these sources were using this information in two different ways to produce two very different chronologies.

Still, is this mere coincidence, or is there more evidence for this phenomenon? An important passage in chapter 66 may give the answer:

> And from the reign of Vortigern to the quarrel between Vitalinus and Ambrosius are 12 years, that is Wallop [*Guollopum*], the battle of Wallop. Vortigern, however, held empire in Britain in the consulship of Theodosius and Valentinian (425) and in the fourth year of his reign the Saxons came to Britain in the consulship of Felix and Taurus (428).[12]

What is initially of interest here is a curious anomaly in this passage. In all other cases in chapter 66, the compiler uses *intervals* to relate when an event occurs. He even does this in the first part of the passage, with the citation of 12 years between Vortigern and the encounter at *Guollopum*. But for some reason we are suddenly told not that 'three years' separate Vortigern and the *Adventus*, but that the latter occurred in 'the fourth year' of Vortigern's reign. There may be a very good reason for the compiler to make this sudden shift to an ordinal number, and we will address it shortly. But for now it is important to remember that *intervals* seem to be the normal way for the compiler to express his dates.

We have no other chronological information about either Vortigern's accession date, or the battle of *Guollopum*. But we do have the earliest known date for the *Adventus*: Bede's date of 450, i.e. the beginning of Valentinian III's reign as senior emperor. It is a citation that pre-dates the *Historia* by a century, and most disciplines devoted to the study of observable reality would consider the earlier reference the one more likely to be correct. If, therefore, we applied a 4-year *interval* to Bede's *Adventus* date, we would get a date of 446 for this version of Vortigern's accession date.

446   Vortigern's accession
         (4 years)
450   *Adventus*/Valentinian III as senior emperor

This again may not seem significant—until we remember that the first date coincides with a very precise consular date given by no less than Gildas himself: 446, the date of Aetius' third consulship.[13] But Gildas uses this not to mark Vortigern's accession but to give the year of a British appeal for aid from the Roman Marshal Aetius. This is a strange phenomenon, and it would be well to investigate whether the two events may (or may not) be connected.

As argued earlier, the very existence of the Appeal citation is curious. With all the violence that Gildas describes, why would a request for Roman aid—a request that was not honoured—be of such importance to British history? One possible explanation often given is that because he is a churchman, and the *De Excidio* is a 'sermon', we should not expect accuracy. His primary aim is to correct the sins of the Britons, and historical accuracy is a low priority.[14] But it is only fair to note that other Late Romans grounded in the ecclesiastical tradition wrote histories that seem to contain valid historical information. Sozomen and Orosius are but two examples. Moreover, by the sixth century clerics were the intellectual elite of western Europe. It was they who kept the Easter Tables and noted important events. Further, the fact that the *De Excidio* is virtually the only piece of British literature preserved from this period indicates that Gildas' audience considered that it was a valid commentary on fifth- and sixth-century events. There is no doubt that Gildas should be treated with great caution. But by his time, if a cleric did not possess a more or less accurate view of Britain's chronology, no one would.

The only real alternative is to see the Appeal as intimately connected with Vortigern's regime. Standing alone, the Appeal has little significance. But when presented as the first act in a *Dux Bellorum*'s rise to power it has immense propagandistic value. Aetius was the greatest general of his age. Yet even he could not save Britain—while Vortigern could. The fact that the *De Excidio* refrains from even mentioning Vortigern's name may also help us to understand why the Appeal is in its present form. Gildas and his milieu could only have remembered Vortigern as the ruler who invited in the Saxon invaders. A reminder that the Proud Tyrant had also once saved Britain would have been deeply distasteful to inhabitants of a sixth-century Britain ravaged by Vortigern's Saxon allies. The best explanation for the Appeal as it stands is that at the time Gildas wrote the *De Excidio* the year 446 was still seen as a date of crucial importance to British history. But mention of the *Dux Bellorum* who came to power in this year was no longer 'politically correct'.

The inaccurate date that the *ASC* gives for the Appeal, 443, is also of interest. Remarkably, in the *ASC* an interval of exactly 12 years separates the Appeal and a battle, just as 12 years separate Vortigern's accession from the *discordia* of *Guollopum*.

> 443—In this year the Britons sent overseas to Rome and asked them for troops against the Picts, but they had none there because they were at war with Attila, King of the Huns...
>
> 455—In this year Hengest and Horsa fought against king Vortigern at a place which is called *Aegelesthrep*.[15]

Aegelesthrep (or *Agaelesthrep*) also happens to be the first recorded battle between Briton and Saxon. Indeed, one of the meanings of the Anglo-Saxon word *threap* is 'strife', a close synonym for the Latin *discordia*.[16] Moreover, in contrast to Hengest's later battles, the *ASC* makes no extravagant claims for Saxon success in this engagement, suggesting that, on this day at least, the British commander was successful, and would thus be anxious to commemorate his victory.

Still, why would we have *two* dates for Vortigern's reign, 446 and 450? The answer is that we have two different systems of timekeeping in operation. One, based on continental regnal years, gives this insular date in terms of the accession of senior emperors. The other, based on yearly consular dates, gives a more refined chronology for the same period. When we take the Saxon dates for Cerdic into account, we seem to be dealing with chronological information from at least *three* different systems of timekeeping.

Despite this, the most striking aspect of the '*Guollopum*' dates is that their intervals agree perfectly with a series of dates in the *ASC*. Moreover, the *ASC* chronology supports Gildas' testimony that the *Adventus* occurred *after* the Appeal.[17] The original source for the insular citations in both the *Historia* and the *ASC* thus appears to have resembled something very like the following:

446   Appeal/Vortigern's accession
       (4 years)   *(12 years)*
450   *Adventus*/Valentinian and Marcian

458   'Strife' of *Aegelesthrep*/*Discordia* of *Guollopum*[18]

If we incorporate the above with the modified 'Decius and Valerius' passage, this would give the following original chronology:

446   Appeal/Vortigern's accession
       (4 years)   *(12 years)*
450   Valentinian and Marcian

452   *Adventus*   *(69 years)*

458   'Strife' of *Aegelesthrep*/*Discordia* of *Guollopum*

521   Consulship of Valerius/Accession of Cerdic in Wessex
       (8 years)
529   Consulship of Decius/Battle of *Ceredicesford*

(Note that it is the *interval* between each event that is important; the *Anno Domini* dates themselves are anachronistic)

The above is probably the nearest we can get to the Late Antique insular chronology that most likely produced both the *ASC* and the *Historia*.

FORTY YEARS MISPLACED

Another question now arises. If Vortigern's accession date is really 446, why did the *Historia Brittonum*'s compiler give it as 425? An explanation provided over half a century ago may answer this question. In 1961 Nikolai Tolstoy argued that the compiler of the *Historia* had chosen the very accurate consular date of Felix and Taurus (428) as the date of the *Adventus* because it was precisely 40 years from the date of the British usurper Maximus' fall in 388. According to Tolstoy, the compiler applied a presumably authentic piece of information, the 'forty years of fear' referred to in chapter 31, and used it to generate the date of 428. Another presumably accurate piece of information, that Vortigern's accession occurred four years earlier, then produced the date of 425.[19]

Yet even if this is the explanation for the *Historia*'s date of 425, why did its compiler reject the date provided by Bede a century earlier? It might be possible that the *Historia*'s author was simply unaware of Bede's work, and used what he had at hand to generate his chronology. However, it has been argued forcefully that the *Historia* displays considerable knowledge of Bede's ideas. Indeed, at times it is even a 'challenge' to the Saxon's views.[20] But all the same, the Venerable Bede was one of the most gifted scholars of his age. Why would the compiler choose to ignore a traditional date that had been accepted for at least a century, and instead generate a completely new year for the *Adventus*?

The answer may lie in what Bede himself says. In both the *History of the English Church and People*, and his *Chronica Maiora*, Bede first gives us the story of the *Adventus* (dated to 449–50). This is followed by the Saxon Revolt. Only then does he recount Saint Germanus' mission to Britain.[21] The *Historia*'s compiler, however, would have known from Prosper's *Chronicle* that Germanus had fought the Saxons in 429—a full 20 years before Bede's *Adventus*.[22] The compiler also tells us that he possessed an alternative *Life* of St Germanus, and this *Life* portrays the Gallo-Roman bishop as present at the *death* of Vortigern—again, some two decades *before* that ruler hired his Saxons in 450. Under such circumstances, the only course for *any* historian to adopt would be to resolve the inconsistencies in his data. One very logical way to achieve this is to reject the 450 *Adventus* date, and attempt to find some date for the arrival and revolt of the Saxons that is before 429. And a genuine insular tradition of 'forty years of fear', if calculated from the fall of Maximus, would provide just such an alternative date. It would 'prove' that Hengest's Saxons came not in 450, but in 428—and thus *before* St Germanus' Alleluia Victory.[23]

The *Historia*'s compiler was not so slipshod as to rely on a single piece of evidence, however. Returning to Prosper's *Chronicle*, he would note that Aetius was reported active as early as 425, and thus 'appealable' well before 446.[24] On a more general level, he could find a plausible reason for such a leap in the 28-year difference between the Victorian and Dionysian systems of timekeeping.[25] While not an exact fit, this could only reinforce his suspicions that Bede had misdated the *Adventus*.

Still, what impelled the *Historia*'s compiler to believe that Vortigern acceded in the same year as Valentinian III, and thus in 425? The short answer is: the same 4-year interval that is found between the Appeal and the *Adventus* in the tentative original chronology we have constructed above. Subtracting 4 from the compiler's new *Adventus* date of 428 would make 424 the year of Vortigern's accession. This is neither the year of the joint consulship of Theodosius and Valentinian, nor of Valentinian III's formal accession, which occurred in 425. But for a compiler anxious to summarize over a century of insular events, it was close enough. Indeed, even if Vortigern acceded in 424, it would still have been true that he 'held empire in Britain in the consulship of Theodosius and Valentinian (425)'.

Moreover, 425 would place the compiler's newly generated *Adventus* date of 428 in the 'fourth year' that Vortigern 'held empire'—an acceptable, if not exact way to express an original citation of an *interval* of four years. And so the *Historia*'s compiler could only see the following as the best way to reconcile the conflicting data he found:

> Vortigern, however, held empire in Britain in the consulship of Theodosius and Valentinian (425) and in the fourth year of his reign the Saxons came to Britain in the consulship of Felix and Taurus (428).[26]

With this, *all* of the dates in chapter 66 are elucidated. Save for the two exact consular dates (most probably generated by the compiler himself from Prosper's *Chronicle*), all of the dates in the *Historia* have an analogue in either the *ASC* or Bede—and were once separated by the same intervals. One, two, or even three such dates and intervals might conceivably be put down as coincidences. But *all* the relevant data in each source behave in this manner, making it highly unlikely that mere chance has any role in this phenomenon.

The hypothesis that exclusively continental sources were used in the *Historia* to fabricate a spurious chronology for fifth-century Britain can never be completely dismissed. But a far simpler and more straightforward explanation for chapter 66 is that its compiler possessed data of insular provenance, and that a related version of this material was also available to the compilers of the *ASC*. But these citations were used in the *Historia* to generate a very different chronology—a chronology specifically designed to resolve the real discrepancies that existed between Bede and Prosper's *Chronicle*.[27] That the compiler's 'correction' would cause great confusion among future researchers, he was not to know.

THE ANGLO-SAXON CHRONICLE

The idea that citations in the *Historia* also exist in the *Anglo-Saxon Chronicle* may give us an insight into just how the latter work was compiled. The orthodox view is that, since the Anglo-Saxons were illiterate until the arrival of Augustine in about 596, all dates prior to this must be highly suspect. They can only be guesses based on 'sagas' and local traditions, and *cannot* preserve authentic chronological data for the fifth and sixth centuries. This of course puts both the Venerable Bede and Alfred the Great in a rather unflattering light, asking us to accept that both knowingly assigned false dates to past events. Not impossible, but certainly not the usual picture we have of either of these two figures. Moreover, the idea that 'sagas' somehow lie behind the *ASC* has been fully discussed above.[28]

The passages elucidated for chapter 66 of the *Historia* give us a far better idea of the provenance of the *ASC*'s citations. If we read chapter 66 carefully, we realize that the earliest citations in the *ASC* are neither sagas nor fabrications—nor are they Saxon. Instead, they are much more likely to reflect Late Antique timekeeping. At bottom they are a series of *intervals* established by the Romano-Britons between known events— precisely the sort of timekeeping used by Gregory of Tours in his sixth-century *History of the Franks*.[29]

Just why the British would do this should be plain enough. As communications between Britain and the continent became more difficult, insular timekeeping still had to be maintained. Many of the *ASC* dates (383, 423, 450) are from a time when communications with the rest of the Roman world would have been at a low ebb. But the fact that these dates have survived indicates that the Britons were still attempting to synchronize their calendars with continental timekeeping. It also strongly suggests that the insular dates provide a fairly accurate chronology for Britain in Late Antiquity. It may be perfectly true that late sixth-century Saxon citations in the *ASC* are inaccurate. But as long as the citation for Valentinian III's accession as senior emperor was part of the earlier sequence of intervals, events in the fifth century (and the early sixth) would remain accurate to within a few years.

That Britons used Late Roman timekeeping is demonstrated by Gildas himself. As the author has argued, his association of *Badon* with a birth date of 43 years and one month can only mean that he calculated this interval from the year 450— Valentinian III's first regnal year. The equation of the Appeal to 'Agitius' with Aetius' third consulship is widely accepted. But it is still best to see these entries as having not a historical, but a *calendrical* significance. A British landowner in the year 494 might care very little about the first regnal year of the emperor Valentinian III—unless he were using it to record the birth date of his grandson. It is only when later writers attempt to use these dates to reconstruct a history of Britain that we begin to see trouble.

TRANSFORMATIONS

The author has postulated 'confusion' between the accession date of Valentinian III as senior emperor and the actual date of the *Adventus*. He has further stated that this is the source of the 3-year 'lag' found in a number of citations in the *ASC*. But is this simply a hypothesis, or can we demonstrate how this actually occurred?

To help answer this question, it is necessary to look not to Britain, but to Ireland. In the *Annals of Ulster* Valentinan III's first regnal year is recorded in a slightly different form, as the beginning of the joint reign of Marcian and Valentinian. But it is also recorded *twice*. One citation gives the year 449 (Bede's date), while another tells us that the two emperors began their joint rule in... 452. Unless we accept that an Irish monk read the *Historia* and correctly guessed who Valerian was, the most likely reason for this is that the 452 date originated in Britain—

and from a time when the *Adventus* and the 'two emperors' citation had already been conflated. This is earlier than Bede (who already reflects the 2-year 'lag' in his 381 citation for Maximus' usurpation). Indeed, it may well be as early as the sixth century. Thus, this 'confusion' between these two events seems to be present in much of the earliest timekeeping found in the British Isles.

But at one time these 'confused' dates were correct. It might therefore be useful to review the hypothetical chronology that the author has generated. If we include the correct date for Maximus' usurpation, the most likely date for the Roman withdrawal, and add Hengest's three remaining battles with their *intervals intact*[30], the original insular entries in the *ASC* would have looked like this:

383	Maximus' usurpation
	(38 years)
421	Roman withdrawal
	(25 years)
446	Appeal/Vortigern's accession
	(4 years) *(12 years)*
450	Valentinian and Marcian
452	*Adventus* *(69 years)*
458	'Strife' of *Aegelesthrep*/*Discordia* of *Guollopum*
	(1 year)
459	Battle of *Crecganford*
	(9 years)
468	Battle of *Wippedesfleot*
	(8 years)
476	Hengest's final battle with the Welsh
521	Consulship of Valerius/Accession of Cerdic in Wessex
	(8 years)
529	Consulship of Decius/Battle of *Ceredicesford*

In considering the above data, it is important to remember something that Bede says about the *Adventus*:

> In the year of our Lord 449 Martian [*sic*] became emperor with Valentinian, the forty-sixth in succession from Augustus, ruling for seven years. In his time the Angles or Saxons came to Britain.[31]

Here we see Bede describing exactly what we see in the above hypothetical chronology. The 'true' date for the *Adventus Saxonum* is not the date of Marcian's accession in 449–50; it is 'in his time', i.e. 452. But whatever the ultimate source of Bede's prescient warning, there is good evidence that by his day the damage had already been done. If we apply the 2-year 'lag' that this discrepancy between 450 and 452 implies, *and maintain the intervals between other insular events*, such as the Appeal and *Aegelesthrep*, we get the following chronology:

381   Maximus' usurpation
        (38 years)
419   Roman withdrawal
        (25 years)
444   Appeal/Vortigern's accession
                                (12 years)
450   [Valentinian and Marcian]
                                        (69 years)
456   'Strife' of *Aegelesthrep*/*Discordia* of *Guollopum*
        (1 year)
457   Battle of *Crecganford*
        (9 years)
466   Battle of *Wippedesfleot*
        (8 years)
474   Hengest's final battle with the Welsh
519   Consulship of Valerius/Accession of Cerdic in Wessex
        (8 years)
527   Consulship of Decius/Battle of *Ceredicesford*

Three of these dates are found either in Bede or in the Parker Manuscript of the *ASC*: the date for Maximus' usurpation (381), and the consulships of Valerius and Decius (519 and 527). Note also that the citation for Marcian and Valentinian would be "free floating," since, unlike the insular citations, its correct date would always be available from continental sources. The date of Maximus' usurpation is of particular interest, for it indicates that by Bede's time the *Adventus* date of 452 had *already* been conflated with the year 450.

The other citations, of course, are one year off from the dates currently found in the *ASC*. The date for the Appeal to Aetius is given in the *ASC* as 443, not 444, and the battle of *Aegelesthrep* is cited as taking place in 455, not 456. A clue as to why an additional year might be introduced into the above dates is found in Bede's citation for the Fall of Rome: 409. This is of course a year earlier than the correct date of 410. But when we remember that for Bede the new year began on 1 September,[32] we begin to understand just why there would be this additional one-year 'lag'. If we apply this to the central section of the hypothetical chronology, we finally get a series of insular dates that are all very familiar:

380	Maximus' usurpation	
	(38 years)	
418	Roman withdrawal	
	(25 years)	
443	Appeal/Vortigern's accession	
		(12 years)
449	[Valentinian and Marcian]	
455	'Strife' of *Aegelesthrep*/*Discordia* of *Guollopum*	
	(1 year)	
456	Battle of *Crecganford*	
	(9 years)	

465   Battle of *Wippedesfleot*
        (8 years)
473   Hengest's final battle with the Welsh

The above also helps to resolve a small discrepancy between the Parker and Laud Manuscripts. While the former gives the date for Maximus' usurpation as 381, the latter provides the year 380 for this event. The best explanation for this is that the Parker Manuscript compiler accepted Bede's 381 date, as set down in the *History of the English People and Church*, while the Laud chronicler applied an additional one-year correction, to give a date of 380. This is the best explanation for the anomaly between the two manuscripts. Both chroniclers, however, appear to have adopted Bede's 'Theodosius' date of 423 without alteration.

That the one-year 'lag' was not applied to the sixth-century dates for Cerdic also suggests the obvious: that Bede's intellectual influence on Kent was far greater than it was on Wessex. Bede is our best witness that his system of timekeeping would have been well known in Kent. His contacts with Albinus are manifest. However, Bede is entirely silent about Cerdic's dynasty, or Wessex affairs in general. His influence was simply not enough to make Wessex change New Year's Day to 1 September.[33]

The above exercise demonstrates in a completely transparent manner how the original material used by both the *ASC* and *Historia* compilers eventually became the fifth and early sixth-century citations that are now found in the Laud and Parker Manuscripts. This process occurred in several stages. Until the time of Gildas, the Britons utilized a combination of regnal, consular, and insular dates in their timekeeping. After the mid-fifth century, dates relevant to Hengest's battles were incorporated into this chronology. Not long after 529, these data were melded with calendrical information relevant to the reign of Cerdic. By Bede's era a traditional Saxon date for the *Adventus* had been confused with the first regnal year of Valentinian III's reign as senior emperor, which altered each citation by two years. Finally, an additional 'lag' of one year was introduced, perhaps by Bede himself, because of the way in which he calculated the New Year.

CONCLUSION

The best explanation for the discrepancies between chapter 66 of the *Historia* and the *ASC* is not that one or both were fabricated, or that they were generated from continental sources. Instead, the compilers of each work drew on a common fund of calendrical information that was first compiled in the fifth and sixth centuries. But the compiler of the *Historia* manipulated the data to correct what were very real discrepancies between his sources. In so doing, he created a chronology significantly different from the one used by Bede and the *ASC*. Ironically, in resolving the inconsistencies in his evidence, the *Historia*'s compiler succeeded only in creating an even greater problem for later generations of historians—a problem that persists to this day.

Maps

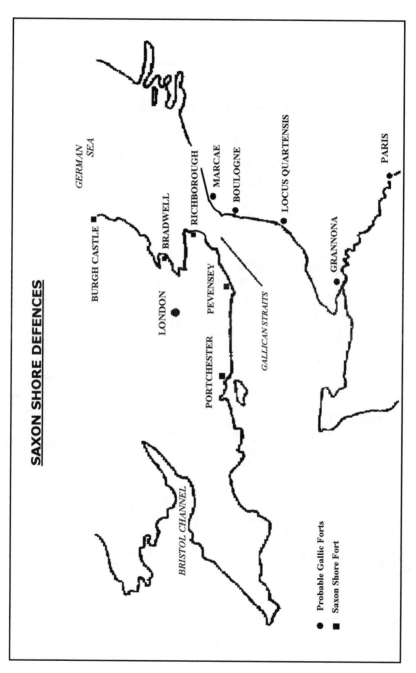

SAXON SHORE DEFENCES

GERMAN SEA

BURGH CASTLE

BRADWELL

RICHBOROUGH

MARCAE

BOULOGNE

LOCUS QUARTENSIS

PARIS

GRANNONA

LONDON

PEVENSEY

PORTCHESTER

GALLICAN STRAITS

BRISTOL CHANNEL

● Probable Gallic Forts

■ Saxon Shore Fort

Map 1

307

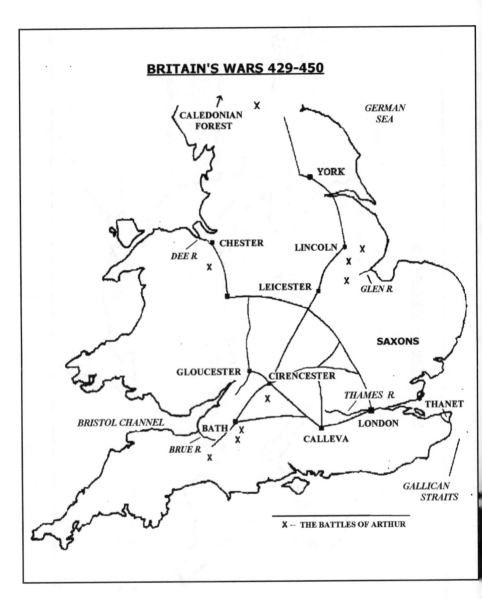

Map 2

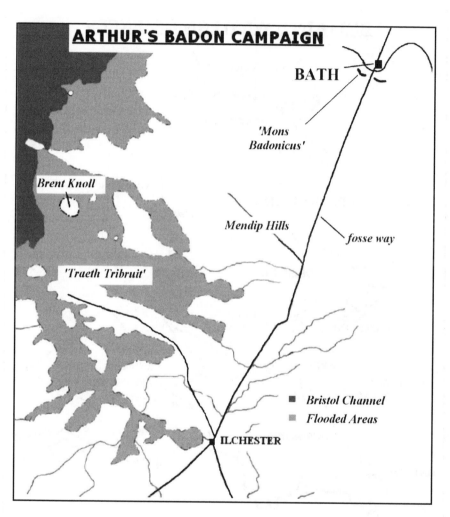

Map 3

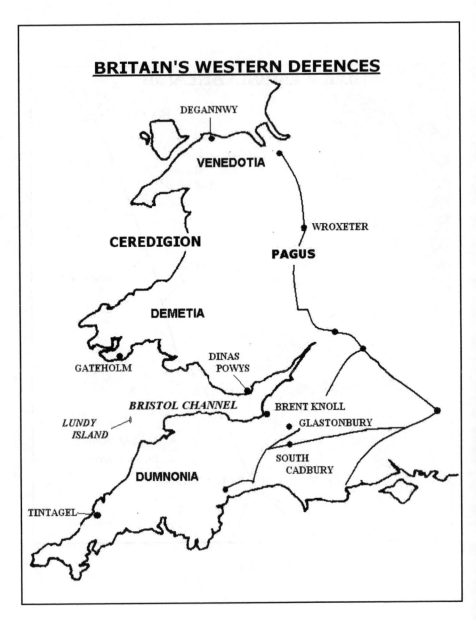

BRITAIN'S WESTERN DEFENCES

DEGANNWY

VENEDOTIA

WROXETER

CEREDIGION

PAGUS

DEMETIA

GATEHOLM

DINAS
POWYS

BRISTOL CHANNEL

BRENT KNOLL

GLASTONBURY

LUNDY
ISLAND

SOUTH
CADBURY

DUMNONIA

TINTAGEL

Map 4

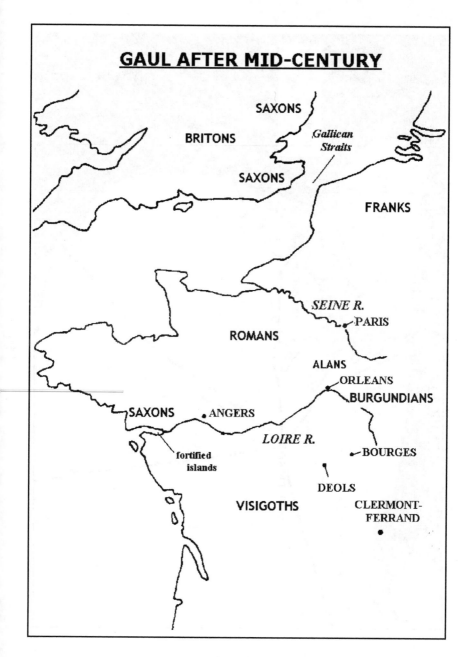

GAUL AFTER MID-CENTURY

SAXONS

BRITONS

*Gallican
Straits*

SAXONS

FRANKS

SEINE R.

PARIS

ROMANS

ALANS

ORLEANS

BURGUNDIANS

SAXONS · ANGERS

fortified
islands

LOIRE R.

· BOURGES

DEOLS

VISIGOTHS

CLERMONT-
FERRAND

Map 5

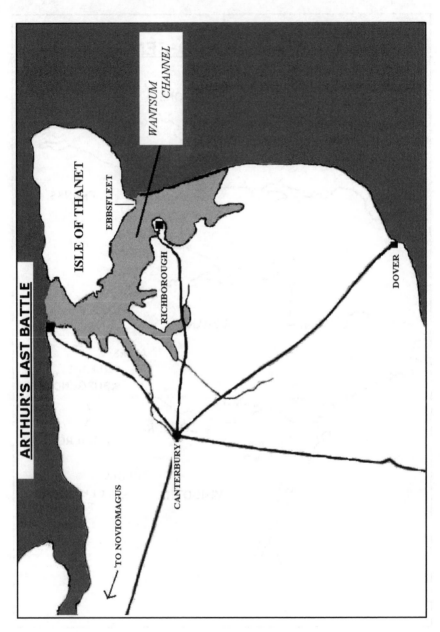

Map 6

REFERENCES

Abbreviations:

AC   *Annales Cambriae*
ASC   *Anglo-Saxon Chronicle*
DEB   Gildas, *De Excidio Britanniae*
HB   *Historia Brittonum*
HE   *History of the English Church and People*
MGH *Monumenta Germaniae Historica*

1. 'CONFLICT WITH THEIR CRUEL ENEMIES'

[1] Sheppard Frere, *Britannia, A History of Roman Britain* (London, 1987), pp. 193–201; K.R. Dark, *Britain and the End of the Roman Empire* (Stroud, 2000), p. 15.

[2] Peter Salway, *Roman Britain* (Oxford, 1984), pp. 516–17.

[3] Ibid., pp. 450, 455; K.R. Dark, *From Civitas to Kingdom: British Political Continuity, 300–800* (London, 1994) pp. 20–1.

[4] Frere, *Britannia*, pp. 201–2, 271;
Dark, *From Civitas to Kingdom*, pp. 25–8.

[5] Frere, *Britannia*, pp. 201–2. It is noteworthy that Heather, while acknowledging that 'the Flight of the Curiales' was a real phenomenon, does not see it as an important factor in Rome's 'decline'. His alternative is that the external barbarian threat was a major factor in the disappearance of the western empire. Peter Heather, *The Fall of the Roman Empire* (London, 2005), pp. 110–19.

[6] Frere, *Britannia*, pp. 365–7; A.S.E. Cleary, *The Ending of Roman Britain* (London, 1989), pp. 130–45.

[7] Salway, *Roman Britain*, pp. 378–82, 401–9, 440, 662; Frere, *Britannia*, p. 201.

2. 'CAVALRY BY LAND AND MARINERS BY SEA'

[1] Vegetius, trans. N.P. Milner, *Epitome of Military Science* (Liverpool, 1993), III.10, p. 82.

[2] Ibid. IV.7, p. 116. Vegetius explicitly states that this is the responsibility of 'the landowners'.

[3] Ibid. III.3, p. 65.

[4] Zosimus, trans. Ronald T. Ridley, *New History* (Canberra, 1982), I.6; Bernard Bachrach, *History of the Alans in the West* (Minneapolis, 1973), pp. 28, 33–7.

[5] Zosimus VI.6; Edward Gibbon, *Decline and Fall of the Roman Empire* (6 vols, London, 1910), vol. 3, XXVII, pp. 66–72; Bachrach, *History of the Alans*, pp. 33–5.

[6] Gibbon, *Decline and Fall*, vol. 3, XXVII, p. 97; Bachrach, *History of the Alans*, p. 34.

[7] Herodotus, trans. George Rawlinson, *The Persian Wars* (New York, 1942) IV.62; Ammianus Marcellinus, trans. C.D. Yonge, *The Roman History of Ammianus Marcellinus* (London, 1894), XXXI, 2, xxii–xxiii.

[8] Priscus, fragment 3, in R.C. Blockley, *The Fragmentary Classicising Historians of the Later Roman Empire*, vol. II (2 vols, Liverpool, 1981).

[9] Vegetius, *Epitome*, II.13, p. 44.

[10] Helmut Nickel, 'The Dawn of Chivalry', in *Metropolitan Museum of Art Bulletin* 32 (1975), pp. 150–2.

[11] Sidonius Apollinaris, trans. W.B. Anderson, *Sidonius: Poems and Letters* (2 vols, London, 1934), IX, xiii, 5.

[12] M. Henig, 'Late Antique Book Illustration', pp. 23, 38, quoted in Dark, *From Civitas to Kingdom*, pp.187–8.

[13] Vegetius, *Epitome*, IV.45, p. 141.

[14] While the *Notitia Dignitatum* does not specifically mention naval assets, it is important to note that this document was probably compiled *after* Britain's break with Rome. It is not at all certain that it reflects the organization and equipment of Britain's forces in the fourth century. Please see the discussion of Constantius' reconquest in chapter 5.

[15] *DEB*, in J.A. Giles, *Six Old English Chronicles* (London, 1848), II.17, p. 306.

[16] Claudianus, trans. William Barr, *Panegyric on the Fourth Consulate of Honorius* (Liverpool, 1981), II, 31–3.

[17] *Chronica Gallia a CCCCLII, Auctores Antiquissimi*, t. 9.2, *MGH* (1892), p. 646; Claudianus, trans. Maurice Platnauer, *Claudian* (London, 1922), 'On Stilicho's Consulship', 'Against Eutropius'.

[18] The *Annals of the Kingdom of Ireland* specifically state that Niall was killed at 'Muir-n-Icht', the 'sea between France and England'. *Annals of the Kingdom of Ireland by the Four Masters from the earliest period to the year 1616*, ed. John O'Donovan (New York, 1966), vol. I, p. 127.

[19] *Chronica Gallia a CCCCLII*, pp. 646–64.

[20] Frere, *Britannia*, pp. 230–7.

3. 'LEFT WITHOUT A SHEPHERD'

[1] A.H.M. Jones, *The Later Roman Empire* (3 vols, Baltimore, 1964), vol. I, pp. 182–5.

[2] Ibid., vol. I, pp. 186–7.

[3] Ibid., vol. I, pp. 184–7.

[4] Orosius, trans. I.W. Raymond, *Seven Books of History against the Pagans* (New York, 1936), VII.40.

[5] Bernard Bachrach, *Warfare and Military Organization in Pre-Crusade Europe* (Aldershot, 2002), pp. 178, 180.

[6] Harold Mattingly and W.P.D. Stebbing, *The Richborough Hoard of 'Radiates'* (New York, 1938), pp. 11–12.

[7] Sozomen, trans. C.D. Hartranft, *The Ecclesiastical History of Sozomen* (New York, 1886), IX, 13; Olympiodorus, fragment 16, in Blockley, *The Fragmentary Classicising Historians*; Orosius, *Seven Books*, VII, 43.

[8] Sozomen, *Ecclesiastical History*, IX, 12.

[9] Ibid., IX, 13.

[10] Ibid., IX, 14.

[11] Jones, *Later Roman Empire*, vol. I, p. 187–8; Cleary, *The Ending*, p. 138.

[12] *Historia Brittonum, Chronica Minora, Saec. IV, V, VI, VII, Auctores Antiquissimi*, Vol. III, t. 13.2, *MGH* (1894–98); *HB* 49. The 'Guitaul' listed as Vortigern's father in his genealogy is generally considered to be a Welsh version of the Latin name Vitalis. But it is also noteworthy that Guital and Catel are linguistically very similar. The 'C' in a number of early Welsh words eventually transmuted to a 'Gu' sound (cf. Cat = Gueith). Note also Kirby's calculation that the *Historia*'s genealogy would place Catel in the fifth century. D.P. Kirby, 'British dynastic history in the pre-Viking Period', *Bulletin of the Board of Celtic Studies* 27, p. 1 (Nov. 1976), p. 106.

[13] *HB* 33–35; Edmond Faral, *La Légende arthurienne: Etudes et documents* (Paris, 1929), pp. 55–6. As argued in chapter 16, the son of Catel Durnluc can only be the *Dux Bellorum*, the literal Brythonic meaning of Cattegirn. Moreover, since the days of Diocletian, sons had been required to follow the trade of their father. A Late Roman or post-Roman officer almost certainly comes from a military family.

4. 'THE PROUD TYRANT'

[1] Christopher Gidlow makes an interesting analogy with Napoleon's great antagonist, the Duke of Wellington, drawing attention to the various titles by which the latter was known, and demonstrating that if we knew as little about the hero of Waterloo as we do about the fifth century, we would never

connect the various citations about the 'Iron Duke' with one and the same person. Christopher Gidlow, *The Reign of Arthur* (Stroud, 2005), p. 130.

[2] Barbara Yorke, 'The origins of the Anglo-Saxon kingdoms: The contribution of written sources', in *Anglo-Saxon Studies in Archaeology and History* 10 (1999), p. 25; Dark, *Britain and the End of the Roman Empire*, p. 43.

[3] One popular scholarly theory argues that nearly all genuine information in chapter 66 of the *Historia* actually comes from continental sources. However this relies on the contention that over half of the '69 years' citation has been somehow lost, and that the original used intervals of 4 and 89 years respectively. David Dumville, 'Some aspects of the chronology of the *Historia Brittonum*', *Bulletin of the Board of Celtic Studies* 25 (1972–74), pp. 440–5. Please see Appendix III for an alternative explanation of the '69 years', as well as the probable link between the *Historia* and the *ASC*.

[4] Gildas, I.23, 24.

[5] Bede, trans. Leo Sherly-Price, *Bede: A History of the English Church and People* (Harmondsworth, 1968), I.15.

[6] *DEB*, I.20, in.Giles, *Six Old English Chronicles*, p. 308.

[7] *HB* 37–46.

[8] The *Historia*'s alternative date of 428 for the *Adventus* is unconvincing on several counts. Bede's testimony *precedes* that of 'Nennius' by a century. We know that St Germanus was fighting Saxons in 429, a year after this supposed *Adventus*, allowing the Saxons no time to defeat the Picts, let alone revolt. Finally, 'Nennius' could never have accepted an *Adventus* of 450, for the simple reason that he would then have been unable to use the spurious *Life of St Germanus* in his work. Using Bede's chronology, a four-year interval between Vortigern's accession and the *Adventus* would have Vortigern coming to power in 446. In that year St Germanus would not even have been alive, let alone in Britain to deliver his climactic cursing on the Proud Tyrant. It is well to remember that the House of Powys claimed descent from Vortigern and were also rivals of Nennius' patron Merfyn of Gwynedd. To leave out the calumnies found in the spurious *Life* would have been unthinkable. See Appendix III.

[9] The 'Gallic Chronicle of 452' most likely uses the regnal years of the senior emperor as a basis for its chronology, i.e. at precisely the time that Arthur would have flourished. It is also significant that Valentinian III's first regnal year gives a very round date from the Incarnation (CCCCL), and that the date is found *twice* in the *Annals of Ulster*. Michael E. Jones and John Casey, 'Gallic Chronicle restored: A chronology for the Anglo-Saxon invasions and the end of Roman Britain', *Britannia* XIX (1988), pp. 368–73.

[10] Leslie Alcock, *Arthur's Britain: History and Archaeology* (London, 1973), pp. 27–8.

References

[11] Toby Griffen, *Names from the Dawn of British Legend* (Felinfach, 1994), pp. 80–90.

[12] *DEB*, I.26, in Giles, *Six Old English Chronicles*, p. 313.

[13] Michelle Ziegler, 'Artúr mac Aedan of Dalriada', *The Heroic Age,* Issue 1, Spring/Summer (1999).

[14] It might be possible to argue for an original Arthur flourishing after 535 and before 550. But this was precisely the time of a worldwide famine brought on by a volcanic eruption in 535, and of a pandemic of bubonic plague in the 540s. It is very doubtful that any large-scale battles would have been taking place in this period. David Keys, *Catastrophe: An Investigation into the Origins of the Modern World* (London, 1999), pp. 125–35.

[15] *DEB*, I, 26, in Giles, *Six Old English Chronicles*, p. 313. Please see the discussion of Gildas' date for the battle of Badon in Appendix II.

5. 'THE ROMANS THEREFORE LEFT THE COUNTRY'

[1] St Patrick, trans. A.B.E. Hood, *St Patrick: His Writings and Muirchu's Life* (London, 1978), 'Declaration', 1, p. 41.

[2] *HB* 31, in Giles, *Six Old English Chronicles*, p. 396.

[3] St Patrick, *His Writings*, 'Letter to Coroticus'.

[4] Dark, *From Civitas to Kingdom*, pp.10–12; Cleary, *The Ending*, p. 139.

[5] Cleary, *The Ending*, pp. 141–2, 145.

[6] Ibid., pp. 130–45.

[7] Dark, *Britain and the End of the Roman Empire*, p.17.

[8] Dark, *From Civitas to Kingdom*, pp.15–17.

[9] Dark, *Britain and the End of the Roman Empire*, p. 57.

[10] Alcock, *Arthur's Britain,* p. 192.

[11] Dark, *Britain and the End of the Roman Empire*, pp. 146–7, 183.

[12] Frere, *Britannia*, pp. 366–7. The observation that Gildas nowhere mentions villas in his narrative, and thus indicates that they had disappeared long before his time, is also of interest.

[13] Katherine Forsyth, *Language in Pictland* (Utrecht, 1997), pp. 28–38.

[14] John Bannerman, *Studies in the History of Dalriada* (Edinburgh, 1974), pp. 151–4.

[15] John Haywood, *Dark Age Naval Power* (London, 1991), pp. 93–105.

[16] Ibid., pp. 93–110.

[17] St Patrick, 'Declaration', 23.

[18] A.O. Exquemelin, trans. Jack Beeching, *The Buccaneers of America* (Baltimore, 1969), pp. 67–8, 77–80, 143–5.

[19] *DEB* I.19, in Giles, *Six Old English Chronicles*, p. 307.

[20] Ibid., I.18, p. 307.

[21] Zosimus, trans. Ronald T. Ridley, *New History* (Canberra, 1982), VI.5.

[22] There is a very real question as to whether the famous 'imperial rescript' issued by Honorius applied to Britain or to Bruttium in Italy. Since direct contact between the empire and Britain was virtually impossible anyway until 418, the question as to which region was ordered to 'defend itself as best it could' is largely irrelevant. It is certainly not an order to withdraw Roman troops who were in open revolt against Honorius himself. Zosimus, *New History*, VI.5.

[23] Zosimus, *New History*, VI.5, 6.

[24] Pat Southern and Karen Dixon, *The Late Roman Army* (London, 1996), pp. 68, 69, 86.

[25] Mahan, *The Influence of Sea Power upon History* ([1890] New York, 1987), pp. 49–53. Of no little interest, Mahan was attempting to goad American public opinion into re-creating the antebellum American merchant marine, which had been devastated by a Confederate raiding strategy in some ways similar to that of Britain's seaborne enemies.

[26] *DEB* I.18, in Giles, *Six Old English Chronicles*, p. 306.

[27] *DEB* I.18, in *Gildas: The Ruin of Britain and Other Works,* trans. M. Winterbottom (Chichester, 1978), p. 22.

[28] Orosius, *Seven Books*, VII.43.

[29] Jones, *Later Roman Empire,* vol. I, pp. 175–6.

[30] The idea of a Roman reoccupation of Britain after 418 is far from new. Among others, Collingwood argued forcefully for it, citing the *Notitia* as evidence: R.G. Collingwood and J.N.L. Myres, *Roman Britain and the English Settlements* (Oxford, 1936) pp. 296–301. Jones's comment that we lack *any* information about Gaul for this period is also significant. Jones, *Later Roman Empire,* vol. I, p. 188. For a full listing of the *Notitia*, see his appendix on this subject.

[31] Although there are no naval assets reported in the *Notitia* for Britain, note Vegetius' complaint about *contemporary* naval practice, i.e. *after* Britain's break with Rome. 'The Roman People... used not to fit out the fleet on the spur of the moment.' In other words, the naval assets used by Constantius are likely to have been *ad hoc* formations, and not a formal *classis*. Vegetius, *Epitome*, IV.31, p. 132.

[32] Horst Wolfgang Böhme, 'Das Ende der Römerherrschaft in Britannien und die Angelsachsische Besiedlung Englands im 5. Jahrhundert', *Jahrbuch des Römisch-Germanischen Zentralmuseums Mainz* 33 (1986), pp. 468–574.

[33] John Morris, *The Age of Arthur* (London, 1973), p. 56.

[34] *HB* 14.

[35] Asser 54, quoted in N.J. Higham, *King Arthur, Mythmaking and History* (London, 2002), p. 172. It is noteworthy that in the Caribbean of the seventeenth century Tortugas and Port Royal both had a similar role.

[36] *DEB* I.17, in Giles, *Six Old English Chronicles*, p. 306.

[37]Olympiodorus, fragments 33, 34, in Blockley, *The Fragmentary Classicising Historians,* vol. II.

[38] J.B. Bury, *History of the Later Roman Empire* (2 vols, London, 1923), vol. I, pp. 208–9.

[39] *Anglo-Saxon Chronicle,* trans. G.N. Garmonsway (London, 1972), pp. 10–11.

[40] For example, the *Chronicle*'s date for Aetius' third consulship is 443, not the generally accepted date of 446. Similarly, the date for Maximus' usurpation is given as 380 in the Laud Manuscript, and 381 in the Parker Manuscript, not the genuine date of 383. *The Annals of Ulster* actually gives *two* dates for the beginning of the joint rule of Marcian and Valentinian: 449 and 452, reflecting this same gap in time. The *Annals of Ulster*, 449, 452, pp. 42–5. See Appendix III for the author's explanation of this phenomenon.

[41] Bury, *Later Roman Empire*, vol. I, pp. 208–9, 222; Jones, *Later Roman Empire,* vol. I, p. 189.

6. 'FORTY YEARS OF FEAR'

[1] Jones, *Later Roman Empire,* vol. I, p. 191.

[2] Sidonius, *Poems and Letters*, VIII, xvi, 1.

[3] Ammianus, *Roman History*, XXIII, 5, xi, pp. 326–7.

[4] Constantius, 'Germanus of Auxerre', in *The Western Fathers. Being the lives of SS Martin of Tours, Ambrose, Augustine of Hippo, Honoratus of Arles, and Germanus of Auxerre,* ed. and trans. F.R. Hoare (London, 1954), 2, 4, 28.

[5] Constantius, 'Germanus', 13, 17.

[6] E.A. Thompson, *Saint Germanus of Auxerre* (Woodbridge, 1984), pp. 53–4.

[7] Constantius, 'Germanus', 15.

[8] Salway, *Roman Britain*, pp. 466–7.

[9] Constantius, 'Germanus', 17, p. 300.

[10] Constantius, 'Germanus', 17, 18, pp. 300–1.

[11] Thompson, *Saint Germanus*, pp. 41–2.

[12] On the Pillar of Eliseg, the descendants of Vortigern explicitly claim this ('Guarthi que bene German'): V.E. Nash Williams, *Early Christian Monuments of Wales* (Cardiff, 1950), p. 123.

[13] *HB* 35. This appears to be a response by the rulers of Gwynedd to the Powysian claim on the Pillar of Eliseg. Note in particular how the humble status of Catel's family is stressed—in sharp contrast to the martial career of Cunedda and *his* sons.

[14] Sidonius, *Poems and Letters*, II, ix, 7–9, pp. 459–61.

[15] Cleary, *The Ending,* pp.200–2.

[16] *DEB* I, 20, p. 308.

[17] S.P. Dark, 'Paleoecological Evidence for Continuity and Change in Britain, ca. AD 400–800', p. 39, in K.R. Dark, *External Contacts and the Economy of Late Roman and Post-Roman Britain* (Studies in Celtic History, 16). (Woodbridge, 1996).

[18] A parallel tendency existed in another unsettled time and place: the American frontier of the eighteenth and nineteenth centuries. Partly descended from Lowland Scots who had suffered constant raiding in the sixteenth century, American frontiersmen initially expended no more than a minimum of effort on insubstantial log dwellings that might quickly have to be abandoned because of Native American raiding. This was a 'folk-way' that they arguably brought with them from Scotland. David Hackett Fischer, *Albion's Seed* (New York, 1989), pp. 655–62.

[19] Böhme, 'Das Ende der Römerherrschaft', pp. 558–9; Peter Salway and John Blair, *The Oxford History of Britain: Roman and Anglo-Saxon Britain* (Oxford, 1984), p. 62.

[20] Böhme, 'Das Ende', pp. 468–574.

[21] That these East Anglian settlers were somehow the first Saxon federates is unconvincing for several reasons. These barbarians still practised pagan rites like cremation of the dead. The East Anglian coast is of far less importance militarily than the littoral further south, yet Saxons appear in strategic areas like Kent and the Isle of Wight only a quarter of a century later. Moreover, the Kentish Saxons are culturally quite distinct from the East Anglian group. This also makes it extremely doubtful that the material differences between the two groups is proof that Britain was divided into independent polities based on the old provinces. Böhme's characterization of the East Anglian group as 'migrants', and the Kentish group as 'federates', fully explains the differences seen in the archaeology. Böhme, ibid.

[22] David Dumville, 'Sub-Roman Britain: History and legend', *History* 62 (1977), p. 185.

[23] Sidonius, *Poems and Letters*, VIII, ix, 5.

[24] H.B. Elllis Davidson, *Gods and Myths of Northern Europe* (Baltimore, 1964), p. 62. Not surprisingly, after the Anglo-Saxons were Christianized the word came to mean 'witch'.

[25] Sidonius, *Poems and Letters*, VIII, ix, 5; VIII, vi, 15.

[26] John Morris, *Arthurian Sources* (6 vols, Chichester, 1995), vol. 4, p. 53.

[27] Sidonius, *Poems and Letters*, VIII, 6, 13.

[28] Morris, *Arthurian Sources*, vol. 4, p. 53.

[29] The less hierarchically differentiated Comanches of nineteenth-century North America enjoyed a similar reputation. T.R. Fehrenbach, *Comanches: The Destruction of a People* (New York, 1974), pp. 60–81.

[30] The fact that St Guthlac could meet Brythonic speakers in the Fens as late as 700 indicates that Romano-British peasants were at the very least tolerated by their Saxon neighbours. Frere, *Britannia*, p. 367.

[31] Collingwood and Myres, *Roman Britain*, pp. 394–5; Böhme, 'Das Ende', pp. 468–574.

7. 'THEY LEFT THEIR CITIES'

[1] Jones, *Later Roman Empire,* vol. I, pp. 242–3.

[2] Collingwood and Myres, *Roman Britain*, pp 394–5.

[3] Böhme, 'Das Ende', pp. 468–574; Dark, *Britain and the End of the Roman Empire*, pp. 75–8. One of the most astute discussions of this question is in Haywood, *Dark Age Naval Power*, pp. 81–4.

[4] Dark, *Britain and the End of the Roman Empire*, pp. 97–103.

[5] Valentinian III became senior emperor in 450; Marcian became the new eastern emperor in the same year. Note also that the *Anglo-Saxon Chronicle* gives an incorrect, earlier date of 449 for this. It also incorrectly gives the two rulers as 'Mauricius' and 'Valentines', suggesting that these are the two names that Albinus gave to Bede, who then made the correct identification. Alcock, *Arthur's Britain*, p. 108. In other words, the *ASC* date *precedes* Bede, and the fact that almost all citations prior to Valentinian III's first regnal year have nothing to do with Germanic immigrants is strong evidence that fifth-century Britons were using regnal years in their timekeeping. Jones and Casey, 'Gallic Chronicle restored'.

[6] According to David Dumville, Gildas *intends* to say that the Appeal to Aetius precedes the *Adventus*. David Dumville, 'The Chronology of the *De Excidio Britanniae*, Vol. I', in *Gildas: New Approaches,* eds. Michael Lapidge and David Dumville (Woodbridge, 1984), p. 83. Also, in his 'table of contents' in chapter 2 Gildas explicitly places the two events in this order.

[7] *DEB* I.19, in Giles, *Six Old English Chronicles*, p. 307.

[8] *DEB* I.23, in Giles, ibid., pp. 307–8. While the actual name in the Appeal is 'Agitius', this is almost certainly Aetius, who actually was consul for the third time in 446. Any doubt about this is silenced when we read a list of Roman 'kings' in Gaul dated to Merovingian times. The last three 'kings' are listed as Egetius, Egegius and Syagrius: i.e. Aetius, Aegidius and Syagrius.

Agitius/Egetius is simply the way Late Romans pronounced the name Aetius. *Scriptorum Rerum Merovingicorum.*, t. 7, p. 854, *MGH*.

[9] Salway actually accepts that the Appeal is for help against Saxons attacking westward, and that the Thanet Saxons were a different group from those in East Anglia. However, he still conflates the 441 attack with the Revolt, which Gildas reports came 'a long time' after 446. Salway, *Roman Britain*, p. 479.

[10] The fact that Gildas mentions three *cyuls* makes it overwhelmingly likely that this is the earliest recorded mention of Hengest's arrival in 450. Again, it is strong evidence that Saxon citations in Bede and the *ASC* date from at least the early sixth century. *ASC*, Garmonsway, pp.12–13.

[11] *DEB* I, 19, Giles, *Six Old English Chronicles*, p. 307.

[12] *DEB* I, 20, Giles, ibid., p. 308.

[13] Jones, *Later Roman Empire*, vol. I, pp. 176–7.

[14] Jones, *Later Roman Empire*, vol. I, pp. 188–9; *The Chronicle of Hydatius and the Consularia Constantinopolitana*, ed. and trans. R.W. Burgess (Oxford, 1993), pp. 92–5; Sidonius, *Poems and Letters*, pp. xv–xvi.

[15] Steven Muhlberger, *The Fifth Century Chroniclers* (Leeds, 1990), p. 104.

[16] *Chronica Gallia a CCCCLII*, op. cit., p. 660; Bachrach, *History of the Alans*, pp. 133–40.

[17] Didier-Georges Dooghe, *Les Saxons de Gaule* (Lille, 1974), p. 14.

8. 'THEY OVERTHREW THEIR ENEMIES'

[1] *HB* 56, in *Nennius: British History and The Welsh Annals*, p. 35.

[2] Alcock, that great champion of a late fifth-century *Dux Bellorum*, argued that Gildas fails to mention Arthur because the good cleric is 'altogether sparing with names'. Alcock, *Arthur's Britain*, pp. 27–8. This actually implies that Arthur was of less importance than either Vortigern or Ambrosius, both of whom Gildas *does* name. The notion that Gildas somehow 'missed' Arthur has also left the door open for the many amateur studies that have 'found' Arthur, using almost no hard evidence. That *these* Arthurs are also invariably insignificant ironically moves the explanation for his notoriety back into the unverifiable realm of bardic genius.

[3] *DEB* I.20, in Giles, *Six Old English Chronicles*, p. 308.

[4] C. Scott Littleton and Linda A. Malcor, *From Scythia to Camelot* (New York, 2000), pp. 62–3.

[5] N.J. Higham, *King Arthur, Mythmaking and History* (London, 2002), p. 146.

[6] Bernard Bachrach, 'The question of King Arthur's existence, and of Romano-British naval operations', *The Haskins Society Journal* 2 (1990), p. 19.

[7] *DEB* I.20, in Giles, *Six Old English Chronicles*, p. 308.

[8] *DEB* I.21, in Winterbottom, *Gildas: The Ruin of Britain*, p. 24.

[9] It is right to use 'cohorts' here. Even in the next century we find a Briton using this term: Eleuther Cosgord Maur, 'Eleutherius of the Great Cohort'. Faral, *La Légende arthurienne*, vol. II, p. 53. Also, Vegetius mentions that each cohort would have its own dragon standard. Vegetius, *Epitome*, II.13, p. 44.

[10] *HB* 56, in *Nennius: British History*, p. 35.

[11] Gidlow portrays Arthur as an insular *Magister Militum*, with the kings as his subordinates. Gidlow, *Reign of Arthur*, p. 126.

[12] 'Pa Gur', in *The Four Books of Ancient Wales*, trans. W.F. Skene (New York, 1982), pp. 262–3. In the poem Cai's enemies are described as *cinbin*, i.e. 'dogheads', and one scholar argues that this is 'a calque on the classical *Cynocephali,* mythical inhabitants of India'. However, as the author himself concedes, just why these particular *Cynocephali* would be so far from India is very unclear. Patrick Sims-Williams, 'The Early Welsh Arthurian Poems', in Rachel Bromwich, A.O.H. Jarman and B.F. Roberts (eds), *The Arthur of the Welsh* (Cardiff, 1991), pp. 41–2. An alternative is that this is an abusive term for the inhabitants of northern Britain. Very significantly Gildas shows great contempt for the appearance of both Pict and 'Scot', complaining of how they were 'eager to shroud their villainous faces in bushy hair'. *DEB* I.19, in Giles, *Six Old English Chronicles*, p. 307.

[13] Helmut Nickel, 'Wer Waren König Artus' Ritter? Über die geschichtliche Grundlage der Artussagen', in *Zeitschrift der historischen Waffen-und Kostümkunde* 1 (1975), p. 12.

[14] G. Afanasivev, 'The Burtasses', in P. Puchkov (ed.), *Peoples that Vanished* (Moscow, 1989), pp. 81–91.

[15] This was the Anglo-Saxon name for the old Roman roads: *her* means 'army'. Joseph Bosworth, *Anglo-Saxon Dictionary* (Oxford, 1898).

[16] Vegetius, *Epitome*, III.3, p. 65.

[17] *DEB* I.21, in Giles, *Six Old English Chronicles*, p. 308.

[18] *DEB* I.21, in Giles, ibid., pp. 308–9.

[19] Dark, *Britain and the End of the Roman Empire,* pp. 97–103.

[20] *DEB* I.22, in Giles, *Six Old English Chronicles*, pp. 309–10. Just why sixth Century Britons like Gildas would see Badon as a battle against Saxons is perfectly logical, when we remember that these former Irish foes were now good citizens (and even rulers) of what was left of Roman Britain. With Saxons as the main threat in the sixth century, the greatest victory against the

'pagans' can only have been against a Saxon foe. Gildas is perfectly correct on Badon's date, just mistaken on which of Britain's many foes were defeated on that day. For a fuller discussion, see Appendix III.

9. 'A PROTECTION TO THEIR COUNTRY'

[1] Nikolai Tolstoy's explanation for these last four battles remains the best by far, and the author readily acknowledges his debt. It is important to note, however, that in Tolstoy's opinion this was not an Irish-Pictish landing in 450, but a Saxon landing circa 500. Nikolai Tolstoy, 'Nennius, chapter fifty-six', *The Bulletin of the Board of Celtic Studies* 19 (1961), pp. 140–6.

[2] The complement of the majority of Morgan's ships was on average no more than that of a Saxon *cyul*. Exquemelin, *Buccaneers*, p. 128.

[3] Barri Jones and David Mattingly, *An Atlas of Roman Britain* (Oxford, 1990), p. 10. The map for Arthur's *Badon* campaign is a simplified version of the map cited in this work.

[4] Interestingly, even in the nineteenth century J.A. Giles saw Somerset as a possible venue for both *Tribruit* (the River Brue) and Mount *Agned*. Giles, *Six Old English Chronicles*, pp. 409, ff., 1 and 2. Moreover, the 'Pa Gur' contains the following very significant passage: 'Did not Manawyd bring / Perforated shields from Trywruid?' Manawyd is, of course, the warrior in the *Mabinogion* who brings back Bran the Blessed's head after the fatal conflict in Ireland, and then takes it to London for burial. This strongly suggests that in Late Roman and post-Roman times *Tribruit* was considered a logical landfall for anyone coming from Ireland on the way to London. The Brue is one very likely candidate for this. Skene, *Four Books*, 'Pa Gur', pp. 262–3.

[5] Ibid.; Tolstoy, 'Nennius, chapter fifty-six', p. 159.

[6] Skene, *Four Books*, 'Chair of the Sovereign', p. 259.

[7] *Nennius: British History and The Welsh Annals*, p. 45.

[8] The contention that the list is a pastiche of various British victories thrown together because of a supposed need to create a 'British Joshua' fails to answer one pertinent question: just why would the *Historia*'s compiler feel the need to complement a genuine account of a 'Mosaic' St. Patrick (based on sources he can only have considered to be authentic, i.e. Tirechan and Muirchu) with a *completely fabricated* account of an 'Arthurian' Joshua? Moreover, that Arthur's victory at Chester is somehow either the seventh-century British *disaster* of that name, or, alternatively, the *synod* at Chester is unlikely in the extreme. Finally, the very idea that the *Historia*'s compiler had a 'biblical agenda' is suspect. The *Historia* uses almost no Holy Scripture. Indeed, 'biblical agendas' are much more typical of Late

Antiquity—most especially of the 'Biblical Style' of writers like Gildas. Higham, *King Arthur*, 146–50.

⁹ *Nennius: British History and The Welsh Annals*, p. 45.

¹⁰ Alcock, *Arthur's Britain*, p. 71.

¹¹ *HB* 56, in *Nennius: British History and The Welsh Annals*, p. 35.

¹² It is important to remember that Bede gives us the earliest date for the *Adventus*, but it is by no means exact. He merely says that when Marcian became emperor in the east (i.e. Valentinian III's first year as senior emperor), the Saxons came 'in his time', i.e. sometime during the next seven years: *HE* I.15. For the author's argument that the most likely date for the 'Jutish' *Adventus* is 452, see Appendix III.

10. 'TO FIGHT IN FAVOUR OF THE ISLAND'

¹ *HE* I.15, trans. Sherly-Price, *Bede*, p. 56.

² Dark, *Britain and the End of the Roman Empire,* pp. 49–53, 59, 97–103.

³ Garmonsway, *ASC*, pp. 12–13.

⁴ Collingwood and Myres, *Roman Britain*, pp. 394–5.

⁵ *HB* 31.

⁶ Garmonsway, *ASC*, pp. 12–13.

⁷ Dark, *Britain and the End of the Roman Empire,* pp. 75–8.

⁸ This is no oversight. Bede does the same thing in his *Chronica Maiora. Bedae: Chronica Maiora, ad a. DCCXXV, Chronica Minora, Saec. IV, V, VI, VII, Auctores Antiquissimi*, Vol. III, t. 13.2, *MGH* (1894–98), p. 304. The logic is actually impeccable. If no Germans were in Britain prior to 450, St Germanus must be fighting them *after* that date. Unlike 'Nennius', Bede does not seem to have had access to Prosper's *Chronicle*.

⁹ Barbara Yorke, 'Fact or fiction? The written evidence for the fifth and sixth centuries AD', *Anglo-Saxon Studies in Archaeology and History* 6 (1993), p. 47.

¹⁰ J.R.R. Tolkien, *Finn and Hengest*, ed. Alan Blair (London, 1982), pp. 61–71.

¹¹ *DEB* I.21, in Winterbottom, *Gildas*, p. 24.

¹² *HB* 38, in Giles, *Six Old English Chronicles*, p. 400.

¹³ David Dumville, 'Historical value of the *Historia Brittonum*', in *Arthurian Literature* 6 (1986), pp. 11–14.

¹⁴ Ibid., pp. 11–13.

¹⁵ John Morris, *The Age of Arthur* (London, 1973) pp. 57–62. Morris's account of Vortigern's Saxons remains one of the most insightful analyses of how these federates were probably used—and why they were of such critical importance to the Britons. Only his chronology is at fault.

¹⁶ Jordanes, *The Origins and Deeds of the Goths*, trans. C.C. Mierow (Princeton, 1905), 36, p. 60.

¹⁷ Sidonius, *Poems and Letters*, C. VII, 388–95, p. 151. Interestingly, Avitus' reward was one even grander than the one we have hypothesized for Arthur: elevation to the rank of emperor.

¹⁸ Collingwood and Myres, *Roman Britain*, p. 356.

¹⁹ Morris, *The Age of Arthur*, p. 56.

²⁰ Dark, *Britain and the End of the Roman Empire,* p. 50.

11. 'KINGS WERE ANOINTED'

¹ St Patrick, op. cit., 'Letter to Coroticus', 2, 3, 14, 19, pp. 55–9.

² *Nennius: British History and The Welsh Annals*, p. 45.

³ St. Patrick, op. cit., 'Letter to Coroticus', 2, p. 59. Tolstoy notes that because the Picts are labelled as 'apostate', this incident could have taken place no later than 458, when the Pictish ruler Nectan accepted Christianity. Nikolai Tolstoy, 'Who was Coroticus?' *The Irish Ecclesiastical Record* XCVII, No 1 (1962), pp. 146–7.

⁴ Dark, *Britain and the End of the Roman Empire,* pp.145–6.

⁵ K.R. Dark, 'Centuries of survival in the west', *British Archaeology* 32 (1998), pp. 8–9.

⁶ Here and elsewhere, the terms 'Wales' and 'Welsh' are purely geographic. Both derive from the Germanic *Weala*, used by many barbarians to describe the Romans. Walloon, Wallachia, and Vlach all arguably derive from this word.

⁷ One meaning was as a subdivision of a British tribe. Frere, *Britannia*, pp. 197–8.

⁸ Dark, *Britain and the End of the Roman Empire,* p. 162.

⁹ Dark, *From Civitas to Kingdom,* pp. 92–3. Dark's mention of Irish influence in these areas is best explained as the replacement of Saxon federates by Irish federates following the Saxon Revolt.

¹⁰ Tolstoy has argued persuasively that the apparent ancestor named 'Protector' in Vortipor's genealogy was actually part of the gloss for this particular genealogy. Nikolai Tolstoy, 'Early British history and chronology', *Transactions of the Honourable Society of Cymmrodorion* (1964), pt. 2, p. 262; quoted in Thomas D. O'Sullivan, *The De Excidio of Gildas: Its Authenticity and Date* (Leiden, 1978), p. 105.

¹¹ Faral, *La Légende arthurienne*, vol. II. p. 51.

¹² *DEB* II.31, in Winterbottom, p. 31.

¹³ Although by no means certain, the fact that St Germanus meets an official with 'tribunic powers' on his visit to Britain argues that 'tribune' was

a title used in post-Roman times. Constantius, 'Germanus', 15. Note also the later ruler with the name 'Triphun'.

[14] Philip Rahtz, 'Glastonbury Tor', in Geoffrey Ashe, *The Quest for Arthur's Britain* (London, 1968), p. 201.

[15] Dark, *Britain and the End of the Roman Empire,* pp. 133–4; Alcock, 'Wales in the Arthurian Age', in Ashe, *The Quest for Arthur's Britain*, p. 91.

[16] *DEB* I.17, in Giles, *Six Old English Chronicles*, p. 306.

[17] *HB* 62, in Winterbottom, p. 37.

[18] Dumville, 'Sub-Roman Britain', pp, 182–3; Higham, *King Arthur, Mythmaking and History*, pp. 116–36.

[19] Compare with the Pictish tribe of the Venicones.

[20] *DEB* II.33.

[21] Faral, *La Légende arthurienne*, vol. II, p. 51.

[22] The reason that the *Historia* gives such a wildly inflated duration between Maelgwn and Cunedda is easily explained. The fact that Cunedda's dynasty owed its existence to the Proud Tyrant's good offices would have been a political liability after Arthur's fall. With no other British leader of any stature available to invite Cunedda in, the only alternative was to place the invitation in Roman times. Indeed, when we remember that British tradition saw the usurper Maximus (383–88) as both the founder of several Welsh dynasties, and the ruler who first settled Armorica with Britons, the motive is clear. The Venedoti could not come to Wales at the behest of a traitor like the Proud Tyrant; they could only come at the invitation of the great *British* emperor Maximus. See also Dumville, 'Sub-Roman Britain', p. 182.

[23] Ibid., and fn. 42. Note, however, that Dumville does not consider either date as historically valid.

[24] Kirby, 'British dynastic history', p. 89; Faral, *La Légende arthurienne*, Vol. II, pp. 56–7.

[25] Henry Morgan had a similar career path in the West Indies of the seventeenth century, going from pirate to governor of Jamaica: Exquemelin, *Buccaneers*, p. 225. As to the Pictish connection, it is of interest that in the sixth century we find people bearing names that may well be Pictish in origin, in particular 'Drustan' and 'Erbin', both of which display a strong similarity to those of the famous Pictish King Drust and his father, Erp.

[26] Tolstoy makes a very good point when he stresses that the only other plausible candidate for Coroticus, 'Ceretic Guletic', is little more than a name on a Strathclyde regnal list. Indeed, Tolstoy's assertion that the 'two Ceretics' may really be identical, and that Ceretic may not actually be Cunedda's son, indicates that Arthur was recruiting a number of different federates from northern Britain. Tolstoy, 'Who was Coroticus?' p. 141.

[27] St Patrick, op. cit., 'Letter to Coroticus', 2, p. 55.

[28] Morris, *Arthurian Sources*, vol. 3, p. 68.

[29] Dark, *Britain and the End of the Roman Empire*, p. 191.

[30] Gibbon, *Decline and Fall*, XXXV, pp. 384–93.

[31] Ibid., XXXVI, pp. 407–13.

[32] Gregory of Tours, *The History of the Franks*, trans. Lewis Thorpe (Harmondsworth, 1974), II.12, pp. 128–9.

[33] Sidonius, *Poems and Letters*, C. VII, 1–3, 588, pp. 107, 169.

[34] Jones, *Later Roman Empire*, vol. I, pp. 240–2.

12 'A MOST EXTRAORDINARY PLENTY'

[1] *DEB* I, 21, in Giles, *Six Old English Chronicles*, p. 308.

[2] Ibid. The displacement of thousands of Britons in the 440s would make a subsequent plague well-nigh inevitable. Malnourished Britons would have been the perfect hosts for deadly diseases, and their wanderings would have spread contagion to all corners of the diocese.

[3] Dark, *Britain and the End of the Roman Empire*, pp. 99–100.

[4] Ibid., p. 55.

[5] Christopher Snyder, *An Age of Tyrants* (University Park, 1989), pp. 245–7.

[6] Courtenay Stevens, *Sidonius Apollinaris and His Age* (Oxford, 1933), p. 70.

[7] Dark, *From Civitas to Kingdom*, pp. 187–91.

[8] *Conciliae Galliae a. 314–a. 506*, ed. C. Munier (Turholti, 1963).

[9] Sidonius, *Poems and Letters*, IX, ix, 6–16.

[10] Faral, *La Légende arthurienne*, vol. II, pp. 53–6.

[11] Sidonius, *Poems and Letters*, IX, xiii, 5.

[12] One of the earliest Welsh poems, *The Lament for Gereint*, speaks of 'Arthur's men', and may be the first extant literary mention of something resembling the Knights of the Round Table.

[13] Gidlow, *Reign of Arthur*, p. 108. The name of his son, Cynric, is also probably Brythonic, meaning 'Hound King'. Note also the *British* king Cerdic whom Bede mentions: *HE* IV.23.

[14] Dark, *Britain and the End of the Roman Empire*, pp. 57–60.

[15] Garmonsway, *ASC*, pp. 14–17.

[16] Cleary, *The Ending*, pp. 201–3. Cleary raises the possibility that at least some Britons may actually have possessed Saxon items.

[17] *DEB* I, 23. For one model of how the Late Roman *foedus* may have operated, see Walter Goffart, *Barbarians and Romans AD 418–584: The Techniques of Accommodation* (Princeton, 1980), pp. 53–4.

[18]Christopher Sparey-Green, 'Poundbury, Dorset: Settlement and economy in Late and post-Roman Britain', in Dark, *External Contacts and the Economy of Late Roman and Post-Roman Britain,* pp.137–42.

[19] Rachel Bromwich, *The Welsh Triads* (Cardiff, 1961), p. 154.

[20] Nash Williams, *Early Christian Monuments*, p. 123.

[21] Both Cuneglassus and Vortipor are accused of setting aside their wives. The fact that Gildas accuses Vortipor of 'raping' his daughter *could* be the origin of the *Historia*'s account of Vortigern's incest with his own daughter. *DEB* II.31, 32.

13. 'A HUMBLE MAN'

[1] It is worth noting that Gildas' phrase about the Proud Tyrant may also be a sarcastic reference to the *Dux Bellorum*'s humble birth as the son of Catel. The statement about Ambrosius' humility would then put him in the best possible light: a man humble even though his birth is noble, and thus in no way like the arrogant parvenu who preceded him.

[2] *HB* 66, *Nennius: British History and the Welsh Annals*, p. 39.

[3] It is noteworthy that one source of the scepticism about the *ASC* is based not on anomalies concerning events in the fifth century, but on the suspiciously regular intervals of citations for the sixth. A number of passages from the latter are at regular four-year intervals, suggesting that an Easter Table was 'backdated' with legends about much earlier times. Since the earliest section of the *ASC* for the fifth century concerns purely British matters, and even those passages about the Kentish Saxons show great irregularity, this suggests that the earlier material was compiled in a very different manner from later Saxon citations. Indeed, the best explanation is that these are citations from Late Antiquity, and therefore much more reliable than those of the next century. Alcock, *Arthur's Britain*, p. 116.

[4] David Dumville, 'The West Saxon genealogical regnal list and the chronology of early Wessex', *Peritia* 4 (1985), pp. 39–60.

[5] Yorke, 'The origins of the Anglo-Saxon kingdoms', p. 25.

[6] Procopius, *History of the Wars*, trans. H.B. Dewing (London, 1914), VIII, 20.

[7] Garmonsway, *ASC*, pp. 12–13.

[8] Garmonsway, *ASC*, pp. 12–13. Doubts about the reliability of the *ASC* rely mainly on the supposed illiteracy of the Saxons. There is a generally held belief among scholars that it is very doubtful that 'illiterate' Saxons would have been able to preserve accurate records over two centuries: Dark, *Britain and the End of the Roman Empire*, pp. 43–5. Yet scholars also assert that independent, presumably literate, British kingdoms existed in eastern Britain

within a century of Augustine's arrival. They also leave open the possibility that many Christian Britons—and perhaps even Christian Saxons—existed in Saxon Britain prior to Augustine: Dark, *Britain and the End of the Roman Empire*, pp. 78–85. Since illiterate Germanic rulers found literate Gallo-Romans very useful in their administration during the fifth century, it would be at least useful to have an argument that would state clearly why illiterate Germanic rulers on the opposite side of the Channel would not have followed the same course. Sidonius, *Poems and Letters*, IV, xxii; VIII, iii; VIII, vi. The fact is that the sources for sixth-century Saxon England are so scanty that there is practically no evidence *either way* as to what records were (or were not) being kept in Saxon England. To say we have no evidence for a Saxon capability to preserve their past is simply to default to a very nineteenth-century image of these people. For the probable use by sixth-century Saxons of Roman consular dates, see Appendix III.

[9] The order of the battles in the *Historia* is not clear, but the author would argue that the following match-up between the two sources makes *Guollop* by far the best choice for the first battle:

HB	ASC
No Name	*Aegelesthrep* (Aylesford?)
'on the river Darenth'	*Crecganford* (Crayford)
Rhyd yr Afael (Episford)	*Wippedsfleot*
No name ('Stone by Gallic Sea')	No name

The *Historia*'s claim that Vortimer besieged the Saxons three times on the Isle of Thanet also strongly suggests that the first time this occurred was as a result of *Guollop*: *HB* 44.

[10] Nikolai Tolstoy first saw the *Historia*'s *Guollop* citation as occurring in the year 458, *twelve years* after what he asserted was the date of Vortigern's accession: 446. This offers a crucial insight into the true relationship between the *Historia* and the *ASC*—as well as between Vortimer and Ambrosius. Note, however, that in Tolstoy's opinion *Guollop* marked the *end* of Vortigern's power, and thus the beginning of the rise of Ambrosius. Tolstoy, 'Nennius, chapter fifty-six', pp. 153–4.

[11] The provenance of the name Vortigern and other Brythonic 'superlative kingly' names is a complicated issue, and scholars sometimes take a some-what anachronistic view of it, supporting their assertions with Celtic names that may actually be from later periods. O. Padel, 'Recent work in the origins of the Arthurian legend: A comment', in *Arthuriana* 5:3 (Fall 1995). While it is certainly true that in western Britain we find many such names in the sixth century, our knowledge of naming practices in Lowland Britain in the fifth is much more fragmentary. Nash Williams's comment about the 'alien

derivation' of the Class I stones of the sixth century suggests that some of these names may ultimately derive from Ireland, and that Vortigern may well be the name that the Irish used for the Proud Tyrant. Nash Williams, *Early Christian Monuments*, pp. 170–1, 213.

[12] The idea that accurate insular historical information is unlikely earlier than a 'horizon' in the late sixth century is unproven. It is important to note that if a work of 110 chapters, such as Gildas' *De Excidio*, could be accurately preserved down to the ninth century, it is also likely that other British accounts could be similarly transmitted. In particular, the inhabitants of the British (and therefore presumably literate) polity that existed in the London area until the dawn of the sixth century would almost certainly have preserved accounts of the events that so transformed neighbouring Kent. Dark, *Britain and the End of the Roman Empire,* pp. 97–103.

[13] *HB* 49.

[14] Gibbon, *Decline and Fall*, XXVII, p. 99.

[15] The Pillar of Eliseg's testimony that Britu was the son of Sevira and Vortigern suggests that he may have been born later than Ambrosius. If Pascent was a product of Arthur's first marriage, all three siblings would thus have had only one parent in common—a plausible enough reason for discord within the family.

[16] *HB* 43, *Nennius: British History and the Welsh Annals*, p. 31.

[17] Garmonsway, *ASC*, pp. 12–13.

[18] Dark, *Britain and the End of the Roman Empire,* p. 59.

[19] *HE* I.25.

[20] *HB* 38.

[21] Garmonsway, *ASC*, pp. 12–13.

[22] *DEB*, I.23, in Winterbottom, p. 26.

[23] Significantly, Guoyrancgonus is not a name, but a title: in this case merely the Brythonic word for 'governor'. As with 'the Tribune', once again we see a fifth-century conflation of personal names and political titles. *HB* 37.

[24] It is also of interest that the *Historia* tells us that Vortigern had a number of wives. *HB* 47.

14. 'MOST KINGLY'

[1] Sidonius, *Poems and Letters*, C. V, 201–3, p. 77.

[2] Ibid., C. V, 583–91, p. 113.

[3] Jones, *Later Roman Empire,* vol. I, p. 241.

[4] Ibid., vol. I, pp. 240–3.

[5] Ibid., vol. I, pp. 241–2; Sidonius, *Poems and Letters*, p. xxv.

[6] Gregory, *History of the Franks*, II, 12.

[7] Ibid., II, 18.

[8] Cleary, *The Ending*, pp. 136, 160. Also of no little interest, one of Aegidius' ancestors seems to bear the name of 'Alanus': Faral, *La Légende arthurienne*, vol II, p. 83.

[9] Eugippius, *The Life of Saint Severinus*, 44, pp. 103–6; Jones, *Later Roman Empire*, vol. I, p. 246; Heather, *Fall of the Roman Empire*, pp. 411–12.

[10] Jordanes, *Goths*, 45, p. 75.

[11] Collingwood and Myres, *Roman Britain*, p. 356. Gildas does speak of Britons leaving for the continent, but this is *after* the Revolt, which, as we shall see occurred only in 469.

[12] The author would very much welcome *any* comprehensive, well-documented argument for Riothamus as a refugee Breton warlord, or even for the existence of a mid-fifth century Breton state. Also, use of such terms as the 'relatively obscure Riothamus' begs the question: relative to what other *better-documented* fifth-century British ruler? The fact that three separate sources mention Riothamus is our best indication that he was the most significant Briton of his age. Higham, *King Arthur, Mythmaking and History*, p. 76.'

[13] Gibbon, *Decline and Fall*, XXXVI, p. 445; Geoffrey Ashe, *The Discovery of King Arthur* (New York, 1985), pp. 53–9.

[14] It is of interest that one important study of Gildas' implied chronology finds that the probable interval between the *Adventus* and the Revolt involved 'at least' a decade. Dumville, 'The chronology of the *De Excidio Britanniae*', pp. 72–3.

[15] Cleary, *The Ending*, pp. 200–1.

[16] *Nennius: British History and The Welsh Annals*, p. 45.

[17] It is worth noting that if 44 years are added to the *ASC*'s date for the last battle between Hengest and Vortimer, 473, we arrive at a date of 517 for the battle of Badon. This is almost precisely the date found in the *Annales Cambriae (AC)*, and could indicate that the *AC*'s compiler saw Gildas as having been born 44 years after Ambrosius' last battle. This anticipates the argument that O'Sullivan makes by some 1500 years: O'Sullivan, *The De Excidio of Gildas*. For a thoughtful alternative explanation for this, see Howard Wiseman, 'The derivation of the date of the Badon entry in the *Annales Cambriae* from Bede and Gildas'.

[18] The author's hypothesis owes much to the one advanced by Geoffrey Ashe in his *The Discovery of King Arthur*. In the author's estimation Ashe's theory remains one of the most important twentieth-century insights into this issue. It is also interesting to compare Arthur with the more modern figure of Napoleon. Texts about the latter might call him Buonaparte, First Consul,

Emperor, 'the Little Corporal', or even 'Boney' in English sources. If our sources were as fragmentary as those of fifth-century Britain there would be no way to connect all these names to a single person.

[19] Very significantly, no name resembling Riothamus or Riocatus is found in any inscription from the Roman period: R.G. Collingwood and R.P. Wright, *The Roman Inscriptions of Britain* (Gloucester, 1990). For the most careful dating of names of this pattern in western Britain, please see Nash Williams, *Early Christian Monuments*, pp. 170–1, 213.

[20] We have already seen an example of this in the sixth-century ruler of Dyfed known as 'Triphun', the Brythonic version of the Latin title 'tribune'. It is very doubtful that either Triphun or Riothamus were given these elevated names at birth.

[21] *Gregorii Turonensis: Historiarum Libri X, Scriptores Rerum Meroving-icorum,* t. 1, p. 1, fasc. 1, *MGH* (1894–98), II, 18, p. 65.

[22] Morris, *Arthurian Sources,* vol. 3, p. 166.

[23] Eugippius, *Saint Severinus,* 7, p. 45.

[24] Hydatius, *The Chronicle of Hydatius*, pp. 171, 194.

[25] Gregory, *History of the Franks*, II, 18.

[26] Ibid., II, 19.

[27] Jones, *Later Roman Empire,* vol. I, p. 242.

[28] Sidonius, *Poems and Letters*, C II, 193–211.

[29] Ibid., C II, 10–20, p. 7.

[30] Ibid., C II, 537–548, pp. 55–57. Heather stresses the naval dimension to this panegyric: Heather, *Fall of the Roman Empire*, p. 401.

[31] Damascius, *The Philosophical History*, trans. Polymnia Athanassiadi (Oakville, CT, 1999), p. 145.

[32] Walter Goffart, 'Rome, Constantinople and the barbarians in Late Antiquity', *American Historical Review* 76 (1981), pp. 275–306.

[33] Gibbon, *Decline and Fall*, XXXVI, pp. 448–51.

[34] Ibid., XXXVI, p. 437.

[35] Heather, *The Fall of the Roman Empire,* pp. 402–4; Jones, *Later Roman Empire,* vol. I, p. 222; Sidonius, *Poems and Letters*, p. xxvii.

[36] Sidonius, *Poems and Letters*, VII, vi, 6–9.

[37] Hydatius, *The Chronicle of Hydatius*, pp. 120–3.

[38] Peter Brent, *The Viking Saga* (London, 1995), pp. 49–51, 59.

[39] Raymond Chevallier, *Roman Roads*, trans. N.H. Field (London, 1976), p. 161.

15. 'BY WAY OF OCEAN'

[1] It is worth comparing Riothamus with a genuine local Breton warlord of

the sixth century, Waroch, who was a constant thorn in the side of the Franks. After decades of Breton immigration, Waroch's forces carried out a series of savage raids—that extended only as far as Nantes. Gregory, *History of the Franks*, IX.18.

[2] Brent, *Viking Saga*, pp. 49, 59.

[3] Sidonius, *Poems and Letters*, III, ix, 1, pp. 35–7.

[4] Ibid., III, ix, 2, p. 37.

[5] Ibid., I, vii, 1–3, pp. 367–9.

[6] Ibid., I, vii, 5, p. 371.

[7] Stevens, *Sidonius Apollinaris*, p. 106.

[8] Sidonius, *Poems and Letters*, I, vii, 5, p. 371.

[9] Herwig Wolfram, *History of the Goths*, trans. Thomas Dunlap (Berkeley, 1988), p. 130.

[10] Jordanes, *Goths*, 45, p. 74.

[11] Sidonius, *Poems and Letters*, C. V, 402–416, p. 97.

[12] Jordanes, *Goths*, 45, p. 74.

[13] Gregory, *History of the Franks*, II.18.

[14] Ibid., II.18.

[15] Jones, *Later Roman Empire*, vol. I, p. 243; Bury, *Later Roman Empire*, vol I, pp. 342–3.

[16] Gregory, *History of the Franks*, II.19.

[17] Theophanes, *The Chronicle of Theophanes Confessor*, trans. Cyril Mango and Roger Scott (Oxford, 1997), p. 243.

[18] Eugippius, *Life of St Severinus*, 32, pp. 86–74.

[19] Interestingly, Odovacer's coup was precipitated by a dispute with Italian landowners over what percentage of the harvest would go to the largely barbarian army—the same issue that initiated the Saxon Revolt. However, in contrast to Britain, the barbarians simply took over. This suggests that in 469 there was a genuine civil war that involved Britons on both sides, not simply a mercenary revolt. This is precisely the scenario that *Camlann* implies. Jones, *Later Roman Empire*, vol. I, p. 244.

16. 'THE FIRE OF VENGEANCE'

[1] Sidonius, *Poems and Letters*, VIII, vi, 13–18, pp. 429–33.

[2] *The Annals of Ulster*, pp. 50–1.

[3] Sidonius, *Poems and Letters*, IX, ix, 6–9.

[4] *HB* 44, in Giles, *Six Old English Chronicles*, p. 404.

[5] Garmonsway, *ASC*, pp 12–15.

[6] Reginald Lane-Poole, *Chronicles and Annals* (Oxford, 1926) pp. 16–20.

[7] *The Mabinogion*, trans. Gwyn Jones (London, 1974), p. 128.

References

[8] Skene, *Four Books*, 'Pa Gur', pp. 262–3.

[9] Geoffrey of Monmouth, *History of the Kings of Britain*, trans. Lewis Thorpe (Harmondsworth, 1966), p. 257.

[10] Bromwich, *The Welsh Triads*, p. 144.

[11] Jones and Mattingly, *Atlas of Roman Britain*, p. 12. The map for Arthur's *Camlann* campaign is a simplified version of the map cited in this work.

[12] From his spurious Life of St Germanus the author of the *Historia* would have 'known' that the Proud Tyrant died not from wounds gained in battle, but from heavenly fire. From the Harleian genealogies he would have learned that Cattegirn was a member of the Powysian dynasty founded by Vortigern. Since the Proud Tyrant could not die twice, the only plausible identity for this Cattegirn who dies at *Wippedsfleot*, and thus *before* Vortigern, would have been as a *son* of the Proud Tyrant.

[13] Skene, *Four Books*, 'The Verses of the Graves', pp. 312–16, 'Pa Gur', pp. 262–3.

[14] *HE* I, 25.

[15] *Geiriadur Priofysgol Cymru, A Dictionary of the Welsh Language*, 4 vols (Caerdydd, 1968–87), pp. 2095–6. Also 'flood', 'influx'.

[16] Vegetius, *Epitome*, III, 20, p. 101.

[17] *HB* 44., in *Nennius: British History and The Welsh Annals*, p. 31.

[18] Skene, *Four Books*, 'The Verses of the Graves', pp. 312–16.

[19] Plutarch. *Moralia* (London, 1936), Vol. XII, 'Concerning the Face that Appears in the Orb of the Moon', pp. 943–52.

[20] One strong candidate for the origin of the name Avalon is the old British god of the underworld, Avallach or Aballach. Indeed, the Welsh name for Avalon is *Ynys Avallach*. This deity even appears as one of the ancestors in several British dynastic lists. Roger Sherman Loomis, 'The Legend of Arthur's Survival', in R.S. Loomis (ed.), *Arthurian Literature of the Middle Ages* (Oxford, 1959), p. 66. Procopius tells a curious story that ties in with this. He says that Thanet was a kind of 'Isle of the Dead', where souls from mainland Europe congregated: Dark, *Britain and the End of the Roman Empire*, p. 28. This story may be a garbled reference to Avallach's position as god of the underworld, since Thanet would be the first landfall for anyone sailing from the continent, living or dead. The fact that Thanet bears more than a passing resemblance to the Greek word for death, *thanatos*, may also have reinforced this view among Procopius' informants. Procopius, *History of the Wars*, VIII, 20.

[21] *DEB* I.24, in Giles, *Six Old English Chronicles*, p. 311.

[22] Ibid., I.25, in Giles, ibid., p. 312.

[23] Ibid., II.27.

²⁴ The *Annales Cambriae* (*AC*) tell us that Arthur and Medrawt died at *Camlann. Nennius: British History and The Welsh Annals,* p. 45. Curiously, in other Welsh literature Bedwyr is given a 'patronymic' of *Pedrawc* or *Pedrawt.* In medieval Welsh the labials 'm' and 'p' are often conflated, and it is possible that Pedrawt is merely a later corruption of Medrawt. Moreover, Medrawt is sometimes described as a Welsh version of the Latin name Moderatus, and it is possible that, as with Arthur and other Romano-Britons of this period, Medrawt/Pedrawt may simply be Bedwyr's Latin name. In other words, the *AC may* be telling us that Bedwyr was one of the twelve British nobles that the *ASC* reports fell at *Wippedsfleot.* Sims-Williams, 'Early Welsh Arthurian Poems', p. 43.

²⁵ *HB* 48.

²⁶ *HB* 44., in *Nennius: British History and The Welsh Annals,* p. 31.

APPENDIX II: HAPPY BIRTHDAY, GILDAS!

¹ *DEB* I.26. This particular version is from Dr. H.W. Wiseman's 'The derivation of the date of the Arthurian entries in the *Annales Cambriae* from Bede and Gildas'.

² *HE* I.16.

³ *HE* I.23, II.14, and V.23.

⁴ *HE* I.15, in Sherly-Price, *Bede,* p. 55.

⁵ Jones and Casey, 'Gallic Chronicle restored', pp. 370–6.

⁶ *HE* I.23, II.14, and V.23. Note that in each case he explicitly says that these are approximate intervals from the *Adventus.*

⁷ *Nennius: British History and The Welsh Annals,* p. 45.

⁸ *DEB* I.26. Gildas' complete silence on the 'years without summer' in 535–37 also makes it unlikely that he was writing at any time after 535. This global occluding of the sun would have produced widespread famine, and a providentially minded Gildas would undoubtedly have mentioned it if he had actually lived through it. Keys, *Catastrophe,* pp. 125–35.

⁹ *DEB* I.26. O'Sullivan's explanation for Gildas' passage is ingenious, as are most explanations for this passage. However, it ignores the fact that nowhere does Gildas say that there were *two* distinct counter-attacks by the British after the Revolt, which, moreover, were separated by forty-three years and one month. Indeed, if *Badon* had been fought so recently, this makes the *De Excidio* superfluous. Many of Gildas' readers would have had vivid memories of those times, and the 'white-haired' Vortipor would have been old enough to have taken part in the fighting. Much of the '*Badon* generation' would have still been in power, and thus well aware of the Saxon threat. It

also remains unclear why anyone would bother to record that forty-three years *and one month* separated Ambrosius' last victory (unnoted by Gildas) from the battle of *Badon*. O'Sullivan, *The De Excidio of Gildas*, pp. 134–81.

APPENDIX III: THE *HISTORIA* AND THE *CHRONICLE*: THEIR COMMON ORIGINS

[1] *HB* 66, in *Nennius: British History and The Welsh Annals*, p. 39. Garmonsway, *ASC*, pp. 12–13.

[2] Constantius, *Life of St Germanus*, 17–18.

[3] *DEB* I.20.

[4] *HE* I.15.

[5] Dumville 'Some aspects of the chronology of the *Historia Brittonum*', pp. 439–45.

[6] *HB* 66, in Giles, *Six Old English Chronicles*, p. 416.

[7] Ibid., fn 2, p. 440.

[8] Jones and Casey, 'Gallic Chronicle restored', pp. 368–73.

[9] Note that this is *insular* timekeeping, from a period when Britain was outside the empire. This is not the very strict assignment of a whole year to one or the other emperor, as seen in the *Gallic Chronicle of 452*. Note how Jones and Casey stress that although Honorius actually died in October of 423, Theodosius II's first regnal year did not begin until January 424, so his reign would count as 27 and *not the expected 28 years*. But if both Stilicho/Honorius and Theodosius II share the same year, each reign would possess 28 years. Jones and Casey, 'Gallic Chronicle restored', pp. 370–1. Bede, of course, assigns a total of 28 regnal years for Honorius, in tandem with first Arcadius (13) and then Theodosius the Younger (15). *Bedae: Chronica Maiora*, op. cit., p. 300.

[10] *HB* 66, in *Nennius: British History and The Welsh Annals*, p. 39.

[11] Moreover, this may also give some insight into a puzzling anomaly in the Laud Manuscript of the *ASC*, which reads:

> 519—In this year Cerdic and Cynric obtained the kingdom of the West Saxons and the same year they fought against the Britons at a place now called *Cerdicesford*.

> 527—In this year Cerdic and Cynric fought against the Britons at the place which is called *Cerdicesford*.

That Cerdic fights the Britons *twice* in the same place would be best explained if the compiler of the Laud *Chronicle* MS had a citation very like the one in chapter 66, and assumed that Decius and 'Valerian' were *co-consuls* in the *same* year, 519. He would then conclude that the information about Cerdic's accession and his battle at *Cerdicesford* both applied to the same year. Thus, two separate entries would be combined into one for the year 519, while the original citation for 527 would also be retained. Garmonsway, *ASC*, pp. 15–17.

[12] *HB* 66, in *Nennius: British History and The Welsh Annals*, p. 39.

[13] Arguments that the 'Agitius' mentioned in Gildas is somehow not Aetius ignore the fact that continental sources call Aetius by an almost identical name: 'Egetius'. *Scriptorum Rerum Merovingicorum*, t. 7, op. cit., p. 854. It is therefore highly unlikely that this is the later Roman warlord Aegedius, who was never a consul, and who is most likely the 'Egegius' mentioned in this source. 'Agitius, consul for the third time' is thus a precise consular date that also has an analogue in the *ASC*.

[14] Higham, *King Arthur, Mythmaking and History*, pp. 45–58.

[15] Garmonsway, *ASC*, pp. 12–13.

[16] Bosworth, *Anglo-Saxon Dictionary*, p. 1067. This is the only early Saxon battle which is described as a *threap*. Moreover, all the others appear to be associated with place-names.

[17] Note that Gildas gives the same sequence of events in both chapter 2 and chapter 20. The ordering is very deliberate. *DEB* I.2, 20.

[18] Nikolai Tolstoy first drew attention to the crucial insight that 446 would be Vortigern's accession date, and 12 years afterward (458) would come the battle of *Guollopum*. Tolstoy, 'Nennius, chapter fifty-six', pp. 152–4.

[19] Ibid.; *HB* 31, *Nennius: British History and The Welsh Annals*, p. 26. That this would be used to calculate a new *Adventus* date suggests that the *Historia* compiler considered it an authentic piece of information for fifth-century Britain, and did not simply fabricate it. Dumville, 'Some aspects of the chronology of the *Historia Brittonum*', p. 444. Note also that the *Historia* compiler saw 388 as a highly significant date. He calculated this as the date when Cunedda and his sons came into Britain, and had Maglocunus reigning exactly 146 years later. Dumville, 'Sub-Roman Britain', p. 182 and fn. 42.

[20] David Dumville, '*Historia Brittonum*: an insular history from the Carolingian Age', in A. Scharer and G. Scheibelreiter (eds), *Historiographie im fruhen Mittelalter* (Vienna and Munich, 1994), pp. 432–4.

[21] *HE* I.15-21; *Bedae: Chronica Maiora*, op. cit., p. 304.

[22] *Prosper Aquitani: Epitoma Chronicon, Auctores Antiquissimi*, t. 9.2, *MGH*, (1892), p. 472. Just why Bede would place Germanus after the Revolt very likely comes from his reading of Gildas. If the first Saxons arrived only

in 450, then Germanus' Alleluia Victory over Saxons must necessarily come some time after this. That archaeology has discovered Saxon settlement even earlier than 428 neither writer could have known.

[23] Dumville, 'Some aspects of the chronology of the *Historia Brittonum*', p. 444; Tolstoy, 'Nennius, chapter fifty-six', p. 152. Perhaps not coincidentally, a 40-year interval from the date of the usurpation of Constantine III would give a date of 446, while a similar calculation from the date of Honorius' supposed 'rescript' of 410 would give a date of 450.

[24] *Prosper Aquitani: Epitoma Chronicon,* op. cit., pp. 470–2. Significantly, one citation is in the reign of Felix and Taurus.

[25] Lane-Poole, *Chronicles and Annals*, pp. 17–22.

[26] *HB* 66, in *Nennius: British History and The Welsh Annals*, p. 39.

[27] Since the writer has argued that both the *Historia* and the *ASC* drew from the same original sources, an alternative might be that the *ASC*'s chronology is merely a recalculation of more authentic material originally in the *Historia*. However, such a view would require an explanation as to just how the Decius and 'Valerianus' citation could possibly fit in with an *Adventus* in 428. Dumville actually does this—but only to show that the *Historia* contains no authentic insular material. Dumville, 'Some aspects of the chronology of the *Historia Brittonum*', pp. 442–3. Also, with the *ASC* citations two years out of sync with any consular table, it would have been impossible for the *ASC* compilers to derive Cerdic's dates from the *Historia*.

[28] Please see Chapter 13.

[29] Gregory, *History of the Franks*, I.48; II.43; III.37.

[30] Although absent in Bede, the four *ASC* references to Hengest's battles behave in precisely the same manner as all other insular dates in the *ASC*, suggesting that Bede was aware of only some of the information from which the authors of both the *ASC* and the *Historia* drew.

[31] *HE* I.15, in Sherly-Price, p. 56.

[32] Lane-Poole, *Chronicles and Annals*, pp. 16–24.

[33] In his Preface, Bede talks of his association with Albinus, who is an important source for historical details about Kent. But Bede is entirely silent about early events in Wessex. The only Cerdic he seems to be aware of is a *British* king reigning almost two centuries after the founder of Wessex. Bede IV.23. Significantly, Charles W. Jones says: 'Bede did not have satisfactory knowledge of Wessex… therefore, to use Bede as a standard for judging the reliability of the Parker Chronicle is not satisfactory.' Charles W Jones, *Bede, the Schools and the Computus* (Aldershot, 1994), p. 35.

BIBLIOGRAPHY

Abbreviations:
MGH   *Monumenta Germaniae Historica*

PRIMARY SOURCES

Ammianus Marcellinus (1894) *The Roman History of Ammianus Marcellinus*, trans. C.D. Yonge. London: G. Bell.

Aneirin (1988) *Aneirin: Y Gododdin, Britain's Oldest Heroic Poem*, trans. A.O.H. Jarman. Llandysul: Gomer.

Anglo-Saxon Chronicle (1972) trans. G.N. Garmonsway. London: Dent.

Annales Cambriae, in *Nennius: British History and The Welsh Annals* (1980) ed. and trans. John Morris. London: Phillimore.

Annals of the Kingdom of Ireland by the Four Masters from the earliest period to the year 1616 (1966) ed. John O'Donovan. New York: AMS Press.

Annals of Ulster (1983) ed. and trans. Sean MacAirt and Gearold MacNiocail. Dublin: Institute for Advanced Studies.

Bedae: Chronica Maiora ad a. DCCXXV ; *Chronica Minora, Saec. IV, V, VI, VII*, vol. III (1894–98) *Auctores Antiquissimi*, t. 13.2. *MGH*.

Bede (1968) *A History of the English Church and People*, trans. Leo Sherly-Price. Harmondsworth: Penguin.

Chronica Gallia a CCCCLII (1892) *Auctores Antiquissimi*, t. 9.2. *MGH*.

Chronica Gallia a DXI (1892) *Auctores Antiquissimi*, t. 9.2. *MGH*.

Claudianus (1981) *Panegyric on the Fourth Consulate of Honorius*, trans. William Barr. Liverpool: F. Cairns.

Claudianus (1922) *Claudian*, 2 vols, trans. Maurice Platnauer. London: Heinemann.

Conciliae Galliae a. 314–a. 506 (1963) ed. C. Munier. Turholti.

Constantius (1954), in *The Western Fathers. Being the lives of SS Martin of Tours, Ambrose, Augustine of Hippo, Honoratus of Arles, and Germanus of Auxerre*, ed. and trans. F.R. Hoare. London and New York: Sheed and Ward.

Damascius (1999) *The Philosophical History*, trans. Polymnia Athanassiadi. Oakville, CT: D. Brown.

Eugippius, Abbas (1965) *The Life of Saint Severinus*, trans. George W. Robinson. Cambridge, MA: Harvard University Press.

Four Books of Ancient Wales, The (1982) trans. W.F. Skene. New York: AMS Press.

Bibliography

Geoffrey of Monmouth (1966) *History of the Kings of Britain*, trans. Lewis Thorpe. Harmondsworth: Penguin.

Gildas (1978) *The Ruin of Britain and Other Works*, trans. M. Winterbottom. Chichester: Phillimore.

Gregory of Tours (1974) *The History of the Franks*, trans. Lewis Thorpe. Harmondsworth: Penguin.

Gregorii Turonensis: Historiarum Libri X (1894–98) *Scriptores Rerum Merovingicorum*, t. 1, p. 1, fasc. 1. *MGH.*

Herodotus (1942) *The Persian Wars*, trans. George Rawlinson. New York: Random House.

Historia Brittonum (1894–98) *Chronica Minora, Saec. IV, V, VI, VII, Auctores Antiquissimi* vol. III, t. 13.2. *MGH.*

Hydatius (1993) *The Chronicle of Hydatius and the Consularia Constantinopolitana*, ed. and trans. R.W. Burgess. Oxford: Clarendon Press.

Jordanes (1905) *The Origins and Deeds of the Goths*, ed. and trans. C.C. Mierow. Princeton, NJ: Princeton University Press.

Mabinogion, The (1974) trans. Gwyn Jones. London: Dent.

Nennius (1980) *British History and the Welsh Annals*, ed and trans. John Morris. Chichester: Phillimore.

Olympiodorus (1981) in Blockley, R.C., *The Fragmentary Classicising Historians of the Later Roman Empire.* (See below, 'Secondary Sources'.)

Orosius (1936) *Seven Books of History against the Pagans*, trans. I.W. Raymond. New York: Columbia University Press.

Patrick, St (1978) *St Patrick: His Writings and Muirchu's Life*, trans. A.B.E. Hood. London: Phillimore.

Plutarch (1936) *Moralia*, trans. F.C. Babbitt et al. London: Dent.

Priscus (1981) in Blockley, R.C., *The Fragmentary Classicising Historians of the Later Roman Empire.* (See below, 'Secondary Sources'.)

Procopius (1914) *History of the Wars*, trans. H.B. Dewing. London: Heinemann.

Prosper Aquitani: Epitoma Chronicon (1892) *Auctores Antiquissimi*, t. 9.2. *MGH.*

Scriptorum Rerum Merovingicorum, t. VII, *MGH.*

Sidonius Apollinaris (1934) *Sidonius: Poems and Letters*, 2 vols, trans. W.B. Anderson. London: Heinemann.

Sozomen (1886) *The Ecclesiastical History of Sozomen*, trans. C.D. Hartranft. New York: Philip Schaff.

341

Theophanes (1997) *The Chronicle of Theophanes Confessor*, trans. Cyril Mango and Roger Scott. Oxford: Clarendon Press.

Vegetius (1993) *Epitome of Military Science*, trans. N.P. Milner. Liverpool: Liverpool University Press.

Zosimus (1967) Zosimus: *New History, The Decline of Rome*, trans. James J. Buchanan and Harold T. Davis. San Antonio: Trinity University Press.

SECONDARY SOURCES

Afanasivev, G. (1989) 'The Burtasses', in P. Puchkov (ed.), *Peoples that Vanished.*

Alcock, Leslie (1973) *Arthur's Britain: History and Archaeology AD 367–634*. London: Penguin.

Ashe, Geoffrey (1985) *The Discovery of King Arthur*. New York: Doubleday.

Ashe, Geoffrey (ed.) (1968) *The Quest for Arthur's Britain*. London: Pall Mall Press.

Bachrach, Bernard (1973) *History of the Alans in the West*. Minneapolis: University of Minnesota Press.

Bachrach, Bernard (2002) *Warfare and Military Organization in Pre-Crusade Europe*. Aldershot: Variorum.

Bachrach, Bernard (1990) 'The question of King Arthur's existence, and of Romano-British naval operations', *The Haskins Society Journal* 2, 13–28.

Bannerman, John (1974) *Studies in the History of Dalriada*. Edinburgh: Scottish Academic Press.

Blockley, R.C. (1981) *The Fragmentary Classicising Historians of the Later Roman Empire*, 2 vols. Liverpool: F. Cairns.

Böhme, Horst Wolfgang (1986) 'Das Ende der Römerherrschaft in Britannien und die Angelsachsische Besiedlung Englands im 5. Jahrhundert', *Jahrbuch des Römisch-Germanischen Zentralmuseums Mainz* 33, 468–574.

Bosworth, Joseph (1898) *Anglo-Saxon Dictionary*. Oxford: Clarendon.

Brent, Peter (1995) *The Viking Saga*. London: Weidenfeld and Nicolson.

Bromwich, Rachel (1961) *The Welsh Triads*. Cardiff: University of Wales Press.

Bromwich, Rachel, Jarman, A.O.H. and Roberts, B.F. (eds) (1991) *The Arthur of the Welsh*. Cardiff: University of Wales Press.

Bibliography

Bury, J.B. (1923) *History of the Later Roman Empire*, 2 vols. London: Macmillan.

Charles-Edwards, Thomas (1991) 'The Arthur of History', in Bromwich et al. (eds), *The Arthur of the Welsh*.

Chevallier, Raymond (1976) *Roman Roads*, trans. N.H. Field. London: Batsford.

Cleary, A.S.E. (1989) *The Ending of Roman Britain*. London: Batsford.

Collingwood, R.G. and Myres, J.N.L. (1936) *Roman Britain and the English Settlements*. Oxford: Clarendon Press.

Collingwood, R.G. and Wright, R.P. (1990) *The Roman Inscriptions of Britain*. Gloucester: A. Sutton.

Dark, K.R. (1994) *From Civitas to Kingdom: British Political Continuity, 300–800*. London: Leicester University Press.

Dark, K.R. (ed.) (1996) *External Contacts and the Economy of Late Roman and Post-Roman Britain* (Studies in Celtic History, 16). Woodbridge: Boydell Press.

Dark, K.R. (1998) 'Centuries of survival in the west', *British Archaeology* 32.

Dark, K.R. (2000) *Britain and the End of the Roman Empire*. Stroud: Tempus Publishing.

Dark, S.P. (1996) 'Paleoecological Evidence for Continuity and Change in Britain, ca. A.D. 400–800', in K.R. Dark (ed.), *External Contacts and the Economy of Late Roman and Post-Roman Britain*.

Davidson, H.B. Elllis (1964) *Gods and Myths of Northern Europe*. Baltimore, MD: Penguin.

Dooghe, Didier-Georges (1974) *Les Saxons de Gaule*. Lille.

Dumville, David (1972–74) 'Some aspects of the chronology of the *Historia Brittonum*', *Bulletin of the Board of Celtic Studies* 25.

Dumville, David (1975–76) '"Nennius" and the *Historia Brittonum*', *Studia Celtica* 10–11.

Dumville, David (1977) 'Sub-Roman Britain: History and legend', *History* 112, 173–192; also in (1990) *Histories and Pseudo-histories of the Insular Middle Ages*. Aldershot: Variorum.

Dumville, David (1984) 'The chronology of the *De Excidio Britanniae*, vol. I', in Lapidge and Dumville (eds), *Gildas: New Approaches*.

Dumville, David (1985) 'The West Saxon genealogical regnal list and the chronology of early Wessex', *Peritia* 4.

Dumville, David (1986) 'Historical value of the *Historia Brittonum*', *Arthurian Literature* 6.

Dumville, David (1990) *Histories and Pseudo-histories of the Insular Middle Ages*. Aldershot: Variorum.

Dumville, David (1994) '*Historia Brittonum:* an insular history from the Carolingian Age', in A. Scharer and G. Scheibelreiter (eds), *Historiographie im frühen Mittelalter*. Vienna and Munich: R. Oldenbourg.

Exquemelin, A.O. (1969) *The Buccaneers of America*, trans. Jack Beeching. Baltimore, MD: Penguin.

Faral, Edmond (1929) *La Légende arthurienne: Etudes et documents*. Paris: Bibliothèque de l'Ecole des Hautes Etudes.

Fehrenbach, T.R. (1974) *Comanches: The Destruction of a People*. New York: Knopf.

Fischer, David Hackett (1989) *Albion's Seed*. New York: Oxford University Press.

Forsyth, Katherine (1997) *Language in Pictland*. Utrecht: De Keltische Draak.

Frere, Sheppard (1987) *Britannia: A History of Roman Britain*. London: Pimlico.

Geiriadur Prifysgol Cymru: A Dictionary of the Welsh Language (1968–87), 4 vols. Caerdydd: Gwasg Prifysgol Cymru.

Gibbon, Edward ([1776–88] 1910) *Decline and Fall of the Roman Empire*, 6 vols. London: Dent.

Gidlow, Christopher (2005) *The Reign of Arthur*. Stroud: Sutton Publishing.

Giles, J.A. (1848) *Six Old English Chronicles*. London: Bohn.

Goffart, Walter (1980) *Barbarians and Romans AD 418–584: The Techniques of Accommodation*. Princeton, NJ: Princeton University Press.

Goffart, Walter (1981) 'Rome, Constantinople and the Barbarians in Late Antiquity', *American Historical Review* 76.

Griffen, Toby (1994) *Names from the Dawn of British Legend*. Felinfach, Llanerch.

Haywood, John (1991) *Dark Age Naval Power*. London: Routledge.

Heather, Peter (2005) *The Fall of the Roman Empire*. Pan: London.

Higham, N.J. (1994) *The English Conquest: Gildas and Britain in the Fifth Century*. Manchester: Manchester University Press.

Higham, N.J. (2002) *King Arthur, Mythmaking and History*. London: Routledge.

Johnson, Stephen (1976) *Roman Forts of the Saxon Shore*. London: Elek Books.

Bibliography

Jones, A.H.M. (1964) *The Later Roman Empire*, 3 vols. Baltimore, MD: Johns Hopkins Press.

Jones, Barri and Mattingly, David (1990) *An Atlas of Roman Britain.* Oxford: Basil Blackwell.

Jones, Charles W. (1994) *Bede, the Schools and the Computus.* Aldershot: Variorum.

Jones, Michael E. and Casey, John (1988) 'Gallic Chronicle restored: A chronology for the Anglo-Saxon invasions and the end of Roman Britain', *Britannia* XIX.

Keys, David (1999) *Catastrophe: an Investigation into the Origins of the Modern World.* London: Century.

Kirby, D.P. (1976) 'British dynastic history in the pre-Viking period', *Bulletin of the Board of Celtic Studies* 27 (November 1976), p. 1.

Lane-Poole, Reginald (1926) *Chronicles and Annals.* Oxford: Clarendon.

Lapidge, M. (1986) 'Latin learning in Dark Age Wales: Some prolegomena', in E. Evans, J.G. Griffith and E.M. Jope (eds), *Proceedings of the Seventh International Congress of Celtic Studies.*

Lapidge, Michael and Dumville, David (eds) (1984) *Gildas: New Approaches.* Woodbridge: Boydell Press.

Littleton, C. Scott and Malcor, Linda A. (2000) *From Scythia to Camelot.* New York: Garland.

Loomis, Roger Sherman (1959) 'The legend of Arthur's survival', in R.S. Loomis (ed.), *Arthurian Literature of the Middle Ages.* Oxford: Clarendon.

Mahan, A.T. (1987) *The Influence of Sea Power upon History.* New York: Dover.

Mattingly, Harold and Stebbing, W.P.D. (1938) *The Richborough Hoard of 'Radiates'.* New York: The American Numismatic Society.

Miller, Molly (1975) 'Historicity and the pedigrees of the Northcountrymen', *Bulletin of the Board of Celtic Studies* 26 (November), p. 3.

Morris, John (1973) *The Age of Arthur.* London: Weidenfeld and Nicolson.

Morris, John (1995) *Arthurian Sources*, 6 vols. Chichester: Phillimore.

Muhlberger, Steven (1990) *The Fifth Century Chroniclers.* Leeds: F. Cairns.

Nash Williams, V.E. (1950) *Early Christian Monuments of Wales.* Cardiff: University of Wales Press.

Nickel, Helmut (1975) 'The Dawn of Chivalry', *Metropolitan Museum of Art Bulletin* 32.

Nickel, Helmut (1975) 'Wer waren König Artus' Ritter? Über die geschichtliche Grundlage der Artussagen', *Zeitschrift der historischen Waffen-und Kostümkunde* 1.

O'Sullivan, Thomas D. (1978) *The De Excidio of Gildas: Its Authenticity and Date*. Leiden: E.J. Brill.

Padel, O. (1995) 'Recent work in the origins of the Arthurian legend: A comment', *Arthuriana* 5:3 (Fall).

Puchkov, P. (ed.) (1989) *Peoples that Vanished*. Moscow: Nauk.

Rahtz, Philip (1968) 'Glastonbury Tor', in Geoffrey Ashe (ed.), *The Quest for Arthur's Britain*.

Salway, Peter (1984) *Roman Britain*. New York: Oxford University Press.

Salway, Peter and Blair, John (1984) *The Oxford History of Britain: Roman and Anglo-Saxon Britain*. Oxford University Press.

Sims-Williams, Patrick (1991) 'The early Welsh Arthurian poems', in Bromwich et al. (eds), *The Arthur of the Welsh*.

Snyder, Christopher (1989) *An Age of Tyrants*. University Park, PA: Pennsylvania State University Press.

Sparey-Green, Christopher (1996) 'Poundbury, Dorset: Settlement and economy in Late and post-Roman Britain', in K.R. Dark (ed.), *External Contacts and the Economy of Late Roman and Post-Roman Britain*.

Stevens, Courtenay (1933) *Sidonius Apollinaris and His Age*. Oxford: Clarendon Press.

Southern, Pat and Dixon, Karen (1996) *The Late Roman Army*. London: Routledge.

Thompson, E.A. (1982) *Romans and Barbarians*. Madison, WI: University of Wisconsin Press.

Thompson, E.A. (1984) *Saint Germanus of Auxerre*. Woodbridge: Boydell Press.

Tolkien, J.R.R. (1982) *Finn and Hengest*, ed. Alan Blair. London: Unwin.

Tolstoy, Nikolai (1961) 'Nennius, chapter fifty-six', *The Bulletin of the Board of Celtic Studies* 19.

Tolstoy, Nikolai (1962) 'Who was Coroticus?' *The Irish Ecclesiastical Record* XCVII, No. 1.

Tolstoy, Nikolai (1964) 'Early British history and chronology', *Transactions of the Honourable Society of Cymmrodorion* (1964), Pt 2.

Bibliography

Vasiliev, A.A. (1958) *History of the Byzantine Empire.* Madison, WI: University of Wisconsin Press.

Yorke, Barbara (1993) 'Fact or fiction? The written evidence for the fifth and sixth centuries AD', *Anglo-Saxon Studies in Archaeology and History* 6.

Yorke, Barbara (1999) 'The origins of the Anglo-Saxon kingdoms: The contribution of written sources', *Anglo-Saxon Studies in Archaeology and History* 10.

Vermaat, Robert (1999) 'Forty years of fear: Facts, fiction, and the dates for Vortigern in chapter 66 of the *Historia Brittonum*', *The Heroic Age*, Issue 2 (Autumn/Winter) (www.heroicage.org), accessed 20 February 2008.

Wiseman, Howard (2001) 'The Derivation of the Date of the Badon Entry in the *Annales Cambriae* from Bede and Gildas' (www.cit.gu.edu.au/~s285238/DECB/ ParergonArticle.pdf), accessed 20 February 2008.

Wolfram, Herwig (1988) *History of the Goths*, trans. Thomas Dunlap. Berkeley, CA: University of California Press.

Wood, Ian (1984) 'The End of Roman Britain', in Lapidge and Dumville (eds), *Gildas: New Approaches.*

Ziegler, Michelle (1999) 'Artúr mac Aedan of Dalriada', *The Heroic Age*, Issue 1 (Spring/Summer) (www.heroicage.org), accessed 20 February 2008.

Index

Index

Geoffrey of Monmouth 24, 109, 246-8, 260

Genevieve, Saint 171

Gepids, Germainc tribe 171

Germanus, Saint 41, 77-9, 123, 163, 282; winter crossing 78; debate in London 79; leads Britons in battle 80-1; blesses Arthur 83; spurious *Vita* in *Historia Brittonum* 252; Bede's incorrect date for 296-7

Germany 9, 18, 37, 53, 57, 65, 104, 139, 142, 144, 192, 201, 266

Gerontius, insurgent British marshal 34-7, 60, 82, 89, 103, 116, 149, 215; death 35

Gewissei, Thames Saxons 200

Gibbon, Edward 226; view of Riothamus 213

Gildas 2, 26, 56, 127, 161, 165-6, 176, 197; on British military effectiveness 59; agreement with ASC 44; on British counterattack 45; 'present peace' 49, 278; on Roman withdrawal 63-71; reliability 40-2, 68-9, 95-6, 111-12, 124-6, 158, 194-5, 210, 248; misdates *Adventus* 94, 143, 193, 322; criticizes British defensive strategy 98; no mention of Arthur 107; cites Battle List 111-12, 135, 216; 'time of plenty' 122, 174-5; as critic of Arthur 182; confusion of battle lists 195; on Saxon Revolt 246, 258-60; date for Badon 274, 277; birth date 274, 277, 279; uses Valentinian III's first regnal year in timekeeping 277; probable lifespan 279

Glastonbury 161-3

Glein River, *see* Glen River

Glen River, battle on 106, 114

Glevum, see Gloucester

Gloucester (*Glevum*) 100, 102, 105, 112, 131, 149, 153, 164

Gloucestershire 11, 130

Goar, Alanic king 103

Gododdin, *see* Manau Gododdin

Goths *see* Visigoths

Grace, doctrine of 76

Gratia, see grace

Gratian, Roman emperor: Alans in personal guard 21; death 22

Gregory of Tours 211, 219; account of Arthur's Gallic campaign 220, 240; parallels with Romano-British time keeping 299

Gundahari, Burgundian king 65

Guinevere, *see* Gwynhwyfar

Guinnion, see also Cirencester 106, 112, 115, 117, 118, 119, 121, 122, 137, 140, 142, 161

Gunther, *see* Gundahari

Guollop, Discordia or battle of 190-4; Ambrosius' victory 199-201; equation with *Aegelesthrep* 291-5

Guoyrancgonus, fictional British king 203

Gwynedd, *see also* Venedotia 146, 164-8

Gwynhwyfar: 'the three Gwynhwyfars' 187, 204; 'harmful blow' to 248-9, 253

Hadrian's Wall, reported construction in fifth century 64, 67-9

Harleian genealogies 187, 251

Hearward the Wake 87

Hengest 47, 50, 137, 142, 144-5, 191-4, 196, 199, 212-3, 217, 247, 261; as horse god 144; naval mission 143, 145, 212; defeat at Guollop/*Aegelesthrep* 199-201; reinforcements from Germany 201; possible landing at Crayford 202

Hengist, *see* Hengest

Herpath, Saxon name for Roman roads 119

Heruls 171, 223; raids on Spain 220-2; to Italy 242

Historia Brittonum (HB) 2, 42, 46, 67, 83, 111, 167, 177, 187, 203, 210; reliability 42-3, 69, 109, 146-7, 164-5, 190-5, 286; 'forty years of fear' 53, 296; text of Battle List 107; mistakes about Arthur 107-8, 135, 151,